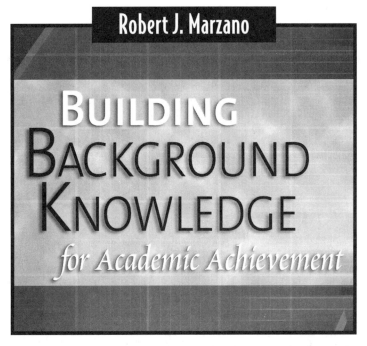

Robert J. Marzano

BUILDING BACKGROUND KNOWLEDGE
for Academic Achievement

Research on What Works in Schools

Association for Supervision and Curriculum Development
Alexandria, VA USA

®

Association for Supervision and Curriculum Development
1703 N. Beauregard St. • Alexandria, VA 22311-1714 USA
Telephone: 800-933-2723 or 703-578-9600 • Fax: 703-575-5400
Web site: http://www.ascd.org • E-mail: member@ascd.org

Gene R. Carter, *Executive Director;* Nancy Modrak, *Director of Publishing;* Julie Houtz, *Director of Book Editing & Production;* Darcie Russell, *Project Manager;* Genevieve Konecnik, *Senior Designer;* Judi Connelly, *Senior Graphic Designer;* Cindy Stock, *Typesetter;* Tracey A. Franklin, *Production Manager*

All Web links in this book are correct as of the publication date below but may have become inactive or otherwise modified since that time. If you notice a deactivated or changed link, please e-mail books@ascd.org with the words "Link Update" in the subject line. In your message, please specify the Web link, the book title, and the page number on which the link appears.

ASCD Member Book, No. FY04-9 (August 2004, P). ASCD Member Books mail to Premium (P), Comprehensive (C), and Regular (R) members on this schedule: Jan., PC; Feb., P; Apr., PCR; May, P; July, PC; Aug., P; Sept., PCR; Nov., PC; Dec., P.

Paperback ISBN: 0-87120-972-1 • ASCD product # 104017 • List Price: $26.95 ($21.95 ASCD member price, direct from ASCD only)
e-books ($26.95): netLibrary ISBN 1-4166-0055-8 • ebrary ISBN 1-4166-0056-6

Library of Congress Cataloging-in-Publication Data

Marzano, Robert J.
  Building background knowledge for academic achievement : research on what works in schools / Robert J. Marzano.
      p. cm.
    Includes bibliographical references and index.
    ISBN 0-87120-972-1 (alk. paper)
  1. Academic achievement—United States. 2. School supervision—United States. 3. Silent reading—United States. 4. Vocabulary—Study and teaching. I. Title.

  LB1062.6.M37 2004
  371.2'03'0973—dc22

                                            2004009792

11 10 09 08 07 06 05   12 11 10 9 8 7 6 5 4 3 2

BUILDING
BACKGROUND KNOWLEDGE
for Academic Achievement

To my grandchildren: Cecilia and Aida

1

The Importance of Background Knowledge

According to the National Center for Education Statistics (2003), every day from September to June some 53.5 million students in the United States walk into classes that teach English, mathematics, science, history, and geography and face the sometimes daunting task of learning new content. Indeed, one of the nation's long-term goals as stated in the *The National Education Goals Report: Building a Nation of Learners* (National Education Goals Panel, 1991) is for U.S. students to master "challenging subject matter" in core subject areas (p. 4). Since that goal was articulated, national and state-level standards documents have identified the challenging subject matter alluded to by the goals panel. For example, in English, high school students are expected to know and be able to use standard conventions for citing various types of primary and secondary sources. In mathematics, they are expected to understand and use sigma notation and factorial representations. In science, they are expected to know how insulators, semiconductors, and superconductors respond to electric forces. In history, they are expected to understand how civilization developed in Mesopotamia and the Indus Valley. In geography, they are expected to understand how the spread of radiation from the Chernobyl nuclear accident has affected the present-day world.

Although it is true that the extent to which students will learn this new content is dependent on factors such as the skill of the teacher, the interest of the student, and the complexity of the content, the research literature supports one compelling fact: what students *already know* about the content is one of the strongest indicators of how well they will learn new information relative to the content. Commonly, researchers and theorists refer to what a person already knows about a topic as "background knowledge." Numerous studies have confirmed the relationship between background knowledge and achievement (Nagy, Anderson, & Herman, 1987; Bloom, 1976; Dochy, Segers, & Buehl, 1999; Tobias, 1994; Alexander, Kulikowich, & Schulze, 1994; Schiefele & Krapp, 1996; Tamir, 1996; Boulanger, 1981). In these studies the reported average correlation between a person's background knowledge of a given topic and the extent to which that person learns new information on that topic is .66 (see Technical Note 1 on p. 127 for a discussion of how the correlation was computed).

To interpret this average correlation, let's consider one student, Jana, who is at the 50th percentile in terms of both her background knowledge and her academic achievement. Envision Jana's achievement at the 50th percentile as shown in the middle of Figure 1.1. (For a more detailed explanation of this example, see Technical Note 2 on pp. 127–129.) If we increase her background knowledge by one standard deviation (that is, move her from the 50th to the 84th percentile), her academic achievement would be expected to increase from the 50th to the 75th percentile (see the bars on the right side of Figure 1.1). In contrast, if we decrease Jana's academic background knowledge by one standard deviation (that is, move her from the 50th to the 16th percentile), her academic achievement would be

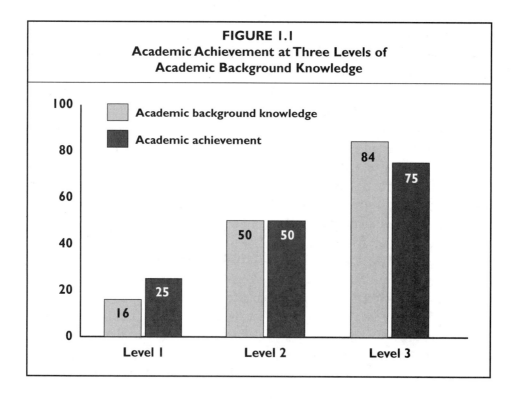

FIGURE 1.1
Academic Achievement at Three Levels of
Academic Background Knowledge

expected to drop to the 25th percentile (see the bars on the left side of Figure 1.1). These three scenarios demonstrate the dramatic impact of academic background knowledge on success in school. Students who have a great deal of background knowledge in a given subject area are likely to learn new information readily and quite well. The converse is also true.

Academic background knowledge affects more than just "school learning." Studies have also shown its relation to occupation and status in life. Sticht, Hofstetter, and Hofstetter (1997) sought to document a relationship between background knowledge and power, with power defined as "the achievement of a higher status occupation and/or the ability to earn an average or higher level income" (p. 2). To test their hypothesis that "knowledge is power" (p. 3), they interviewed 538 randomly selected adults and gave them a test of basic academic information and terminology. They found a significant relationship between knowledge of this academic information and type of occupation and overall income.

This discussion paints a compelling picture of the impact of *academic* background knowledge on students' academic achievement in school and on their lives after school. It is important to note the qualifier *academic*. Two students might have an equal amount of background knowledge. However, one student's knowledge might relate to traditional school subjects such as mathematics, science, history, and the like. The other student's knowledge might be about nonacademic topics such as the best subway route to take to get downtown during rush hour, the place to stand in the subway car that provides the most ventilation on a hot summer day, and so on. The importance of one type of background knowledge over another is strictly a function of context (Becker, 1977; Greenfield, 1998). The background knowledge of the second student is critical to successfully using public transportation in a specific metropolitan area, but probably not very important for success in school. The first student's background knowledge is critical to success in school but not to successful public transit.

This book is about enhancing students' academic background knowledge. This is not to say that other types of background knowledge are unimportant. Indeed, Sternberg and Wagner's (1986) compilation of the research on practical intelligence makes a good case that success in many aspects of life is related to nonacademic types of background knowledge. However, it is also true that in the United States all children are expected to attend school, and success in school has a strong bearing on their earning potential. Figure 1.2 illustrates the dramatic rise in yearly income as the level of education increases. One particularly disturbing aspect of Figure 1.2 is the income level of those who have not graduated from high school—namely, $10,838. This is not much above the official poverty line in the

FIGURE 1.2
Relationship Between Education and Yearly Income

Level of Education	Yearly Income
Not a high school graduate	$10,838
High school graduate	$18,571
Some college, no degree	$20,997
Associate's degree	$26,535
Bachelor's degree	$35,594
Master's degree	$47,121
Professional degree	$66,968
Doctorate	$62,275

Source: U.S. Census Bureau, March 2003

United States, which is $9,359 per year for a single adult (U.S. Census Bureau, September 25, 2003). Students who do not graduate from high school likely condemn themselves to a life of poverty.

Enhancing students' academic background knowledge, then, is a worthy goal of public education from a number of perspectives. In fact, given the relationship between academic background knowledge and academic achievement, one can make the case that it should be at the top of any list of interventions intended to enhance student achievement. If not addressed by schools, academic background can create great advantages for some students and great disadvantages for others. The scope of the disparity becomes evident when we consider how background knowledge is acquired.

How We Acquire Background Knowledge

We acquire background knowledge through the interaction of two factors: (1) our ability to process and store information, and (2) the number and frequency of our academically oriented experiences. The ability to process and store information is a component of what cognitive psychologists refer to as *fluid intelligence*. As described by Cattell (1987), fluid intelligence is innate. One of its defining features is the ability to process information and store it in permanent memory. High fluid intelligence is associated with enhanced ability to process and store information.

Low fluid intelligence is associated with diminished ability to process and store information.

Our ability to process and store information dictates whether our experiences parlay into background knowledge. To illustrate, consider two students who visit a museum and see exactly the same exhibits. One student has an enhanced capacity to process and store information, or high fluid intelligence; the other has a diminished capacity to process and store information, or low fluid intelligence. The student with high fluid intelligence will retain most of the museum experience as new knowledge in permanent memory. The student with low fluid intelligence will not. In effect, the student with the enhanced information-processing capacity has translated the museum experience into academic background knowledge; the other has not. As Sternberg (1985) explains: "What seems to be critical is not sheer amount of experience but rather what one has been able to learn from and do with experience" (p. 307).

The second factor that influences the development of academic background knowledge is our academically oriented experiential base—the number of experiences that will directly add to our knowledge of content we encounter in school. The more academically oriented experiences we have, the more opportunities we have to store those experiences as academic background knowledge. Again, consider our two students at the museum. Assume that one student has an experience like visiting a museum once a week and the other student has experiences like this once a month. The second student might have an equal number of other types of experiences, but they are nonacademic and provide little opportunity to enhance academic background knowledge. In effect, the first student has four times the opportunities to generate academic background knowledge as the second, at least from "museum-type" experiences.

It is the interaction of students' information-processing abilities and their access to academically oriented experiences, then, that produces their academic background knowledge. Differences in these factors create differences in their academic background knowledge and, consequently, differences in their academic achievement.

An examination of the interaction of these factors paints a sobering picture of the academic advantages possessed by some students and not others. Figure 1.3 depicts nine students with differing levels of access to academically oriented experiences and differing levels of ability to process and store information. The darker the box, the more academic background knowledge a student has. Allen has the most background knowledge. He has a great deal of access to experiences that build academic background knowledge and exceptional ability to process and

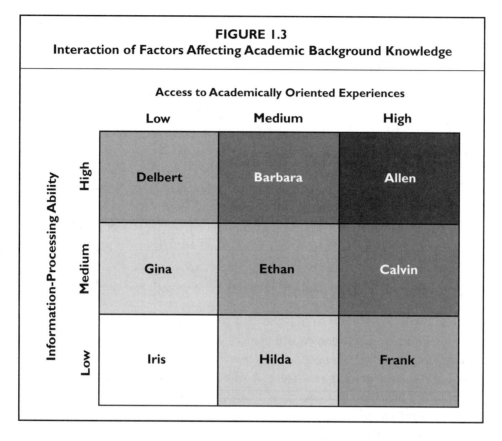

FIGURE 1.3
Interaction of Factors Affecting Academic Background Knowledge

store those experiences. We might say that Allen is doubly blessed because of his ability to process information and his access to many experiences that will be translated into academic background knowledge. Barbara and Calvin are next in order of the amount of academic background knowledge but for slightly different reasons. Barbara has midlevel access to experiences but a highly developed ability to process and store information. She makes maximum use of her academically oriented experiences. Calvin doesn't have Barbara's ability to process and store information, but he has many experiences to draw from. As Figure 1.3 demonstrates, enhanced information-processing ability can offset to some degree lack of access to academically oriented experiences, and vice versa. Figure 1.3 also demonstrates the plight of certain students who—I assert—constitute the academically disadvantaged students in the United States. Consider the three students depicted in the first column of Figure 1.3—Delbert, Gina, and Iris.

Delbert has a moderate amount of background knowledge, but only because he has exceptional ability to process and store information. Even though he has little access to experiences, he stores most of what he experiences. Gina has an average ability to process information, but her limited access to background knowledge plays havoc with her chances of developing a large store of academic background knowledge. Iris is in the worst situation of all. She has diminished information-processing ability and limited access to academically oriented experiences. Limited access to academic background experiences, then, represents "the great inhibitor" to the development of academic background knowledge. We might ask, which students characteristically have limited access to academic background experience? Stated differently, who are Delbert, Gina, and Iris?

The Consequences of Poverty

The plight of Delbert, Gina, and Iris becomes particularly disturbing when we consider the direct relationship between access to academic background experiences and family income. Unfortunately, a great many children attending U.S. schools grow up in poverty. Brooks-Gunn, Duncan, and Maritato (1997) note that "in a given year from 1987 to 1996, about one in five of all American children—from twelve to fourteen million—lived in families in which total income failed to exceed even the Spartan thresholds used to define poverty" (p. 1). Relatively speaking, this is not an insignificant number. As Brooks-Gunn and colleagues explain: "Indeed, the United States has a higher rate of poverty than most other Western industrialized nations . . . and . . . child poverty has increased since the 1970s. . . ." (p. 12).

Even without considering the impact of poverty on access to academically oriented experiences, the relationship between poverty and academic achievement is almost self-evident. To illustrate, Smith, Brooks-Gunn, and Klebanov (1997) analyzed data from two studies: the National Longitudinal Survey of Youth (NLSY) and the Infant Health and Development Project (IHDP). The NLSY involved children of women who were first studied when they were teenagers. The children were tracked beginning in1986 and every year after that. The IHDP followed children born in eight medical centers across the United States each year for the first five years of their lives. Aggregating the findings from both studies as reported by Smith and colleagues dramatizes the impact of family income on academic achievement. Consider two groups of children ages 3–7. The children in one group were born in or near poverty, and those in the other group were not. Assume that children in both categories took an academic test of mathematics, general verbal intelligence, and reading, and that test had an expected passing rate of 50 percent. Figure 1.4 indicates that based on the findings from Smith and colleagues, only 37 percent of those students born in or near poverty would pass the test, whereas 63 percent of those not born in or near poverty would pass. What is most interesting about the findings reported in Figure 1.4 is that they characterize the relationship between poverty and academic success *after controlling for ethnicity, family structure, and mothers' education.* In other words, the relationship depicted in Figure 1.4 is what would be expected if all children in the studies from which the data were taken were equal in terms of their ethnicity, their mother's education level, and whether they came from a single-parent home, a two-parent home, or an intact family. These qualifiers put the impact of family income in sharp perspective. Even if children are equal in these admittedly important factors, the influence of family income creates huge discrepancies in academic success.

Some researchers believe that family income has an even greater impact on achievement than that depicted in Figure 1.4. For example, McLanahan (1997) notes that "income is clearly the most important factor. It explains about 50 percent of the difference in the educational achievement of children raised in one- and two-parent families" (p. 37). Using McLanahan's figures to compute the impact of poverty on students' success on an academic test produces the results reported in Figure 1.5. As the figure shows, only 15 percent of students who grow up in or near poverty are expected to pass a test that we would normally expect half the students to pass and half the students to fail. Regardless of which figure (1.4 or 1.5) depicts the true relationship, the message is clear: Poverty has a profound impact on academic achievement.

The Influence of Poverty on Factors Other Than Academic Achievement

Poverty's negative impact goes well beyond academic achievement. For example, poverty has been associated with an increase in conflicts at home. Conger, Conger, and Elder (1997) explain:

FIGURE 1.4 Relationship Between Poverty and Success on an Academic Test		
Students' Economic Status	**Percent of Students Failing**	**Percent of Students Passing**
Born in or near poverty	63	37
Not born in or near poverty	37	63

Source: Based on data in Smith, Brooks-Gunn, & Klebanov, 1997. For an explanation of how this figure was constructed, see Technical Note 3 on pp. 129–130.

FIGURE 1.5
Relationship Between Poverty and Success on an Academic Test
Using McLanahan's Estimates

Students' Economic Status	Percent of Students Failing	Percent of Students Passing
Born in or near poverty	85	15
Not born in or near poverty	15	85

Source: Based on data in McLanahan, 1997. For an explanation of how these percentages were computed, see Technical Note 3 on pp. 129–130.

> . . . we propose that the psychological stresses and strains associated with economic pressure increase the risk for conflicts between parents about their finances. Spouses who are angered and demoralized by their disadvantaged economic situation and who have to negotiate with one another about the use of scarce resources are living in a situation ripe for conflicts. . . . (p. 302)

It makes intuitive sense that a lack of financial resources puts extraordinary stress on spousal relationships, which translates into more frequent family conflict. Children who are unable to comprehend the dynamics of such conflicts might easily believe that they are somehow responsible for the strife. Also, because wealth is a symbol of success in U.S. society, it is not surprising that poverty is a symbol of failure, leading to a decrease in self-esteem. As Axinn, Duncan, and Thornton (1997) explain:

> Parents' economic resources can influence self-esteem in several ways. Parents' income brings both parents and children social status and respect that can translate into individual self-esteem. Income can also enhance children's self-esteem by providing them with goods and services that satisfy individual aspirations.
>
> Low income and other economic hardships may reduce children's self-esteem by reducing the emotional or supportive qualities of the parents' home. The pressure that limited economic resources can place on marital relationships can, in turn, translate into negative parent-child relations and lower levels of self-esteem. (p. 521)

Some of the more dramatic casualties of poverty are best seen through the lens of language, as demonstrated in a study by Hart and Risley (1995). For two and a half years they observed 42 one- and two-year old children and the manner in which their parents interacted with them. The levels of family income ranged from poverty to affluence. For research purposes, Hart and Risley categorized the families into three basic groups: welfare families, working-class families, and professional families. On the positive side, one of their findings was that quality experiences for children, amount of attention and love shown, had nothing to do with family income:

> We saw quality interactions in families in which the parents had all the advantages of higher education, challenging jobs, substantial incomes, and broad experience; we found quality interactions in middle- and low-income families and in families on welfare limited in both present advantages and future prospects for their children. We saw that quality experience does not depend on parents' material or educational advantages. (p. 91)

However, although children of poverty had equal or better access to loving parents, their access to resources was dramatically different. Whereas those children in working-class or professional families had lives rich in experiences and interactions with others, those on welfare were frequently isolated, sometimes because of the dangers associated with playing in the neighborhood. Additionally, "families too poor to live in public housing put their children through successive moves from one small deteriorating dwelling to another" (p. 69). But this did not stop welfare parents from engaging in heroic acts of sacrifice for their children:

> Particularly striking among the welfare parents was their resilience and the persistence in the face of repeated defeats and humiliations, their joy in playing with their children, and their desire that their children do well in school. They could spend an hour on a bus holding a feverish child and wait longer than that in a public health clinic. They spent their scarce resources on toys for their children. . . . (pp. 69–70)

In spite of these sometimes Herculean efforts by parents in welfare families, their children were exposed to a fraction of the language that children in working-class and professional families were exposed to. This difference was strongly associated with differences in students' academic achievement. Sadly, the use of language also communicated a limited set of expectations:

> In the welfare families, the lesser amount of talk with its more frequent parent-initiated topics, imperatives, and prohibitions suggested a culture concerned with established customs. To teach socially acceptable behavior, language rich in nouns and modifiers was not called for; obedience, politeness, and conformity were more likely to be the keys to survival. Rather than attempting to prepare their children with the knowledge and skills required in a technological world with which the parents had little experience, parents seemed to be preparing their children realistically for the jobs likely to be open to them. . . . (pp. 133–134)

Two of the more dramatic findings of the Hart and Risley study are the discrepancies between the three types of families in the frequency of affirmations and prohibitions. Affirmations are statements by parents that elicit independence and self-efficacy. For example, telling a child to "keep trying, you can do it" while she attempts to tie her shoes is an affirmation. Prohibitions are statements that foster dependence and inhibit self-efficacy. For example, telling a child, "let me do that so that it's done right" is a prohibition. Hart and Risley summarize their findings regarding affirmations and prohibitions in the following way:

> We extrapolated to an average welfare child accumulating experience with 500 affirmatives and 1,100 prohibitions per week and an average working-class child accumulating experience with 1,200 affirmatives and 700 prohibitions per week. To keep the confidence-building experiences of welfare children equal to those of working-class children, the welfare children would need to be given 1,100 more instances of affirmative feedback per week—700 instances to bring the 500 affirmatives up to the 1,200 given an average working-class child plus 400 affirmatives to reduce the 1,100 prohibitions to the 700 of the average working-class child. It would take 26 hours per week of substituted experience for the average welfare child's experience with affirmatives to equal that of the average working-class child. It would take 66 hours of substituted experience per week to lower the average welfare child's experience with prohibitions to that of the average working-class child. Overall, 40 hours per week of substituted experience would be needed to keep the welfare children's ratio of lifetime experience with encouragement relative to discouragement equal to that of the working-class children. (p. 202)

The implications of the Hart and Risley findings are profound. Children who grow up with financial resources have many direct and indirect experiences that children who grow up in poverty do not. By the time children of poverty enter school, they are at a significant disadvantage.

Poverty and Ethnicity

The impact of poverty appears even more sinister when we consider the relationship between poverty and ethnicity. U.S. Census Bureau statistics dated September 26, 2003, indicate that 32.9 million (11.7 percent of the people) in the United States live below the poverty line. Recall that the poverty line for a single individual is $9,359 a year. For a family of two adults, however, the poverty line is $12,047 a year. For a family of two adults and two children, the poverty line is $18,244 a year.

We might say, then, that in the United States, about 12 of every 100 people live at or below the poverty line. For African Americans and Hispanics, however, the percentage is higher. Specifically, 22.7 percent of African Americans and 21.4 percent of Hispanics in the United States live at or below the poverty line, whereas only 9.9 percent of whites live at or below the poverty line. In other words, if you are born African American or Hispanic in the United States, you have twice the chance of living in poverty as you do if you are born white. Further, when poverty is examined across a number of years, the plight of African American and Hispanic children is exacerbated.

To illustrate, Corcoran and Adams (1997) analyzed data from the Panel Study of Income Dynamics that involved about 5,000 families who were studied annually since 1968. They focused on the relationship between poverty and being African American. They noted the following:

• White children's families reported almost twice as much income as did African American children's families.

• About 5 percent of African American children grew up in families whose income was only 50 percent of the poverty level.

• At least two out of three African American children were poor at least one year during the time they were observed. In contrast, only one in seven white children were poor during the time they were observed.

• Forty percent of the African American children were poor for more than half of the time they were observed. In contrast, fewer than 5 percent of the white children were poor for more than half of the time observed.

• More than 60 percent of African American children grew up in households that received welfare at some point, and 17 percent grew up in households that relied on welfare for more than half their income. In contrast, only 25 percent of white children lived in households that ever received welfare, and 4 percent of white children lived in households that relied on welfare for more than 15 percent of their income.

The primary conclusion reached by Corcoran and Adams (1997) was that "black and white children differed considerably in their access to material resources during childhood" (p. 468). The same alarming trends also affect Hispanic children (see Peters & Mullis, 1997; Hernandez, 1997). As Brooks-Gunn, Duncan, and Maritato (1997) explain, "Both single-year and multi-year estimates of poverty indicate that black and Hispanic children are much more likely to be poor, and for longer periods of time, than white children are" (pp. 4–5).

A Clearer Picture of Delbert, Gina, and Iris

With the links made between family income and access to academic experiences and between ethnicity and family income, our pictures of Delbert, Gina, and Iris come into sharp focus. They are most likely to be African American or Hispanic. They are growing up in families at or near the poverty line. They have experienced a fraction of the rich language development opportunities that come so readily to other students. Additionally, they experience twice as many discouraging messages as they do encouraging messages—the opposite ratio of their more affluent counterparts. Finally, they may regularly deal with income-related familial stresses not characteristic of more affluent homes.

These facts are staggering in their implications, and one marvels at the resilience of children who overcome their impact. Yet many if not most of these children will succumb under the weight of these factors without direct and prolonged interventions by schools.

Schools Can Make the Difference

What can and should schools do? Before answering this question, it is important to acknowledge that some people assert that schools can make little difference in overcoming the background factors that negatively affect student academic achievement. At the extreme end of the continuum are theorists like Jensen (1980) and Heurnstein and Murray (1994), who make the case that the differences in knowledge and skill students bring to the classroom are largely due to genetic aspects of aptitude that are impervious to change. However, these arguments dramatically underestimate the importance of nongenetic background factors mentioned in the previous discussion. They also ignore the research indicating that innate intelligence is not as strongly related to academic achievement as once thought.

Previously, I discussed the nature of fluid, or innate, intelligence. A second type of intelligence is referred to as crystallized, or learned, intelligence. Crystallized intelligence is exemplified by knowledge of facts, generalizations, and principles. Although a certain level of innate intelligence is important to academic success, learned intelligence is the stronger correlate of success in school, as demonstrated in a study by Rolfhus and Ackerman (1999). They administered intelligence tests to 141 adults, along with knowledge tests in 20 different subject areas. They then examined the relationship between subject matter test scores and fluid versus crystallized intelligence. They found little relationship between academic knowledge and fluid intelligence, but a strong relationship between academic knowledge and crystallized intelligence. As stated by Rolfhus and Ackerman (1999), these findings suggest that academic "knowledge is more highly associated with [crystallized] abilities than with [fluid] abilities" (p. 520). Madaus, Kellaghan, Rakow, and King (1979) have reported similar findings.

Interestingly, it might even be the case that fluid intelligence can be altered. This is dramatically illustrated in the book *The Rising Curve: Long-Term Gains in IQ and Related Measures* (Neisser, 1998), which seeks to explain the worldwide phe-nomenon in industrialized countries of rising IQ scores:

> Scores on intelligence tests are *rising* [emphasis in original], not falling; indeed, they have been going up steeply for years. This rapid rise is not confined to the United States; comparable gains have occurred all over the industrialized world . . . Perfor-mance on broad-spectrum tests of intelligence has been going up about 3 IQ points per decade ever since testing began. (pp. 3–4)

What is most interesting about this rise in IQ scores is that it is at least as strong in terms of fluid intelligence as it is in terms of crystallized intelligence. That is, a systematic increase has occurred in the type of intelligence that is assumed to be innate as well as in the type that is assumed to be learned. Although researchers have posed a number of explanations for these increases, one of the strongest can-didates is the influence of effective schooling. To illustrate, Greenfield (1998) reviewed research conducted in Africa and Israel comparing children who had attended school with those who had not. Those who attended school exhibited relatively large IQ gains. Her final conclusion was that "actual performance on intelligence tests is more closely related to years of schooling than it is to chrono-logical age" (p. 89).

The clear message from the research is that schools can make a difference. If the knowledge and skill that students from advantaged backgrounds possess is learned rather than innate, then students who do not come from advantaged backgrounds can learn it too. Indeed, even aspects of intelligence once thought to be genetically based appear to be amenable to change through schooling. To accomplish such a task, schools must be willing to dedicate the necessary time and resources to enhancing the academic background knowledge of students, particu-larly those who do not come from affluent backgrounds. But how does a school do this?

Direct Approaches to Enhancing
Academic Background Knowledge

The most straightforward way to enhance students' academic background knowl-edge is to provide academically enriching experiences, particularly for students whose home environments do not do so naturally. I refer to such efforts as "direct approaches" to enhancing academic background knowledge.

By definition, a direct approach to enhancing academic background knowl-edge is one that increases the variety and depth of out-of-class experiences. Such experiences include field trips to museums, art galleries, and the like, as well as school-sponsored travel and exchange programs. Admittedly, these experiences are powerful, but schools are limited in how many they can provide. In these days of shrinking resources, schools commonly must cut back or even cut out these activities.

Another type of direct approach is to help students establish mentoring relationships with members of the community. A mentoring relationship is a one-to-one relationship between a caring adult and a youth who can benefit from support. Although mentoring relationships can develop quite naturally between students and teachers, relatives, or coaches, planned mentoring relationships are those in which a student is matched with a mentor in a structured format (Brewster & Fager, 1998). Trust appears to be the sine qua non of effective mentoring relationships (Sipe, 1999), but it is not easily established between partners from different socioeconomic or ethnic groups. Although there is no well-established script for an effective mentoring relationship, the following appear to be critical factors (Sipe, 1999):

- Maintain a steady and consistent presence in the student's life.
- Take responsibility for keeping the relationship alive and realize that it will probably be one-sided.
- Involve the youth in decisions about how time will be spent and respect the youth's viewpoint.
- Recognize the youth's need for fun.
- Become acquainted with the youth's family.

Programs that follow this script have demonstrated impressive results. Grossman and Johnson (2002) report the research findings on two popular mentoring programs: Big Brothers Big Sisters (BBBS) and Philadelphia Futures' Sponsor-A-Scholar (SAS). BBBS pairs an adult volunteer with a student from a single-parent household. For at least a year, the volunteer and the student meet two to four times per month with meetings lasting two to four hours. Grossman and Johnson (2002) explain that "BBBS is not designed to ameliorate specific problems or reach specific goals, but rather to provide a youth with an adult friend who promotes general youth development objectives" (p. 8).

Whereas BBBS has general goals, SAS has rather specific goals. Its primary focus is to help disadvantaged students from Philadelphia's public schools "make it" to college. According to Grossman and Johnson: "This goal is sought through a range of support services chief among which are the provision of long-term mentoring and financial help with college-related expenses" (p. 8). Mentors work with students for five years, monitoring their academic progress in high school and helping them apply to college. Grossman and Johnson (2002) report the following outcomes when SAS participants are compared with nonparticipants: higher GPA, higher likelihood to enroll in college, and higher likelihood to persist in college.

In summary, the most direct ways for schools to enhance students' academic background knowledge are to directly provide academically oriented experiences as a regular part of school offerings and to forge mentoring relationships between students and caring adults under the assumption that such relationships will provide more academically oriented experiences. Although I support such efforts wholeheartedly, I believe that a more viable solution is to focus on indirect approaches.

Indirect Approaches: A Viable Answer

If schools had unlimited resources, then the answer to helping Delbert, Gina, and Iris would be straightforward—provide field trips and mentoring programs. These activities would go a long way toward leveling the playing field in terms of the students' academic background knowledge. But in this time of cutbacks in school resources, this solution is unlikely to prevail. So what options do schools have?

I believe that a thorough understanding of the nature of background knowledge and how it is stored in permanent memory demonstrates the usefulness of indirect approaches that schools can implement within the context of the current system and its available resources. I use the term *indirect* because the experiences to which I refer do not rely on students' physically going on trips to the museum or meeting with a mentor. Rather, indirect experiences can be fostered within the regular school day. They represent a realistic and viable approach to providing Delbert, Gina, and Iris with the academic background knowledge possessed by the other students depicted in Figure 1.3, p. 6.

This book provides the rationale for and research behind a systematic, indirect approach to enhancing students' academic background knowledge. I firmly believe that if schools were to implement the suggestions offered in this book, they would make great strides toward ensuring that all students, regardless of background, would develop the background knowledge essential for academic success. I strongly fear that if schools do not implement indirect approaches like those outlined in this book, they will continue to be a breeding ground for failure for those students who grow up in or near poverty.

2

Six Principles for Building
an Indirect Approach

This book is about schools making a profound difference in the academic background knowledge of students by using an indirect approach as defined in Chapter 1. This chapter attempts to provide a reasonably comprehensive review, in nontechnical terms, of the research and theory supporting my recommendations. Six principles form the basis of those recommendations: (1) background knowledge is stored in bimodal packets; (2) the process of storing experiences in permanent memory can be enhanced; (3) background knowledge is multidimensional and its value is contextual; (4) even surface-level background knowledge is useful; (5) background knowledge manifests itself as vocabulary knowledge; and (6) virtual experiences can enhance background knowledge.

Background Knowledge Is Stored in Bimodal Packets

One of the defining features of background knowledge is that it is stored in what can be thought of as "packets" of information. Anderson (1995) refers to these packets as "memory records." Insight into the nature of these packets or records provides clear guidance for indirect approaches to enhancing academic background knowledge.

To understand the nature of the knowledge packets that house our background knowledge, consider a student who has lived his entire life in the inner city of a large metropolitan area but goes on a camping trip for the first time in his life. The experience of the camping trip would initially be stored in the student's memory in the form of a description or narrative of what occurred. Linguists and cognitive psychologists (e.g., Kintsch, 1974, 1979; van Dijk, 1977, 1980; van Dijk

& Kintsch, 1983) explain that these narrative descriptions are stored as propositions—abstract statements of what occurred. Clark and Clark (1977) explain that there are only eight basic types of propositions:

1. I hiked. (The subject performs an action.)
2. I was happy. (The subject possesses a characteristic.)
3. I drank rainwater. (The subject performs an action on something.)
4. I slept outside. (The subject performs an action in a specific location.)
5. I gave food to the squirrels. (The subject transfers something to someone or something.)
6. Nighttime came quickly. (An action is performed or occurs in a specific manner.)
7. Someone gave me a souvenir. (Someone transfers something to the subject.)
8. The forest impressed me. (Something has an effect on the subject.)

Propositions do not exist in isolation; rather, they are organized as networks. To illustrate, Figure 2.1 shows a partial propositional network of the initial information stored by our inner-city student about the camping trip. (This figure is simplified for easy interpretation. Propositional networks constructed by linguists and psychologists are much more complex and symbolic in nature.)

Linguists explain that propositions represent our deepest level of understanding. In fact, propositions are referred to as the "deep structure" of our understanding. When we speak of our experiences, we translate our deep structure understanding into what is referred to as "surface level language" (Chomsky, 1957, 1965)—language that is actually spoken or written. To illustrate, the propositional network in Figure 2.1 is in "deep structure" form. When the student tells his friends about the camping trip, he translates his deep-structure remembrance of the trip into surface-level language: "I had a great time. We slept outside in the forest. That was amazing. And then . . ." What this tells us is that the packets containing our background knowledge are initially linguistic descriptions of what we have experienced.

Over time, our linguistic descriptions shed their connections to a particular context; instead of describing a specific event, they describe general forms of the event. Over time, our inner-city student's information about the specific camping trip will become general information about camping trips. Like the deep-structure information, this generalized information is stored as propositional networks, as depicted in Figure 2.2. (Again, the figure is simplified for easy interpretation.)

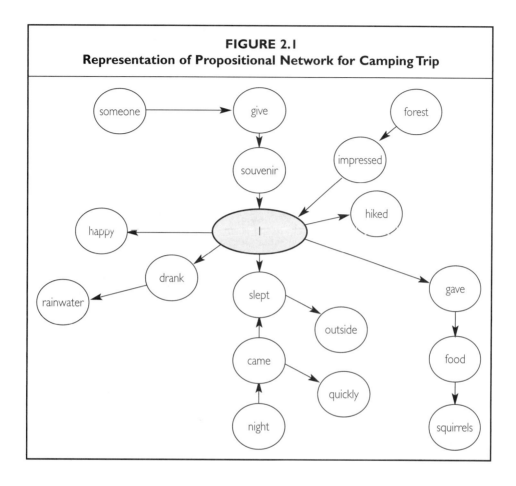

FIGURE 2.1
Representation of Propositional Network for Camping Trip

Psychologist Endel Tulving (1972) explains that the shift from propositional networks depicting a specific event to propositional networks representing decontextualized information is a shift from *episodic memory* to *semantic memory*. One characteristic of the memory packets that constitute background knowledge, then, is that they begin as specific information about specific learning episodes but become more generalized over time.

In addition to a linguistic form, our memory packets have a nonlinguistic form. In other words, our memory packets are *bimodal;* they have a linguistic mode and a nonlinguistic mode. The dualistic nature of memory packets is described in depth in the dual coding theory (DCT) of information storage as described by Paivio and Sadoski (Paivio, 1971, 1990; 1991; Sadoski, 1983, 1985; Sadoski & Paivio, 1994).

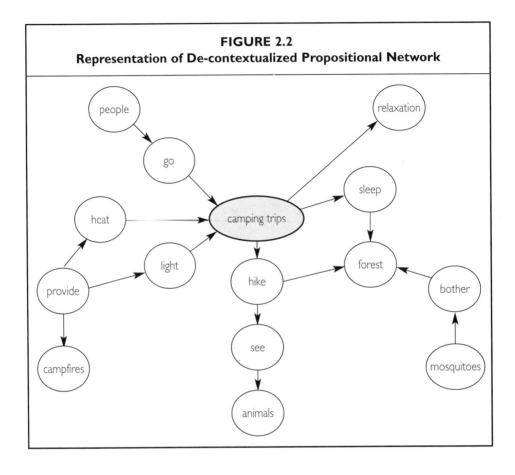

FIGURE 2.2
Representation of De-contextualized Propositional Network

A basic premise of DCT is that all mental representations retain some of the concrete, original qualities of the external experiences from which they derive. These experiences can be linguistic or nonlinguistic. Their differing characteristics develop two separate mental systems, one specialized for representing and processing language (the verbal system) and one for processing information about nonlinguistic objects and events (the nonverbal system). The latter is frequently referred to as the imagery system because its functions include the generation and analysis of mental images in various modalities derived from the senses (i.e., visual, auditory). The verbal and non-verbal systems are separate but connected and can function independently or through a network of interconnections. (Sadoski & Paivio, 1994, p. 584)

Paivio (1990) defines the linguistic and nonlinguistic aspects of DCT in terms of *logogens* and *imagens,* respectively. The term *logogen* is another name for the episodic and semantic propositional networks. Thus, in Paivio's terms, the networks depicted in figures 2.1 and 2.2 are logogens. Imagens are nonlinguistic representations that accompany the propositional networks (the logogens).

Imagens are not just mental pictures. Rather, a fully formed imagen also contains associated sounds, smells, and sensations of touch or movement. Imagens can also have associated emotions (LeDoux, 1996). The size of imagens can vary greatly, and they can be combined and recombined into larger units. To illustrate, within the imagery system, the mental image of a swimming pool can be a single imagen; but this might consist of smaller elements, such as a specific part of the pool or its surrounding area.

Now, let's go back to our inner-city student on the camping trip. We have already seen that he would store information about the trip as propositional networks. Dual coding theory tells us that he would also store images of the experience. He would have images of the first dark and quiet night by the campfire and of waking up at dawn with the sun casting long shadows over the campsite. These images would not be limited to mental pictures. They would include associated smells, tastes, sensations of touch or movement, and even emotions.

The realization that background knowledge is stored in bimodal packets with linguistic and nonlinguistic components greatly informs any attempt to indirectly enhance academic background knowledge. Specifically, such attempts should involve activities designed to enhance students' linguistic representations of the target information and their imagery of the target information.

The Process of Storing Experiences in Permanent Memory Can Be Enhanced

Let's return to the example in Chapter 1 of the two students who go to the museum. Both experience the same things, but one stores the experience in permanent memory and the other does not. The one who has stored it has added to her academic background knowledge. The one who has not stored it has not added to her academic background knowledge. This example underscores the critical importance of storing experiences in permanent memory. Namely, if academically oriented experiences are not stored in permanent memory, they are not added to academic background knowledge. How, then, does experience get into permanent memory to become a functioning aspect of background knowledge, academic or otherwise? To answer this question we must consider the nature of memory.

It is still common to think of two different types of memory—long term and short term. However, Anderson (1995) explains that the long-held distinction between short-term memory and long-term memory has been replaced with the theory that there is only one type of memory, and it has different functions. For this discussion, we will consider three functions of memory: *sensory memory, permanent memory,* and *working memory.* Figure 2.3 depicts their interaction.

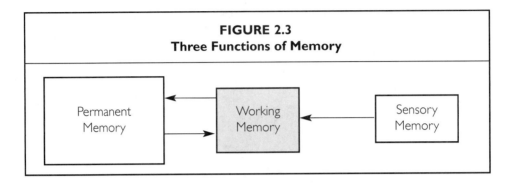

FIGURE 2.3
Three Functions of Memory

Sensory memory deals with the temporary storage of data from the senses. Anderson (1995) describes sensory memory as follows:

> Sensory memory is capable of storing more or less complete records of what has been encountered for brief periods of time, during which people can note relationships among the elements and encode the elements in a more permanent memory. If the information in sensory memory is not encoded in the brief time before it decays, it is lost. What subjects encode depends on what they are paying attention to. The environment typically offers much more information at one time than we can attend to and encode. Therefore, much of what enters our sensory system results in no permanent record. (p. 160)

Sensory memory, then, is a (very) temporary repository for information from our senses. However, we cannot process all of the information from the senses. Rather, we pick and choose.

As its name indicates, *permanent memory* contains information that has been stored in such a way that it is available to us. In simple terms, all that we know and all that we understand is stored in permanent memory. Stated in terms of the topic of this book, permanent memory is the repository of our background knowledge, academic and nonacademic. One interesting aspect of permanent memory is that the information it contains is frequently activated even without our awareness. Anderson (1983, 1990, 1995) addresses this phenomenon in his "spreading activation theory." In brief, he explains that memory packets in permanent memory are activated by any related item in working memory. To illustrate, reconsider the semantic propositional network in Figure 2.2, p. 20. Notice that it contains information about campfires, forest, mosquitoes, and so on. According to Anderson's spreading activation theory, whenever the student has an experience that involves any of this information, his memory packets for camping trips will be active, albeit below his level of consciousness. This theory explains why our sample student might walk by a grove of pine trees in a forest and subsequently remember his camping trip a year earlier. The smell of the pine trees in the forest activates any memory packets containing forests—one of which involves camping trips. Again, we are not aware of all the memory packets that are activated by the information in working memory. However, this doesn't negate the fact that they are activated. In itself, this phenomenon provides a fairly strong argument for the importance of background knowledge—once information resides in permanent memory, it is useful to us even when we are not aware of it. Students who have a great deal of background knowledge are making connections even when they are not consciously trying to do so.

Working memory is the third type of memory. As depicted in Figure 2.3, working memory can receive data from sensory memory (where it is held only briefly), from permanent memory (where it resides permanently), or from both. The amount of time data can reside in working memory has no theoretical limit. As long as we focus conscious attention on the data in working memory, it stays active (Dennett, 1991). To this extent, working memory can be considered the "seat of consciousness." That is, our experience of consciousness is actually our experience of what is being processed in working memory at any given point in time (Dennett, 1969, 1991). All things being equal, it is the quality and type of processing that occurs in working memory that dictates whether that information makes it to permanent memory. If processing goes well in working memory, information makes it to permanent memory. If processing does not go well, information does not make it to permanent memory. What, then, are the characteristics of working-memory processing that facilitate the storage of information in permanent memory?

At least three interacting dynamics of working-memory processing dictate whether information makes it into permanent memory. One is strength of the "memory trace," or the pathway to the information. As Anderson (1995) explains: "Memory records are assumed to have a property called strength, which increases with repeated practice" (p. 193). In simple terms, the more times we engage information in working memory, the higher the probability that it will be embedded in permanent memory. In educational terms, the more times a student processes information, the more likely the student will remember it. This was the basic conclusion of Nuthall (1999) when he studied what middle school students did and did not remember from science and social studies lessons. Building on the work of Rovee-Collier (1995), Nuthall found that students require about four exposures to information to adequately integrate it into their background knowledge. Nuthall also notes that these exposures should be no more than about two days apart: "We found that it took a minimum of three or four exposures with no more than a two-day gap or 'time window' (Rovee-Collier, 1995) between each one, for

[handwritten margin notes: "how to get into perman. memory"; "4X in 2 days"]

these experiences to become integrated as a new knowledge construct" (p. 305). However, sheer repetition of information in working memory is not enough to ensure that it will be stored in permanent memory. In a dramatic illustration, Neisser (1982) relates the story of a professor at Stanford who estimated that he had read specific prayers at dinner some 5,000 times over a 25-year period. However, when he tried to recall these prayers without reading them, he could not.

Depth of processing is the second aspect of effective processing in working memory. Craik and Lockhart (1972) explain depth of processing in terms of detail. Deep processing of information adds detail to our understanding of information. For example, our student is processing information about camping trips deeply if he tries to identify the defining characteristics of camping trips.

Elaboration is the third aspect of effective processing of information in working memory. Elaboration deals with the variety of associations we make with information. Although depth of processing and elaboration are related, depth of processing refers to going into more detail; elaboration, on the other hand, refers to making new or varied connections (Bradshaw & Anderson, 1982). For example, our student is elaborating on his understanding of camping trips if he associates it with sleepovers and trips to his grandmother's house.

In summary, information must make it to permanent memory to become part of our background knowledge, and the quality of processing in working memory enhances or inhibits the likelihood that information will reach permanent memory. Effective processing of information in working memory depends on certain critical activities: the information is processed multiple times, detail is added, and associations are made with other information. Consequently, any program that seeks to enhance academic background knowledge should present the target information in a way that allows it to be processed with these features of working memory in mind.

Background Knowledge Is Multidimensional and Its Value Is Contextual

Background knowledge is inherently multidimensional. An individual might have a great deal of background knowledge in one area and very little in another. Our inner-city student might have little background knowledge related to camping trips but a lot related to getting around the city on the subway. Consequently, he would have difficulty learning and integrating new information about camping trips but would find it easy to learn new information about transportation via subway systems. No general set of background knowledge helps us learn in every situation.

Even within the academic subject areas, we can have a great deal of knowledge in one area and little in another. This was demonstrated in the study by Rolfhus and Ackerman (1999) cited in Chapter 1. They administered tests of knowledge in 20 academic subject areas to 141 adults. If subject matter knowledge has a common core of knowledge, then we would expect their scores to be correlated quite highly from subject area to subject area. However, Rolfhus and Ackerman found that knowledge within the 20 subject areas was more independent than initially thought. That is, knowledge of biology did not transfer to knowledge of economics, which, in turn, did not transfer to knowledge of U.S. history. This finding is important to keep in mind for any attempt to enhance academic background knowledge—enhancement must be done subject by subject.

Even though research supports the intuitively obvious notion that a person can be knowledgeable in one subject area and not in another, many people have tried to identify that "core" body of knowledge that provides the basis for all academic learning (see Ogden, 1932; Becker, Dixon, & Anderson-Inman, 1980; Burger, 1984). Among these many efforts, that of E. D. Hirsch (1987) has been the most popular in recent years. Given its popularity, it is important to consider it in some detail. I address it briefly here and again in Chapter 6, where the Hirsch list of information is contrasted with the list provided in the Appendix of this book.

In 1987, Hirsch started a national discussion of the need for a common core of academic background knowledge with the publication of his book *Cultural Literacy: What Every American Needs to Know*. He noted:

> To be culturally literate is to possess the basic information needed to thrive in the modern world. The breadth of that information is great, extending over the major domain of human activity from sports to science. It is by no means confined to "culture" narrowly understood as an acquaintance with the arts. Nor is it confined to one social class. (p. xiii)

Hirsch's general point was well taken—that background knowledge plays a critical part in a person's ability to communicate within a culture and learn the information considered important within a culture. As an aid to the development of cultural literacy in K–12 students, Hirsch identified 4,546 terms and phrases listed in alphabetic order along with six dates. For Hirsch and his colleagues, knowledge of these terms and phrases was necessary for full participation in U.S. society. This is implied in the subtitle of his book—*What Every American Needs to Know*. The point was made explicit in one of his later works:

> Although it is true that no two humans know exactly the same things, they often have a great deal of knowledge in common. To a large extent this common knowledge or collective memory allows people to communicate, to work together, and to live

together. It forms the basis for communities, and if it is shared by enough people, it is a distinguishing characteristic of a national culture. The form and content of this common knowledge constitute one of the elements that make each national culture unique. (Hirsch, Kett, & Trefil, 1993, p. ix)

Hirsch went on to say that the academic background knowledge of students had declined dramatically in the late 20th century, and that decline was in no small part due to the failure of public education:

> The decline of American literacy and the fragmentation of the American school curriculum have been chiefly caused by the ever growing dominance of romantic formalism in educational theory during the past half century. We have too readily blamed shortcomings in American education on social changes (the disorientation of the American family or the impact of television) or incompetent teachers or structural flaws in the school systems. But the chief blame should fall on faulty theories promulgated in our schools of education and accepted by educational policymakers. (p. 110)

As popular as Hirsch's argument has become, it has some flaws and omissions. First, his basic assumption that the academic background knowledge of students has declined is questionable. Those who support this position commonly cite studies like that reported in Ravitch and Finn's 1987 book *What Do Our 17-Year-Olds Know?* Specifically, the book details the result of a 1986 National Assessment of Educational Progress (NAEP) study involving more than 7,000 17-year-old students who were given tests of their knowledge of history and literature facts. The history test included items dealing with the following facts:

1. The Underground Railroad was a secret network to help slaves escape.
2. Woodrow Wilson appealed for the U.S. entry into the League of Nations.
3. The Missouri Compromise admitted Maine as a free state and Missouri as a slave state.
4. "Reconstruction" refers to the readmission of Confederate states into the Union.

The study found that 88 percent of students correctly answered the first item, 60 percent correctly answered the second item, 43 percent correctly answered the third item, and 21 percent correctly answered the fourth item. The literature test included items dealing with facts such as the following:

1. In Greek mythology, the ruler of gods is Zeus.
2. Dickens's novel *A Tale of Two Cities* occurs during the French Revolution.
3. Walt Whitman wrote *Leaves of Grass*, which includes the line "I celebrate myself, and sing myself."
4. Henrik Ibsen wrote *Hedda Gabler, A Doll's House, An Enemy of the People.*

The study found that 87 percent of the students correctly answered the first item, 59 percent correctly answered the second item, 40 percent correctly answered the third item, and 20 percent correctly answered the fourth item.

Overall, U.S. 17-year-olds correctly answered 54.4 percent of the history items and 51.8 percent of the literature items. Ravitch and Finn (1987) described these findings in the following way:

> Observers looking for the bright side might suggest that the proverbial glass is half full rather than half empty. Another way of characterizing these results, however, is in the terms traditionally used by teachers: a score of less than 60 percent is failing. (p. 1)

It was this latter interpretation that Ravitch and Finn preferred. In fact, they portrayed the results as a form of report card on the background knowledge of U.S. students: "[I]f there were such a thing as a national report card for those studying American history and literature, then we would have to say that this nationally representative sample of eleventh grade students earns failing marks in both subjects" (p. 1). These findings were publicized widely and accepted by many as an indication that the history and literature knowledge of U.S. students had declined. However, this conclusion is based on the assumption that 17-year-olds in earlier decades would have had average scores higher than the 54.5 percent and 51.8 percent posted by the 1986 sample. Apparently, this is not the case. Whittington (1991) articulated the problems with Ravitch and Finn's conclusions as follows:

> In other words, the study provided no indication whether 17-year-olds in the mid-1980s knew any more or less than anyone else living in the United States today. Nor can the test's results tell us how much 17-year-olds of the mid-80s knew compared to 17-year-olds of the past. The study's validity rested solely on the author's judgment that (a) all the questions in their test represented basic information about history, geography, and literature; (b) all students should have been instructed in the content covered by this test and have it permanently ingrained in their memory; (c) a test of factual knowledge, while not ideal, could adequately determine what America's 17-year-olds have and have not learned about history and literature; and (d) in order to "pass" the test, students needed to answer 60 percent of its questions correctly. (p. 763)

To examine the validity of the test used by Ravitch and Finn, Whittington sought out history and social studies tests administered from 1915 to the early 1990s and equated them as closely as possible to the NAEP tests. In general, Whittington found that students in the Ravitch and Finn study were less knowledgeable than students in the past on about one-third of the items and more knowledgeable on about one-third of the items. Commenting on Whittington's findings, Berliner (1992) notes: "When compared to historical records, the data in Ravitch and

Finn's study do not support their charge that today's seventeen-year-olds know less than they ever did" (p. 19).

Another problematic aspect of Hirsch's argument is that it does not adequately acknowledge the validity and importance of other types of background knowledge that students might possess. Zahler and Zahler (1989) made this point rather humorously in their book *Test Your Countercultural Literacy,* in which they developed a list of information that makes up what they referred to as countercultural literacy. To understand Zahler and Zahler's basic point, contrast the questions in Figure 2.4 that are constructed from Hirsch's list with the questions constructed from Zahler and Zahler's list. Given that the information in Zahler and Zahler's list was not on Hirsch's 1987 list, one might ask, is it more important to know about Spiro Agnew than about Cesar Chavez? Is it more important to know about limericks than about the *I Ching?* Although presented in a tongue-in-cheek fashion, Zahler and Zahler's point is well taken—the importance of one type of knowledge over another may be simply a matter of culture, not a matter of the inherent worth of the information itself.

The research on the multidimensional nature of background knowledge and the work of Hirsch and others provide some useful guidelines and cautions for efforts to develop academic background knowledge like those described in this book. First, to develop background knowledge that will enhance success in specific academic subjects, the information critical to those specific academic areas must be the target of instruction. Second, educators must keep in mind that all

---

FIGURE 2.4
Cultural Literacy and Countercultural Literacy Items

Cultural Literacy Items	Countercultural Literacy Items
Who wrote *Macbeth?*	Who was Cesar Chavez?
What is a limerick?	What is the *I Ching* used for?
What does *nouveau riche* mean?	How did Janis Joplin die?
What is a non sequitur?	What does *macrobiotic* mean?
What is a carnivore?	What countries were in SEATO?
Who was Spiro Agnew?	Who was Timothy Leary?

Sources: The cultural literacy items are from Hirsch, 1987. The countercultural literacy items are from Zahler & Zahler, 1989.

students have background knowledge even though not all of them have the *academic* background knowledge necessary to do well in school. The background knowledge that is not germane to academic success may still be highly valuable in other contexts and, as such, should be honored along with the bearers of that knowledge.

Even Surface-Level Background Knowledge Is Useful

Probably one of the most interesting characteristics of background knowledge is that it does not have to be detailed to be useful. In fact, when we retrieve a packet of information for use in working memory, we initially access its surface-level characteristics only. This was demonstrated in an early experiment by Collins and Quillian (1969), who posited that an individual's knowledge of a given topic is organized in a hierarchy. The top-level knowledge for the word *canary* might include the fact that a canary is yellow and frequently sings. At the next level down, the information might include more general characteristics associated with all birds, such as, it has wings, it can fly, and it has feathers. At an even more general level, the information would include characteristics associated with all animals, such as, it has skin, it eats, and it breathes.

If it is true that information closest to the top of the hierarchy is the most available, then we should remember the top-level information more quickly than the bottom-level information. Collins and Quillian tested this hypothesis by providing subjects with sentences such as the following: "Canaries are yellow." "Canaries can fly." "Canaries breathe." Subjects were asked to determine whether the information in the sentence was true or false. Time taken to validate the accuracy of a sentence was considered an indication of the information's place within the hierarchy. As the researchers had predicted, subjects took less time to validate sentences such as "Canaries are yellow" than they did to validate sentences such as "Canaries can breathe." The study's finding supported the hierarchic hypothesis. Similar findings have been reported by other researchers (Quillian, 1967, 1968; Wilkins, 1971; Just & Carpenter, 1987; Jenkins, Stein, & Wysocki, 1984; Sticht, Hofstetter, & Hofstetter, 1997).

The notion that background knowledge exists at different levels is also strongly supported by the research on vocabulary understanding (Graves, 1984; McKeown & Beck, 1988). Several vocabulary researchers have developed taxonomies of vocabulary understanding. Dale (1965) proposed four stages of knowing a word. Stahl (1985, 1986) and Kame'enui, Dixon, and Carnine (1987) have developed similar taxonomies. Combining these efforts creates a rough description of levels of background knowledge. To illustrate, consider our inner-city student's background knowledge before he went on the camping trip. At the lowest level of background knowledge, our student would have never heard of a camping trip or, at least, would not be able to recall having heard of one. At a level up from this, our student would have heard of the term *camping trip* and have a basic idea of what it entails. At a level higher, he would have an understanding of the key elements of a camping trip. This does not mean that the student has necessarily gone on a camping trip. He might only have heard about camping trips from his friends or have seen movies about camping trips. However, these virtual experiences were stored in permanent memory. At the highest level of background knowledge, our student would know the information at a general or abstract level. The information would have been converted from episodic memory to semantic memory. His knowledge of camping trips would have expanded beyond a specific, direct, or imagined experience to an understanding of the general concept of camping trips.

These levels are not intended as a rigorous categorization scheme for background knowledge. However, they do inform this discussion in that the second level appears to be sufficient for background knowledge to be useful—students must be familiar with the terminology of a given topic and have some general idea as to the terms' meanings. Even this low-level understanding will greatly aid students' comprehension and learning. This phenomenon also occurs with adults. For example, many adults understand the concept of a statistical correlation only at a surface level. They aren't aware that its value ranges from −1.00 to +1.00 or that the size of a correlation tells you little about its significance. However, they have a general sense that a correlation means that as one thing goes up something else goes up (or down). This surface-level understanding, even if it is somewhat inaccurate, still helps them understand reports and discussions that use the term *correlation*.

The fact that even surface-level background knowledge is useful greatly increases the viability of a program that seeks to enhance students' academic background knowledge. The goal of such programs need not be deep conceptual understanding of the target information. Such a goal would require massive resources and time. Rather, the goal should be to develop a surface-level understanding of the target information.

Background Knowledge Manifests Itself as Vocabulary Knowledge

The strong relationship between vocabulary knowledge and background knowledge is implicit in much of the previous discussion. Our inner-city student who went on the camping trip no doubt came back with new knowledge packets and

SES = socioeconomic status

new terms to represent those knowledge packets (e.g., campfire, lean-to, douse a fire). The relationship between vocabulary and background knowledge is also explicit in the research. For example, a great deal of research indicates that vocabulary knowledge is highly correlated with family income or socioeconomic status (SES), which, as we have seen, is highly correlated with background knowledge. Nagy and Herman (1984) found a consistent difference in vocabulary knowledge between students at different levels of family income. They estimated a 4,700-word difference in vocabulary knowledge between high- and low-SES students. Similarly, they estimated that mid-SES 1st graders know about 50 percent more words than do low-SES 1st graders. Graves and Slater (1987) found that 1st graders from higher-income backgrounds had about double the vocabulary size of those from lower-income backgrounds.

4,700 word diff !

Hart and Risley (1995) found that the differences in vocabulary development due to family status start at a very early age. They computed the correlation between vocabulary knowledge and family income to be .65 (p. 168). To interpret this correlation, consider a student who comes from a family that is at the 50th percentile in income. Also assume that the student is at the 50th percentile in vocabulary development. A correlation of .65 implies that an increase in the student's family income of one standard deviation would be associated with an increase of 24 percentile points in the student's vocabulary development. That is, if we could change the student's family income from the 50th percentile to the 84th for the rest of the student's life, we would expect the student's vocabulary knowledge to move from the 50th to the 74th percentile (see Technical Note 2 on pp. 127–130 for a more detailed discussion).

Hart and Risley also computed the differences in vocabulary development in children from 10 to 36 months old in welfare families, working-class families, and professional families. They found 36-month-old children from welfare families have about 70 percent of the vocabulary of children from working-class families and only about 45 percent of the vocabulary of children from professional families. What is even more disturbing is the differential rates of vocabulary development in children from the three types of families. This means that the differences in vocabulary knowledge will be even greater as the children grow older. As Hart and Risley note: "We saw a widening gap beginning as early as age 24 months" (p. 234).

The relationship between vocabulary knowledge and academic achievement is also well established. As early as 1941, researchers estimated that for students in grades 4 through 12, a 6,000-word gap separated students at the 25th and 50th percentiles on standardized tests (see Nagy & Herman, 1984). Using a more advanced method of calculating vocabulary size, Nagy and Herman estimated the difference to be anywhere from 4,500 to 5,400 words for low- versus high-achieving students.

Finally, researchers have also shown that vocabulary and intelligence are highly correlated. Anderson and Freebody (1981) note: "The strong relationship between vocabulary and general intelligence is one of the most robust findings in the history of intelligence testing" (p. 77). Jenkins, Stein, and Wysocki (1984) explain that "vocabulary knowledge is one of the best predictors of overall verbal intelligence, yielding correlations in the neighborhood of .80" (p. 767). To illustrate, consider Figure 2.5, which reports correlations between vocabulary knowledge and intelligence from some landmark studies. Given that the upper limit of a correlation is 1.00, those reported in Figure 2.5 are quite high.

Clearly, vocabulary knowledge has a strong, documented relationship with a variety of factors that have been shown to be related to background knowledge—family income or SES, academic achievement, and intelligence. A logical question is, why? An examination of the nature of vocabulary terms provides the answer.

What Is a Word?

When we hear or read a word, we reference the meaning of the word stored in permanent memory. Stated in terms of the previous discussion, a word is the label associated with a packet of knowledge stored in permanent memory. For example,

FIGURE 2.5
Reports of Correlations Between Vocabulary and Intelligence in Various Studies

Study	Correlation
Terman (1918)	.91
Mahan & Whitmer (1936)	.87
Spache (1943)	.92
Elwood (1939)	.98
McNemar (1942)	.86
Lewinski (1948)	.82
Wechsler (1949)	.78
Raven (1948)	.93

a word = representation of a packet of knowledge

when we read or hear the word *cat,* we reference our stored packet of knowledge regarding cats. Interestingly, no inherent reason explains why a given word relates to a given packet of knowledge. As Drum and Konopak (1987) explain:

> A word, an acoustic configuration of speech sounds and a written rendition (more or less) of these sounds, comes or is assigned to refer to things, events, and ideas arbitrarily. There is no inherent connection between a word and its referent; a "tree" could be called a "drink" and vice versa. (p. 73)

The actual words we know, then, are tags or labels for our packets of knowledge. Thus it makes intuitive sense that the more words we have, the more packets of knowledge, and, hence, the more background knowledge we have. The understanding that a word is the representation for a packet of knowledge enhances our understanding of vocabulary and greatly expands its usefulness. In fact, from this perspective it becomes evident that the traditional conception of vocabulary has been artificially limited in its scope. To illustrate, consider the study by Nagy and Anderson (1984), who examined the vocabulary found in "printed school English"—those vocabulary items students encounter in the material commonly read in grades 3 through 9. They excluded from their count derivative forms such as regular and irregular plurals, regular and irregular inflected forms, and regular and irregular comparisons and superlatives. This makes good sense. All of these forms relate to the same basic packet of knowledge. We might conclude, then, that vocabulary researchers and theorists have rightfully excluded, as vocabulary terms, items that refer to the same basic packet of knowledge but vary in their form. However, Nagy and Anderson also excluded proper names in their word count. Thus, using the Nagy and Anderson criteria, *runner* would be considered a vocabulary term, but *Carl Lewis* would not. This is a common convention in vocabulary research, and it seems to be consistent with Vygotsky's (1962) notion that a word is a label for a class of knowledge packets as opposed to a single packet: "A word does not refer to a single object, but to a group or to a class of objects. Each word is therefore already a generalization" (p. 6). Whereas the word *runner* refers to a variety of packets, the term *Carl Lewis* applies to only one—that stored knowledge about a particular individual.

Nagy and Anderson are vocabulary researchers. Psychologists and linguists also distinguish between terms that apply to single packets of knowledge versus classes of packets. Just and Carpenter (1987) explain that terms that refer to a single element are called *singular terms,* whereas those that refer to a class of elements are called *general terms* (p. 199). *General terms* have a one-to-one relationship with *concepts* in that *concepts* are generally thought to encompass classes of elements (Turner & Greene, 1977). Using this terminology, we might conclude that vocabulary instruction has traditionally been limited to *general* as opposed to *singular* terms because the former are more conceptual in nature.

Although the exclusion of terms with singular referents might be defensible from a research perspective, it does not make sense from the perspective of understanding the relationship between vocabulary and background knowledge. In fact, from the perspective of background knowledge, it makes better sense to treat singular and general terms the same way. To illustrate, a good deal of evidence indicates that individuals naturally tend to think of specific referents even for general terms (Anderson & McGaw, 1973; Rosch, 1975; Smith & Medin, 1981). That is, we seem to treat all terms as singular from the perspective of processing in working memory. Thus, when we hear the word *bird*, we tend to think in terms of a specific type of bird (for example, a robin) or a stylized prototype of a bird as opposed to the general characteristics associated with the concept *bird*. Unless the surrounding context specifically directs us, we think of a specific type of bird or stylized prototype when reading or hearing a sentence such as "The bird landed on the ground."

This phenomenon is important to understanding the relationship between vocabulary knowledge and background knowledge. In terms of background knowledge, there is little distinction between the words *runner* and *Carl Lewis,* or between the words *state* and *Colorado.* The mind of the learner treats proper nouns that apply to singular elements the same as common nouns that apply to sets of elements. Interestingly, even though they excluded proper nouns in their count of words in printed school English, Nagy and Anderson (1984) acknowledged the importance of teaching proper nouns:

> One could argue, however, that there is at least a subset of proper names that should be counted as part of a general vocabulary. . . . Lack of knowledge of familiar geographical names such as *Washington, Florida, Alaska* or *Panama,* for example, could contribute to comprehension failure in exactly the same way that ignorance of the meaning of other words in the text might. (p. 316)

This perspective on how the mind understands vocabulary items also expands the notion of vocabulary terms made up of more than one word. That is, the process we use to access the referents of some word combinations appears to be the same as the process we use to access the referents of single words (Just & Carpenter, 1987; Potter & Faulconer, 1979). This is the case with word combinations that are so common that they function as a single unit. Some word combinations become compounds with repeated use (*heartbeat, landslide*). Others do not. However, even when word combinations are not expressed as compounds, many function as single units in terms of reference (*drummer boy, food poisoning, killer shark*).

Linguists have identified various types of these word combinations, including subject and verb combinations (*bee sting*) and verb and object combinations (*book review*) (see Quirk, Greenbaum, Leech, & Svartvik, 1972).

Understanding the relationship between vocabulary and background knowledge provides a useful perspective on programs that seek to enhance academic background knowledge. Specifically, the research and theory strongly suggest that teaching vocabulary is synonymous with teaching background knowledge. The packets of information that constitute our background knowledge all have labels associated with them. This is true for singular terms, general terms, and even commonly used phrases. Thus, teaching background knowledge about whales, killer whales, and Shamu the killer whale all can be approached from a vocabulary perspective.

background knowledge = vocab knowl.

Virtual Experiences Can Enhance Background Knowledge

As discussed in Chapter 1, direct experience is the most straightforward way to enhance academic background knowledge. However, schools are limited in the quality and quantity of direct experience they can provide for students. Fortunately, virtual experiences can be as powerful as direct experiences in enhancing background knowledge.

To understand the concept of a virtual experience, consider again the three types of memory—sensory, working, and permanent—and their interactions. When we have a direct experience like going on a camping trip, our sensory memory records the sights, sounds, tastes, smells, and kinesthetic sensations we experience. As we have seen, sensory memory lasts only a few moments. To be processed and subsequently stored in permanent memory, information from sensory memory must be translated into working memory. In working memory, information is a selective *representation* of what we are experiencing through the senses; it is not a direct analog of what we experience through our senses.

From this understanding we might conclude that we are frequently one step removed from sensory experiences. As we move about the forest on our camping trip, we experience it as much in working memory as we do in sensory memory. We view the scene around us, but then we "think about" what we have directly experienced through our senses. When we are thinking about what we are experiencing, we are attending not to the forest around us but to our representation of the forest in working memory. This is one of the great paradoxes of human experience. We experience the world around us far more indirectly than we might expect (Dennett, 1969, 1991). The fact that we experience much of life through working memory opens the door to alternative ways of generating background experiences. Anything that creates representations in working memory is a potential source of background knowledge. What, then, are some ways that we can generate academically oriented experiences virtually in working memory even if they are not experienced directly? Here we consider three.

Reading as a Form of Virtual Experience

Reading is one of the most straightforward ways to generate virtual experiences. When we read about a camping trip, as opposed to directly experiencing one, our sensory memory is filled with images of the words on the page. However, based on our understanding of these words and the conventions of the written language (all of which are stored in permanent memory), we create a virtual representation of the camping trip in working memory. In working memory, the virtual experience of the camping trip is for all practical purposes the same as the direct experience.

Reading, then, can be a powerful way to generate virtual experiences. Even though these experiences might not be as robust as direct experiences, they will suffice to significantly increase background knowledge. Indeed, many adults who do not have the resources to travel extensively know a great deal about other countries because they read about them. Although it is a cliché, it is accurate to think of reading as a "magic carpet" to new places and experiences that are otherwise out of our reach. Although all students do not have the opportunity to go to Africa to see elephants meandering across the Serengeti, all students do have the opportunity to read about them. Although all students do not have the opportunity to visit the NASA space center in Houston, Texas, all students do have the opportunity to read about it. In short, reading provides the promise of every student's having a rich array of virtual experiences. As explained by Galda and Cullinan (2003), reading provides

> windows on other worlds and experiences, windows that become virtual experiences as we read. These virtual experiences are then added to children's knowledge of the world. This increase in knowledge, in turn, increases the possibilities for responding to the world. . . . Reading extensively . . . increases [students'] . . . storehouse of experiences. (p. 642)

Although reading offers the promise of providing all students with a rich array of virtual experiences, there is, unfortunately, a great discrepancy in the amount of reading students do. This strong differential is probably due largely to the relationship between the amount of reading one does and one's skill at reading. A great deal of research supports this position.

Stanovich (1986) has discussed in detail how skill at reading is both a cause and a consequence of voluminous reading. The more children read, the more skilled they become at reading; this, in turn, makes reading easier and consequently increases the chances that they will read more. In his studies of 1st graders, Allington (1984) found that the total number of words read during a week of school reading sessions ranged from a low of 16 for one child who was classified as a poor reader to a high of 1,933 for a child classified as a good reader. Commenting on these findings, Stanovich (1986) notes: "The average skilled reader reads approximately three times as many words in the group reading sessions as the average less skilled reader" (p. 380). Similarly, Nagy and Anderson (1984) estimate that

> the less motivated children in the middle grades might read 100,000 words per year while the average children at this level might read 1,000,000. The figure for the voracious middle grade reader might be 10,000,000 or even as high as 50,000,000. If these guesses are anywhere near the mark, there are staggering individual differences in the volume of language experience, and, therefore, opportunity to learn new words. (p. 328)

wow!

Anderson, Wilson, and Fielding (1986) studied the reading of 5th grade students outside of school and came to slightly different conclusions. They estimated that students read an average of 650,000 words of text per year. The avid reader, however, encounters 5.85 million words per year. More pointedly, they noted that students at the 90th percentile in terms of the volume of their reading encounter 200 times more words than students at the 10th percentile.

Not surprising, the differences in students' exposure to reading has a documented impact on the development of their background knowledge. Stanovich and Cunningham (1993), in a study involving 268 college students, examined the relationship between exposure to print and a number of factors, including general knowledge—what I am referring to as background knowledge. They computed the correlation between reading and background knowledge to be .61. This means that an increase of one standard deviation in reading or exposure to print information is associated with an increase of 23 percentile points in background knowledge (see Technical Note 2 on pp. 127–129). What is most interesting about this correlation is that it was computed after controlling for GPA, general intelligence, math ability, reading comprehension, and exposure to television. That is, the 23-point increase is what would be expected if all the subjects were equal in terms of all these other factors.

The research on sustained silent reading (SSR) programs also supports the positive impact reading can have on background knowledge. Pilgreen (2000) undertook a comprehensive review of the research on SSR programs. She explains that SSR programs have been in existence since the 1950s under a variety of names: Free Voluntary Reading (FVR), Uninterrupted Sustained Silent Reading (USSR), Sustained Quiet Reading Time (SQUIRT), Drop Everything and Read (DEAR), High Intensity Practice (HIP), Positive Outcomes While Enjoying Reading (POWER), and Fun Reading Every Day (FRED), among others. According to Pilgreen, the research on the impact of SSR programs on student learning is compelling. Pilgreen was able to identify 32 studies on the impact of SSR. She explains:

> Within the thirty-two studies, there were forty-one experimental groups that were engaged in free reading programs. Of these, ten were successful in attaining statistically significant results in reading comprehension; seven were successful in attaining statistically significant results in reading motivation; and fifteen were successful in attaining "observable" growth in reading motivation—that is, improvement which could be quantified but not interpreted through the use of inferential statistics. . . . For each experimental group that reached statistical significance, a comparable control group operated; in the case of the groups that made only observable growth, there were no control groups. Interestingly, in the cases where the experimental groups did not do significantly better than the control groups, they did just as well, with the exception of two groups. (pp. 5–6)

Given Pilgreen's description of the search methods used to identify the studies she reviewed, we can reasonably assume that they represent a fairly exhaustive list of the studies conducted on the topic. When the results of these studies (as reported by Pilgreen) are subjected to meta-analysis techniques as described by Bushman (1994), they indicate that SSR has an estimated effect size of .40 on student comprehension. (For an explanation of how this estimate was computed, see Technical Note 4 on pp. 130–131.) To understand the interpretation of this effect size, consider two students, A and B, who are both at the 50th percentile in their comprehension ability. However, student A is placed in an SSR program and student B is not. At the end of the SSR program, student A will be at the 66th percentile in terms of comprehension ability, but student B will still be at the 50th percentile. (For a discussion of how effect sizes are interpreted, see Technical Note 5 on p. 131.)

Krashen (2000) has also analyzed the research on SSR. He summarizes the findings as follows:

> There is overwhelming evidence that free voluntary reading makes a powerful contribution to language and literacy development, and that it helps developing readers beyond the very beginning level improve: It is good for children, teenagers, and first and second language acquirers. . . . It has been shown to work all over the world, including in the United States . . . in England . . . in Japan . . . in the Fiji Islands . . . in Ireland . . . in Singapore . . . and Hong Kong. . . . (p. vii)

In summary, although schools might not have the resources to provide direct experiences for students, they do have the resources to engage students in prolonged reading activities through programs like SSR. Reading, however, is not the only way to generate virtual experiences.

Language Interaction as a Form of Virtual Experience

Just as reading generates virtual experiences in working memory, so, too, can language interaction—talking and listening to others. When we describe our camping trip to a friend, that friend translates our words into working memory representations. The more we talk to our friend about our camping trip, the more our friend's background knowledge of camping trips expands. Stated in general terms, the more students talk and listen to others, the more virtual experiences are generated.

Unfortunately, there are great discrepancies in the amount of language experience students from different backgrounds have. Additionally, these differences start at an early age. To illustrate, consider again the study by Hart and Risley (1995). Recall that they conducted in-depth observations of 42 families for two and a half years. They found that by the time children in welfare homes are 1 year old, they have only about 50 percent of the language experience of children from working-class families and only about 30 percent of the language experience of children from professional families. The situation gets worse as children get older. As described by Hart and Risley, in four years the average child in a professional family would

> have accumulated experience with almost 45 million words, an average child in a working-class family would have accumulated experience with 26 million words, and an average child in a welfare family would have accumulated 13 million words. By the age of 4, the average child in a welfare family might have 13 million fewer words of cumulative experience than the average child in a working-class family. (pp. 197–198)

Hart and Risley further explain that "to keep the language experience of welfare children equal to that of working-class children, the welfare children would need to receive 63,000 words per week of additional language experience" (p. 201).

Given these discrepancies in language experience, it is hard to imagine closing the gap between children from welfare families and those from other families without schools overtly stimulating language interactions. Consequently, an indirect approach designed to enhance academic background knowledge of students would place great emphasis on language interaction.

Educational Television as a Form of Virtual Experience

Educational television is a third form of virtual experience. An interesting secondary finding in the Stanovich and Cunningham (1993) study discussed earlier was that television viewing seemed to add nothing to the development of background knowledge once the findings were controlled for GPA, general intelligence, math ability, and reading comprehension. This finding suggests that television might not be the great equalizer of exposure to experiences, as some have hypothesized (see Stanovich and Cunningham, 1993, for a discussion). However, a follow-up study by Hall, Chiarello, and Edmonson (1996) found that the type of television viewed moderates the relationship with background knowledge. Specifically, there was no relationship between watching general television programs designed primarily for entertainment and the development of background knowledge. However, watching educational television significantly enhanced the development of such knowledge. Hall and colleagues found that watching educational television had a correlation of .45 with background knowledge. This indicates that an increase of one standard deviation in watching educational television is associated with an increase of 17 percentile points in background knowledge (see Technical Note 2 on pp. 127–130).

The Hall, Chiarello, and Edmondson study is quite consistent with a study conducted in 1947 by Hall and Cushing. It found that watching a movie on a topic had the same effect on students as listening to a lecture or reading about the topic. These findings greatly expand the possibilities for schools that want to generate virtual experiences. In addition to reading and language experience, schools might use educational television or programs that have been recorded on DVDs or videotapes. Schools, then, have a wide variety of options for generating virtual experiences to build academic background knowledge.

Summary

Six research-based principles underlie many of the recommendations made in this book. The six principles suggest an approach for enhancing student background knowledge even without enhanced direct experience. This is not to say that direct experiences such as field trips and mentoring relationships should be avoided. Indeed, the more of them the better. However, schools are limited in their ability to make such offerings. They can, however, offer a comprehensive set of indirect approaches. Such approaches would have the following characteristics:

• They would have the goal of installing background knowledge in permanent memory.

• To facilitate the storage of information in permanent memory, they would ensure that students have multiple exposures to the target information.

• They would focus on the development of surface-level but accurate knowledge across a broad spectrum of subject areas.

• The instructional techniques they use would focus on the linguistic and nonlinguistic aspects of background knowledge.

• They would focus on developing labels for packets of experiential knowledge in the tradition of direct vocabulary instruction.

• They would rely on the generation of virtual experiences in working memory through wide reading, language interaction, and educational visual media.

3

Tapping the Power of Wide Reading and Language Experience

In Chapter 2 we noted that reading accompanied by language interaction (talking and listening to others) may compensate for the lack of direct experiences by providing a variety of virtual experiences. We also discovered that students from different environments vary widely in the amount of reading they do and the amount of language they experience. This chapter describes an approach to adapting sustained silent reading (SSR) so that it enhances the academic background knowledge of students through extensive reading and language interaction.

Sustained Silent Reading

As described in Chapter 2, SSR programs have a proven track record of enhancing students' knowledge and skills. To be effective, however, the SSR program must have specific characteristics. One of those characteristics is that it must be continuous over many years. To illustrate, Krashen (2000) organized the studies in SSR into three categories based on how long the programs were in place: less than seven months, seven months to one year, and more than one year. Again, I used meta-analytic techniques described by Bushman (1994) to analyze these data (for an explanation of the process used, see Technical Note 4 on pp. 130–131). When I analyzed the impact of SSR programs that were used for less than seven months or for seven months to one year, I found no significant effect. In other words, statistically there was no difference between the students who went through SSR programs and those who did not in terms of their comprehension ability. For the studies in which SSR was used for more than a year, however, the estimated effect size was .87. To interpret this, consider two students who are both at the 50th percentile in terms of their comprehension ability. (For a more detailed discussion of how to interpret an effect size, see Technical Note 5 on p. 131.) One student is placed in an SSR program that lasts for more than a year and the other student is not. At the end of that period, the student who has gone through the extended SSR program will be at the 81st percentile and the student who did not will remain at the 50th percentile.

Based on these findings, I recommend that an SSR program used to enhance academic background knowledge be continuous over many years. Why? My emphasis is on building academic background knowledge, which is, by definition, a cumulative process. Students who have grown up in economically disadvantaged backgrounds have not had the many opportunities other students have had to accumulate critical academic background knowledge. Righting this situation will not happen in a year or two. Indeed, past efforts to help such students have demonstrated that interventions lasting only a year or two might provide initial gains in student learning, but these gains fade when the programs cease. For example, speaking of the efforts in the early 1960s to wage a "War on Poverty," Hart and Risley (1995) explain that it was not enough to remove barriers and to offer early intervention programs for children in poverty before they entered formal schooling (p. 15). Given the disparity in oral language and reading experiences between students from families with differing financial resources, compensatory programs must be sustained and intense and must span many school years. I recommend that a modified SSR program as described in this chapter be implemented through grade 10. Such a program should also conform to the eight factors identified by Pilgreen (2000): access, appeal, conducive environment, encouragement, staff training, nonaccountability, follow-up activities, and distributed time to read.

Access refers to the ease with which students acquire reading materials. Pilgreen defines access as follows: "trade books, comics, newspapers, and other reading materials [are] provided directly to the students in a variety of ways instead of requiring the students to bring something from home to read" (p. 8). To provide adequate access, SSR classrooms commonly have a large stock of books. For example, Pilgreen notes that in the studies she reviewed, some schools checked out books from local libraries and housed them in the classroom during the time students were initially selecting books. In other studies, students had opportunities to visit the school library and local libraries. When access to school and local libraries was not sufficient, students received help acquiring books through interlibrary loans. Pilgreen further explains that the key to providing access in all of the successful SSR programs was that the burden did not fall on the students to locate their own reading materials outside school. The teachers ensured that all students found something suitable to read.

Appeal means that students are free and encouraged to read information that they find highly interesting. This factor is not as straightforward as it seems. In addition to being interesting to students, the selected books should be at appropriate levels of reading difficulty. As Pilgreen explains:

> The goal is to be sure that everyone has access to materials that they not only want to read—but **can** [emphasis in original] read. Materials that will pique everyone's interests must be available so that the least proficient to the most proficient readers in the classroom can enthusiastically engage in free reading. (p. 9)

Conducive environment refers to the atmosphere provided for reading. Ideally, it is relaxed and comfortable because this is a natural characteristic of personal reading. As Pilgreen explains: "Whenever we find something good to read, it is logical that we are drawn to comfortable, quiet places. . . ." (p. 10). In SSR classrooms, teachers commonly arrange the classroom to make it more like the typical environment for personal reading—for example, by placing a comfortable chair or couch in one corner of the room. Other teachers may allow students to go to some area of the school that has comfortable seats. Pilgreen notes that even when students simply sit in their regular seats they should be protected from noise and interruptions.

Encouragement refers to providing students with positive feedback regarding their topic selection and their involvement in the reading process. This commonly occurs in three ways. First, the teacher demonstrates interest in what students are reading; for example, by asking students questions about what they have read or providing students with supplemental information or resources. Teachers also provide encouragement by being excited about their own personal reading. Teacher enthusiasm is highly contagious. Finally, teachers provide encouragement by allowing students to share what they have read with their peers. In fact, according to Pilgreen, researchers in the successful programs mentioned the importance of peer interaction as a way of legitimizing the SSR process for students. Seeing their peers enthusiastic about reading made it safe for students to be personally excited.

Staff training involves providing information and training that engage all members of a school's staff in the success of an SSR program. Pilgreen identifies some of the unsuccessful SSR programs as those that did not adequately explain the purposes of their SSR program and enlist the support of all staff members—not just those who were enthusiastic about the program from the outset. Programs do not fare well if they simply set aside time for students to read but do not take time to ensure that teachers learn about the philosophy underlying SSR and the mechanics of a well-functioning program.

Nonaccountability is a critical factor in the success of an SSR program, Pilgreen believes. In fact, she makes the case that violating this factor can totally subvert the positive impact of an SSR program. In discussing those SSR programs she found successful, she notes:

> The key to non-accountability, as indicated by these successful groups, is to omit any activity that gives students the message that they are responsible for completing a task, comprehending a particular portion of their reading, or showing they have made improvement in some way. In order to get the most enjoyment possible from their reading, they should feel no obligation associated with it. (p. 15)

By definition, then, nonaccountability rules out testing students' knowledge of what they have read. However, it does not rule out activities that ask students to interact with the text and with one another in complex ways. In the context of SSR, such activities are referred to as *follow-up activities.*

Follow-up activities are those that allow and encourage students to interact about the information they have read. This might involve students' interacting with one another or with the information they have read in some personal way. At first blush, this factor looks like it conflicts with the factor of nonaccountability. It is true that follow-up activities include some activities that might be used to hold students accountable, such as answering questions about the information and reviewing the information. The distinguishing feature is that these activities are *recommended,* not *required.* Additionally, the purpose of follow-up activities is to help students better understand and interact with the information they have read, not to test their knowledge or track their performance.

Distributed time to read involves systematically and frequently providing students with SSR time. Pilgreen explains:

> In fact, it wasn't the range of time that varied so much as the frequency with which free reading time was provided. In ninety-seven percent of the successful programs, the researchers offered free reading time to the students at least twice per week. This frequency pattern became the yardstick for what I called the "distributed time programs." And, more than half of these programs offered SSR on a daily basis. I noticed that students were sometimes given time to read for longer stretches of time, but on a monthly, bi-monthly, weekly, or bi-weekly basis, so I characterized these cases as "massed time to read"—or "all at once" programs. (p. 18)

From Pilgreen's comments we can conclude that SSR time should be provided at least twice per week. Other discussions of SSR programs (National Institute of Child Health and Human Development, 2000; Holt & O'Tuel, 1989; Pilgreen & Krashen, 1993) typically recommend a 20- to 30-minute SSR period.

A Five-Step Process

The eight principles identified by Pilgreen coupled with the principles discussed in Chapter 2 can be accommodated in a simple five-step process. As mentioned previously, I recommend using this process through grade 10 to enhance students' academic background knowledge. As explained in Chapter 4, I also recommend that a program of *direct vocabulary instruction* be implemented through grade 10. These two interventions working in tandem would constitute a comprehensive, indirect approach to enhancing student academic background knowledge. (Chapters 4 through 7 address the direct vocabulary instruction program in depth.)

In keeping with Pilgreen's principles of staff training, staff members should thoroughly understand and agree to the five steps presented here before an SSR program is implemented. I recommend that teachers in a school investigate the nature and purpose of SSR programs before adopting one. To this end, Pilgreen's text, *The SSR Handbook* (2000), is a valuable source. If and when all teachers agree to support SSR, then the following five steps can be implemented.

Step 1: Students Identify Topics of Interest to Them

Appeal is one of the factors Pilgreen identified as critical to the success of an SSR program. For Pilgreen, appeal involves ensuring that each student reads something of interest that is at an appropriate level of difficulty. The first step is designed to address this factor, but also to access even deeper levels of motivation in students—levels that are apparently elicited by Macrorie's I-Search process.

More than a decade and a half ago, Macrorie (1988) articulated a remarkably simple but powerful idea for inspiring students to seek out and use new information. He referred to this idea as the I-Search process:

> Teachers around the country and I have been challenging students to do what we call I-Searches—not Re-Searches, in which the job is to search again what someone has already searched—but original searches in which persons scratch an itch they feel, one so marvelously itchy that they begin rubbing a finger tip against it and the rubbing feels so good that they dig in with a fingernail. A search to fulfill a need, not that the teacher has imagined for them but one they feel themselves. (p. 14)

In its basic form, the I-Search process involves students' gathering of information about a topic of great interest to them, synthesizing and organizing this information, and then using it to write a paper that follows the established conventions of writing (e.g., conventions related to spelling, grammar, or footnoting). Since its inception, the I-Search process has been adapted in a variety of ways. For example, Zorfass (1991) recommends a seemingly small but powerful adaptation of the

I-Search process. Instead of a research paper, students may create a variety of end products, including a skit, an oral report, a poster, an experiment, or some other display of knowledge. Based on this simple idea of starting with student interests, Macrorie (1988) has documented impressive growth in students' writing abilities. The most probable explanation for such success is that Macrorie's processes tap into students' *self-systems.*

Psychologists explain that the self-system is a system of thought used by all human beings. By definition, it contains a network of interrelated goals (Markus & Ruvolo, 1990; Harter, 1980, 1999) that help us decide how much energy we will put into a new task. For all practical purposes, the self-system is the center-piece of human motivation. As Csikszentmihalyi (1990) explains:

> The self is no ordinary piece of information. . . . In fact it contains [almost] everything that passes through consciousness: all the memories, actions, desires, pleasures, and pains are included in it. And more than anything else, the self represents the hierar-chy of goals that we have built up, bit by bit over the years. . . . At any given time we are usually aware of only a tiny part of it. . . . (p. 34)

A critical feature of the self-system is that it houses our deep-seated needs and aspirations organized in a somewhat hierarchical structure. This structure pro-vides insight into student motivation.

The notion of a hierarchical structure of goals was first popularized by Maslow (1968, 1971). He proposed five levels of human needs and aspirations:

1. Basic needs that include food and water
2. The need for personal safety
3. Social needs, including the need to belong
4. Esteem needs, including feelings of self-respect and the respect of others
5. Self-actualization, or the need for a sense of personal fulfillment

Although some have criticized Maslow's hierarchy (Wahba & Bridwell, 1976), it still provides us with powerful insights into the nature of human motivation. As Covington (1992) explains, "it provides a useful way of thinking about the factors that activate human beings" (p. 19). Specifically, Maslow's work suggests that we harbor aspirations that in some way define us as whole human beings. These aspi-rations seemingly differ from individual to individual. Whereas one person might aspire to some noteworthy physical accomplishment such as running a marathon, another might aspire to a significant intellectual accomplishment, and yet another might aspire to develop a new product.

The first step in the five-step process taps into this level of motivation in stu-dents. Consequently, this step emphasizes identifying topics in which students are intensely interested. This differs from some SSR programs, in which the availability of books limits student choice. That is, as described previously, in many SSR programs, the books are gathered first and then students select from among them. In this approach, student interest is the initial focus, unconstrained by the books that have been collected.

The following vignettes depict how this first step might play out at three levels: elementary school, middle school and junior high school, and high school.

❖ Elementary School

Classes are self-contained at Stevens Elementary School, so, except for a few special classes like art and physical education, a teacher has a single class for an entire day. Like all the other teachers at Stevens, during the first week of school Mrs. Haystead is introducing her students to the new program entitled Personal Reading and Reacting Time, or PRRT. She explains to her 3rd graders that every day they will be spending time reading and gathering information about something they are personally interested in. She adds that each day they will have 15 to 20 minutes when everyone will read—even the teachers and the principal.

She goes on to explain that they should begin thinking about something they are interested in. This can be a specific book they want to read or a topic they would like to learn more about. She tells students that she also has to identify something and can't quite make up her mind whether to read one of the new Harry Potter books that she has heard so much about, or to read about scuba diving. She explains that she has always wanted to learn to scuba dive. She is very interested in the topic and might spend her PRRT time delving into it more deeply.

Mrs. Haystead assures her students that they don't have to worry about what they pick initially because they can change their minds at any time. She also reassures them that they won't have to take a test on what they read, but she might ask them to write about it and to share what they have learned with their classmates. To help them start thinking about their topics, she passes out a sheet of paper with the following questions:

- What is your favorite TV show?
- What is your favorite movie?
- If you could do anything, what would it be? Why?
- If you could go anywhere, where would that be? Why?
- If you could learn more about any person, who would that be? Why?
- What type of stories do you like to hear? Why?

She gives the students a few minutes to answer these questions, telling them simply to record a few ideas they might have. If they can't think of anything for a particular question, that is fine.

For Aida, the questions are easy to answer. Almost all of her answers have something to do with horses. She loves horses and everything about them. However, she has never mentioned this to anyone in class. She worries that the other students might laugh at her.

Mrs. Haystead then organizes students into groups of three and asks them to share some of the answers to their questions. Students find that the small-group discussions stimulate a lot of ideas about books to read and topics to study. After the small-group interactions, the whole class continues the discussion. Some students share books they want to read and topics they want to study. Aida is too shy to share her interest in horses, but hearing what some of the other children say makes her think that her interest in horses isn't that unusual after all.

❖ Middle School and Junior High School

At Prairie Ridge Middle School, the Silent Reading and Learning time (SRL) is scheduled for 30 minutes, three times per week—Mondays, Wednesdays, and Fridays. All students have reserved a section of their academic notebooks for recording their reactions to what they read. The language arts teacher is the official monitor for the SRL period for each student.

Mr. Loredo is introducing SRL to the new 6th grade students in his language arts class. Although SRL is new to the 6th graders, it is not new to Mr. Loredo; the program was implemented a few years earlier at Prairie Ridge. He starts by explaining the rules that apply to SRL—no talking, no sleeping, no doing homework. He adds that SRL is a time for them to read about something they are interested in. Students ask many questions: "What subject do we have to study?" "Will we have to take a test?" "What if we don't like it?" One student, Andre, asks, "Can I read about Michael Jordan?" Mr. Loredo addresses each of their concerns, although some students are still amazed that they can read about anything they want—even if it doesn't have anything to do with school.

Mr. Loredo gives the new 6th graders a sense of how much leeway they have by providing examples from last year's 6th grade class. He explains that one girl spent the whole year reading about Britney Spears. Another student read five science fiction books, all by different authors. Still another student read four books by the same author. One student spent the entire year reading about top-fuel dragsters. Another student spent the year reading about sharks.

After presenting these examples, Mr. Loredo organizes students into small groups to discuss possibilities. Finally, each student fills out a short form. The form asks students to identify topics they might want to read about or specific books or authors, if they already have one in mind.

❖ High School

MTP (My Topic Period) at O'Dea High School is a regular part of freshman and sophomore English classes that all students must take. To provide the necessary time, these classes are 15 minutes longer than any other classes. Students have MTP three times per week.

Teachers introduce students to MTP during the first week of the first quarter. Students are always a bit incredulous when they are told they can read about anything they wish. Mr. Brooke assures them that he has no hidden agenda or tricks up his sleeve. The rules are clearly spelled out to students regarding no sleeping and no homework. The emphasis is on personal inquiry and enjoyment of reading. Mr. Brooke has all students create a section in their academic notebooks dedicated to MTP. He explains that he won't be checking up on their notebook entries but will expect them to react in written form as well as in other forms regularly.

Finding topics to study and books to read creates an initial problem for some students who assume that their reading has to be related to one of their classes. Mr. Brooke explains that they can read something related to their classes if they like but encourages them to branch out and pick topics, authors, or book titles that they are drawn to. He provides some examples of what students have done in previous years, and that seems to help. He explains that he is going to be reading a James Michener novel. Once students loosen up a bit, they easily start identifying things to read. Henry is interested in jet fighters, so he picks F-18s as his topic. It's a plane that the Navy flies from aircraft carriers, and Henry is fascinated with the entire process.

Step 2: Students Identify Reading Material

Access is one of the factors Pilgreen (2000) associated with successful SSR programs. As stated earlier, most SSR programs address access by purchasing and having available a large number of books for students. Some SSR programs use what is commonly called "book flooding" (Pilgreen, 2000). In such cases, the teacher accumulates so many books it creates a veritable "flood" of titles and authors. In most of the SSR programs reviewed by Pilgreen, these books were primarily fiction.

In contrast, for the approach described here, much of the reading material might be expository in nature, because the emphasis in Step 1 is on student interests as opposed to specific books or authors. To illustrate, consider Aida's interest in horses, or Andre's interest in Michael Jordan, or Henry's interest in fighter planes. All three might choose nonfiction books or articles that discuss these topics. The Internet is also a useful source of information. In addition, some use of educational television might be warranted. Recall the studies reported in Chapter 2 that found that watching educational programs has a significant positive effect on the development of students' background knowledge. This finding implies that students might be allowed to watch some TV programs for a topic they have selected. Such viewing should probably be limited because the emphasis in the approach described here is on reading and language interaction. Yet, television viewing does expand the venues in which students might find information on their topics.

❖ Elementary School

The next day Mrs. Haystead takes the entire class to the library. The previous day she had collected the students' answers to the questions she posed about their interests. She then organized them into categories and gave them to the school librarian, Mr. Baker. When the students enter the library, Mr. Baker shows them specific books and resources on the topics they had chosen. To Aida's delight, Mr. Baker has identified several stories about horses. He also shows her nonfiction books that explain how horses are trained, how horses live in the wild, and what you should do if you own a horse. Mr. Baker even shows her some Web sites where she can obtain information about horses. Aida is thrilled but initially overwhelmed with all her options. She finally settles on a fiction book about a young girl and her horse.

❖ Middle School and Junior High School

The day after students have considered the topics they might study, Mr. Loredo devotes all of language arts class to identifying reading material. He has accumulated a large selection of books in his room. Some students select books to read from Mr. Loredo's cache. Others go to the library, where the librarian has identified sources based on the list of topics generated the day before. These include books by specific authors, fiction books within specific genres, nonfiction books on specific topics, videotapes, and DVDs. By the end of the period, all the students have identified the reading material they will be using during SRL, although some students will change their topics and their material within a few days.

Andre, who asked whether he could read about Michael Jordan, knew right away that this was his topic. He couldn't believe that he was going to be allowed to read about Michael in school. To his surprise, the librarian points him to a book about Jordan's college career. Andre knows a lot about Michael Jordan's career as a professional, but does not know much about his family and college days at University of North Carolina. Andre thumbs through a few pages, looks at the pictures, and decides that the book will do fine.

❖ High School

Mr. Brooke spends time during the next few days helping students identify reading material related to their topics. With the help of the technology specialist in the school and the librarian, students quickly identify books, articles, documentaries on DVD, and Web sites that relate to their topics. To his surprise, Henry finds a book on naval aviation entitled *Earning Your Wings of Gold*. It describes in depth the process necessary to become a navy pilot. Henry likes the pictures of navy jets in action. He also likes how detailed the information about naval aviation is. It turns out to be an easy choice for Henry. But he also finds some DVDs with useful information. He decides to use these also.

Step 3: Students Are Provided Uninterrupted Time to Read

Pilgreen (2000) is fairly directive regarding the time during which students actually read about their chosen topics. Her principle of distributed time applies here. As mentioned previously, I recommend 20- to 30-minute sessions at least twice per week, and ideally more. Additionally, students should experience some version of SSR at every grade level through grade 10.

Of course, SSR is probably implemented differently at elementary schools than at middle, junior high, or high schools. At the elementary level, it is usually easier to have a time when the whole school engages in a period of silent reading. This approach is more problematic at the secondary level because of the differences in schedules, and in large schools because of such things as rotating lunch periods and different starting times. When such scheduling constraints exist, it is probably better to embed SSR in a specific course—commonly a language arts course. Ideally, schools would allocate more time to the course housing SSR to compensate for the instructional time lost.

A conducive environment is also critical to this step. Teachers might dedicate some part of the classroom to SSR by arranging comfortable chairs and cushions that students may choose to use. Students might also be allowed to go to areas of the school that provide comfortable space for silent reading. Of course, such freedom of movement would carry the expectation that students follow all SSR rules, such as these:

- No sleeping
- Homework may not be done
- No talking
- No activities other than silent reading

❖ Elementary School

At least three times per week and some weeks every day, the first 20 minutes after lunch are devoted to PRRT in Mrs. Haystead's class and every other class in the school. Everyone reads—even the principal, the custodian, and the school nurse. No announcements interrupt PRRT. No one talks or does homework. Ms. Haystead even puts some beanbag chairs in the corner of the classroom where students can sit. She also has a large, soft rug on the floor where students can lie down as they read. Students and faculty grow to cherish PRRT. It relaxes everyone and energizes everyone. Because PRRT is scheduled after lunch, the afternoons seem to go very quickly.

❖ Middle School and Junior High School

During SRL period at Prairie Middle School, students sit quietly and read. Some go to the library to look at DVDs related to their topics; others go to the computer lab, where they can access Internet sites that contain information on their topics. Even though Andre enjoys his book about Michael Jordan's college days immensely, every once in a while he spends time on the Internet looking for new information about Michael. Today Andre is reading his book in a quiet section of the library. He likes to spend the SRL period there because it gives him easy access to the other resources about Michael Jordan and nobody bothers him. Sometimes while reading about Jordan's college career or high school career, Andre logs on to the Internet and finds information about the events related in the book. He notices that sometimes the information on the Internet contradicts what he has read in the book. This experience makes him realize that just because information is in a book or on the Internet, it doesn't mean that it is true.

❖ High School

For about 20 minutes a day, three days a week, students read quietly about their topics of choice during MTP. Mr. Brooke does too. Occasionally a student might ask if she can do homework during this time, but Mr. Brooke refuses such requests. Most students enjoy this quiet time. It isn't long before MTP time is considered sacred in terms of any outside interruptions. Henry finds himself looking forward to these periods on Mondays, Wednesdays, and Fridays. He enjoys reading his book *Earning Your Wings of Gold,* but he also likes to watch the DVD. The scenes of planes landing on aircraft carriers inspire him. He begins to plan how he might be a pilot himself some day.

Step 4: Students Write About or Represent the Information in Their Notebooks

As discussed in Chapter 2, background knowledge must reside in permanent memory to be of use. We have also learned of ways to enhance the chances that students will store and be able to retrieve information in permanent memory. These ways involve the processing of information in linguistic and nonlinguistic forms while in working memory, and providing multiple exposures to the information. This step and the next are designed to put these principles into operation. They also increase the language experiences of students in the context of something they are excited about.

To implement the remaining two steps, all students should have an academic notebook with a section devoted to their topic of choice. Some of the vignettes have already referred to this notebook. As we shall see, the notebook has a number of functions, including providing a venue for follow-up activities during SSR. The academic notebook might be thought of as an adaptation of student journals as described by Atwell (1987), Calkins (1986), and Macrorie (1984). Whereas Atwell, Calkins, and Macrorie focus their discussions on using journals for literary response, the purpose of the student academic notebook as described here is to enhance academic background knowledge. The academic notebook is simply a spiral notebook or three-ring binder. One major section is devoted to student SSR topics. As we shall see in the next chapters, other sections of the notebook are reserved for subject area vocabulary.

The work of Rosenblatt (1978) and Iser (1978) is particularly useful in providing guidance for using the notebooks. Briefly, Rosenblatt and Iser both attest to the importance of students' interacting with what they read in a personal way. They refer to such interaction as transactional—the student receives information from the text and brings information to the text. Students who are aware of this relationship have a better understanding of the text and themselves as readers. To facilitate such awareness, the teacher must facilitate students' interactions with or students' responses to what they have read. Such responses fall into two general categories: *free responses* and *structured responses*. It is important to note that these responses should be encouraged without violating Pilgreen's principle of nonaccountability. Perhaps the best way to accomplish this is to make such responses optional.

Free responses are open-ended responses that students record in their academic notebooks after silent reading sessions. This type of response resembles what is commonly referred to as "expressive" writing as described by Sapir (1921) and Britton and his colleagues (Britton, Burgess, Martin, McLeod, & Rosen, 1975).

Britton and colleagues explain that expressive writing is "self-expressive" or "close to the self." It "reveals the speaker verbalizing his consciousness" (p. 90). Discussing the importance of expressive writing and the extent to which it occurs in schools, Fulwiler (1986) notes:

> Expressive writing often looks like speech written down and is usually characterized by first-person pronouns, informal style and colloquial diction. [In a large-scale study of the types of writing done in secondary schools] it accounted for 5.5% of the total sample collected, with no evidence of its use outside of English classes. (p. 24)

Fulwiler goes on to say that the low percentage of expressive writing in the English classroom and its total absence in other classes attest to the lack of importance given to student self-expression and student self-inquiry. This situation is unfortunate because expressive writing is one of the best ways to deepen students' understanding and enhance their language experience. Free-response writing, then, in the academic notebook accomplishes multiple goals that include facilitating the storage of information in permanent memory, enhancing language experience, and promoting self-expression.

Structured responses are so called because the teacher guides students to certain types of responses through specific questions. Again, it is important to keep in mind Pilgreen's principle of nonaccountability. Consequently, structured response queries are best offered to students as activities they *might* engage in as opposed to activities they *must* engage in. One useful type of structured-response question deals with the perceived utility of what students have read and what they like or find interesting about that information. Here are some examples:

- How would you use this information?
- How important is the information to you? Why?
- What do you find most interesting about the information? Why?

Questions like these are designed to tap into the self-system. Recall that the self-system houses all our goals and desires along with our perceptions of ourselves, the world around us, and how we fit into that world. Self-system questions help students not only better understand content, but also better understand themselves.

Structured-response questions that encourage students to represent information in some nonlinguistic manner are also useful and typically do not violate the principle of nonaccountability. Here are some examples:

- Construct a graphic organizer representing something you have found interesting.

• Construct a picture of something you just read about.
• Construct a pictograph of something important to your topic.

As these directions illustrate, nonlinguistic representations that students might use fall into three general classes: graphic organizers, pictures, and pictographs.

Graphic organizers are probably the most common way to stimulate nonlinguistic thinking. In the book *Visual Tools for Constructing Knowledge*, Hyerle (1996) has detailed a wide variety of graphic organizers and their possible uses. Perhaps the most commonly used graphic organizer is the web. It is simply a circle with a topic written inside. Spokes emanate from the topic with details about the topic (see Figure 3.1).

Picture representations are just that—pictures that students draw about the information they have read. The emphasis is not on the artistic qualities of the picture, only the information considered important to the student. One obvious benefit of pictures is that young children can create them. Teachers should also

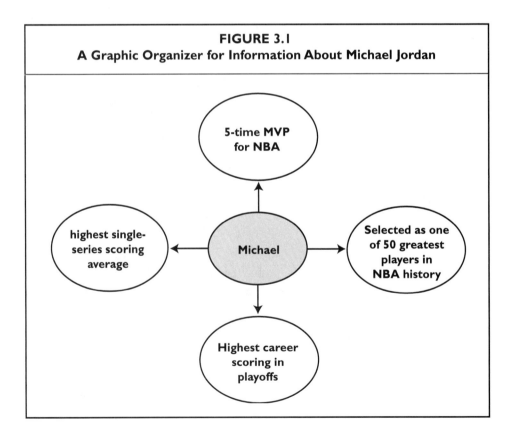

FIGURE 3.1
A Graphic Organizer for Information About Michael Jordan

5-time MVP for NBA

highest single-series scoring average

Michael

Selected as one of 50 greatest players in NBA history

Highest career scoring in playoffs

encourage their use with older students, however, particularly those who might find writing difficult as a form of self-expression.

Pictographs use words and pictures to represent information. Figure 3.2 is a pictograph a student might have drawn after reading about the assassination of President John F. Kennedy. Like pictures, pictographs are easy to construct and do not rely only on language as a form of expression.

In summary, Step 4 is intended to help students process information in linguistic and nonlinguistic ways so that they can store it in permanent memory. Additionally, over time, this step provides the repeated exposure to information that also helps store information in permanent memory and enhances language experience.

FIGURE 3.2
A Student's Pictograph Representing Information
About the Assassination of President Kennedy

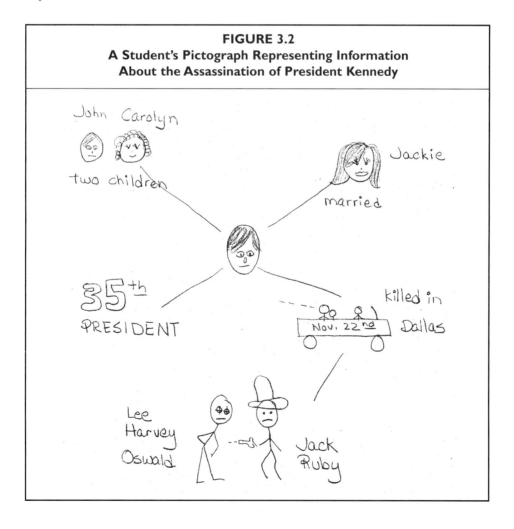

❖ Elementary School

Some days Mrs. Haystead ends silent reading after about 15 minutes. She then encourages students to write something about what they have read. The students write in a three-ring binder that simply has a tab entitled "PRRT." Mrs. Haystead has told students that PRRT stands for Personal Reading and Reflection Time. She explains that the "reading" part of PRRT is done while students read silently, but the "reflection" part is done through writing and discussion. Most of the time Mrs. Haystead does not direct student writing. Rather, students record anything that comes to mind about what they have read. Occasionally Mrs. Haystead directs students to draw a picture about what they have read, or even to draw something that symbolizes what is important to them. Aida always enjoys these types of responses. She usually draws a picture of a horse in a specific setting, and the pictures typically contain details depicting something she has read recently. Sometimes Mrs. Haystead writes specific questions students can answer if they wish. Today she writes the following questions on the board:

- What is the most important thing you have read or learned?
- What is the most unusual thing you have read or learned?
- What are some questions you have about what you have read?
- How is what you have read different from what you thought you knew?

Aida picks the second question because today she has learned some interesting facts about the large white horses called Lipizzan. The foals and young horses have dark coats that gradually turn white.

❖ Middle School and Junior High School

During the last five minutes of each SRL period, Mr. Loredo asks students to write about what they have learned. Sometimes they react to specific questions or prompts he poses. Occasionally he asks them to create a graphic organizer for the information they have read. Today, Andre creates a web graphic organizer about Michael Jordan (see Figure 3.1, p. 56). It's much easier than writing a summary of what he has read, and it's easier for Andre to add information. As time goes on, he will return to his graphic organizer, add more spokes emanating from the center, along with spokes emanating from other spokes.

❖ High School

Today, after students complete their reading during MTP, Mr. Brooke writes the following questions on the board:

- What are some things you read today that contradicted what you thought you knew?
- What are some things you didn't like reading about? Why?

He invites students to answer these questions in the section of their notebook dedicated to MTP. Henry often chooses not to respond to these questions, opting instead to represent what he has read using a picture or a graphic organizer. But today, Henry selects the question dealing with what he didn't like reading about. He has just read that a navy pilot must have 20/20 vision. His eyes aren't bad, but they are not 20/20. As he writes in his notebook, he begins to formulate a plan about how he can improve his eyesight. He has heard about "eye exercises" and plans to look into them.

Step 5: Students Interact with the Information

As we have seen, repeated exposure is required for content to be stored in permanent memory. Step 4 might allow for repeated exposure over time, but the activities suggested in that step are solitary endeavors—students do them alone. A considerable amount of research and theory indicates that a social environment optimizes learning (see Bodrova & Leong, 1996; Martinez & Roser, 2003.) From the perspective of the recommendations in this book, facilitating student interaction not only increases the amount of exposure students have to information, but also dramatically expands their base of language experience. Additionally, dialogue is apparently a natural consequence of developing expertise in a topic (Fish, 1980; Bakhtin, 1986; Lindfors, 1999; Evans, 1996). The more students learn about a topic, the more they have a need to share it with others. This is consistent with Pilgreen's (2000) principle of encouragement. As students hear others become excited about their topics, they feel validated in their own enthusiasm.

Effective student interaction doesn't just happen, though. Hickman (1981) and Kiefer (1986) found that the teacher is a critical factor in eliciting student dialogue. Martinez and Roser (2003) note that the teacher should act as a "nudger" or "helper" in getting students to discuss what they have learned. These findings are consistent with the framework for cooperative learning developed by Johnson and Johnson (Johnson & Johnson, 1999; Johnson, Maruyama, Johnson, Nelson, & Skon, 1981). To be effective, group activities must have explicit structure and purpose. Johnson and Johnson (1999) explain the five critical features of well-run groups:

1. Interpersonal and small-group skills—communication, trust, leadership, decision making, and conflict resolution

2. Group processing—reflecting on how well the team is functioning and how to function even better

3. Positive interdependence—a sense of sink or swim together

4. Face-to-face promotive interaction—helping each other learn, applauding success and efforts

5. Individual and group accountability—each of us has to contribute to achieve the group's goals

Teachers should explicitly teach and practice these elements with students.

The fifth step, then, is not simply a matter of organizing students in groups and asking them to talk. Care must be taken to teach students the skills of group interaction and to organize groups for maximum effectiveness.

❖ Elementary School

About once a week, Mrs. Haystead organizes students into groups of three to five. Earlier she spent time teaching students about group skills such as taking turns and listening to others in the same way they would like others to listen to them. Sometimes Mrs. Haystead gives the groups a question to respond to. Other times she tells them to discuss anything that comes to mind. During these times all students in a group are expected to contribute to the discussion using the strategies they have been taught.

Aida is always amazed at how different her classmates are in terms of what they like to read and what they consider important. Yet every time a student shares a topic, Aida thinks that it makes sense why that particular student selected that particular topic. These small-group sessions typically end with some students volunteering to share their thoughts with the entire class. No one has to respond in front of the class, but over time students take great delight in talking about their topics. Aida is thrilled that her classmates seem to like it when she tells them new information she has learned about horses.

❖ Middle School and Junior High School

On Fridays, the last 10 minutes of SRL are commonly dedicated to students' sharing what they have learned. Sometimes they share in small groups. In such cases, each group member typically has a role to perform, such as facilitator or recorder. Sometimes they share in a large-group format. In such cases, Mr. Loredo typically starts the discussion by sharing what he has learned or found interesting for his topic. Because he is such a history buff, he has selected the Battle of Gettysburg as his topic. He found a new fictionalized account of one of the heroes of Gettysburg, Joshua Chamberlain. Mr. Loredo sometimes gets so enthusiastic about his topic that he takes up too much of the sharing time. However, his enthusiasm for his topic is contagious. Some of the students find themselves equally excited and assertive about telling everyone what they have learned. This is particularly true for Andre. He always has something new to tell about Michael Jordan.

❖ High School

Occasionally Mr. Brooke organizes students into small groups to discuss what they have read and learned. He uses different criteria to organize the groups at various times. Sometimes membership is based on random assignment. Sometimes it is based on reading skills, with each group containing a balance of skilled and not-so-skilled readers. Henry likes it best when the groups are organized by common interests. Two other students in the class have selected topics dealing with aviation, and they have a lot to share with each other. They have learned and practiced a number of group interaction skills under Mr. Brooke's tutelage. They find that their common interest in aviation gives them enough motivation for a useful discussion.

Summary

This chapter has provided the rationale and outline for a five-step approach to using sustained silent reading to enhance academic background knowledge. The approach incorporates the eight principles of an effective SSR program. Although individual students might select fairly narrow topics for SSR, the breadth of knowledge so important to academic success is addressed in the program of direct vocabulary instruction described in the remaining chapters. Consequently, in the SSR program, teachers should allow and encourage students to seek information on whatever topics they desire, regardless of how narrow or specific those topics might be.

4

Building Academic Background Knowledge Through Direct Vocabulary Instruction

In Chapter 2, I discussed the relationship between vocabulary development and background knowledge in some depth. As we have seen, the relationship is strong. Knowledge of specific terms is, for all intents and purposes, synonymous with background knowledge. Given this relationship, I argued that the traditional notion of vocabulary instruction should be expanded to include specific terms such as *Carl Lewis* and *Washington, D.C.,* as opposed to restricting instruction to only general terms such as *athlete* and *city*. This expanded vision of vocabulary instruction has the potential over time to dramatically increase students' academic background knowledge (Marzano, 2004). Indeed, this was one of the primary conclusions from Becker's (1977) analysis of programs designed to fight the War on Poverty in the mid-1960s. Becker noted that to close the gap between students who come from economically disadvantaged backgrounds and those who do not, schools should use systematic programs of vocabulary instruction throughout the grades. Carroll (1971) made the same recommendation as a result of his review of the research on effective practices for the educationally disadvantaged. Finally, recent federal documents have identified vocabulary instruction as one of the essential elements of literacy development for students at risk (RAND Reading Study Group, 2002; NICHD Report of the National Reading Panel, 2000).

With these types of endorsements, we might expect that schoolwide and even districtwide programs of direct vocabulary instruction would be a staple in U.S. education. Unfortunately, this is not the case. Research indicates that uniform and systematic vocabulary instruction is scarce in U.S. schools (McKeown & Curtis, 1987). Indeed, Durkin (1979) noted that in her observation of 4,469 minutes per year of reading instruction using basal readers, only 19 minutes were devoted to direct vocabulary instruction. Roser and Juel (1982) found that on a daily basis, only 1.67 minutes were devoted to direct vocabulary among the 3rd, 4th, and 5th grade teachers they observed. One might legitimately ask, why?

The Case Against Direct Vocabulary Instruction

Strong arguments have been made against direct vocabulary instruction. At the core of many of these arguments are estimates of vocabulary size and the apparent constraints these estimates place on such instruction. As Adams (1990) explains, typical estimates of vocabulary size imply that students learn about 3,000 words per year during the school year. In reaction, she notes: "Even if it [vocabulary] were the only subject taught all day long, every day, the total number of words would barely exceed 3,000. . . ." (p. 149). She states the obvious conclusion of such extrapolation: "While affirming the value of classroom [vocabulary] instruction, we must also recognize its limitations" (p. 148). A host of other researchers have reached similar conclusions. Nagy and Anderson (1984) estimated that the number of words in "printed school English" (i.e., those words that students in grades 3 through 9 will encounter in print) is about 88,500. Obviously, it would be impossible to teach this many words one at a time. Stahl and Fairbanks (1986) summarized this position as follows:

> Since vocabulary-teaching programs typically teach 10 to 12 words a week or about 400 words per year, of which perhaps 75% or 300 are learned, vocabulary instruction is not adequate to cope with the volume of new words that children need to learn and do learn without instruction. (p. 100)

The sheer volume of words students allegedly learn in a year also underlies the suggestion that wide reading might suffice as the primary vehicle for developing vocabulary. This suggestion is based on the assumption that students will learn some percentage, albeit small, of the words they encounter in their reading. For example, Nagy and Herman (1987) assert that if students spend 25 minutes a day reading at a rate of 200 words per minute for 200 days, they will read a million words of text annually and encounter between 15,000 and 30,000 unfamiliar words. If they learn 1 in 20 of these words, their yearly gain in vocabulary will be between 750 and 1,500 words.

On the surface, this logic is compelling and seemingly negates the need for and utility of direct vocabulary instruction. A complete consideration of the research, however, indicates that the arguments for wide reading are not as strong as they appear, and the arguments for direct instruction are much stronger than some would acknowledge.

The Case for Direct Vocabulary Instruction

Three generalizations support the importance and usefulness of direct vocabulary instruction: (1) estimates of vocabulary size vary considerably; (2) wide reading may not enhance vocabulary as much as once thought; and (3) direct vocabulary instruction works.

Estimates of Vocabulary Size Vary Considerably

As we have seen, one pillar of the argument against direct vocabulary instruction is estimates of vocabulary size—the projected vocabulary of students is so large that direct instruction seems woefully inadequate to the task. These estimates, however, are highly problematic in their variability. For example, Jenkins, Stein, and Wysocki (1984) note that estimates of vocabulary size differ by a factor of 12 to 1—high estimates include 12 times as many words as low estimates. Graves (1986) explains that 35 studies were published between 1891 and 1960 estimating average vocabulary size at different age and grade levels. These estimates of vocabulary size for 1st graders ranged from 2,462 to 26,000 and for university graduate students from 19,000 to 200,000. To get a sense of the variability in estimates of vocabulary size, consider Figure 4.1. Depending on the estimate we accept as valid, we get a very different picture of the viability of direct vocabulary instruction. Obviously, the implications for vocabulary instruction are quite different if we assume that 7th graders have a 4,760-word vocabulary rather than a 51,000-word vocabulary. To illustrate, consider two relatively recent but disparate estimates of the number of words known by the average high school senior: 45,000 (Nagy & Anderson, 1984) and 17,000 (D'Anna, Zechmeister, & Hall, 1991). If we assume that the average 4-year-old knows about 800 words (Hart & Risley, 1995), then under the 17,000-word estimate we would calculate that between the ages of 5 and 18, the average student learns about 1,150 words per year (although it is probably true that more words are learned the older a student becomes). Under the 45,000-word estimate, we would calculate that the average student learns about 3,150 words per year. If students learn 1,150 words per year, then direct instruction can carry a significant amount of the load. However, if students learn about 3,150 words per year, the probable impact of direct vocabulary instruction is not very great.

Wide Reading May Not Enhance Vocabulary as Much as Once Thought

A second pillar of the argument against direct vocabulary instruction is the perceived utility of wide reading. As the argument goes, reading develops vocabulary so well that direct instruction is not necessary. However, estimates of the number

FIGURE 4.1
Estimates of Vocabulary Size from Landmark Studies

Grade Level	Study	Estimated Number of Words in Student's Vocabulary
1	Dolch (1936)	2,703
	Ames (1964)	12,400
	Smith (1941)	17,000
	Shibles (1959)	26,000
3	Dupuy (1974)	2,000
	Terman (1916)	3,600
	Brandenburg (1918)	5,429
	Cuff (1930)	7,425
	Smith (1941)	25,000
7	Dupuy (1974)	4,760
	Terman (1916)	7,200
	Brandenburg (1918)	11,445
	Cuff (1930)	14,910
	Bonser, Burch, and Turner (1915)	26,520
	Smith (1941)	51,000

of words learned through reading also vary greatly. To illustrate, Graves (1986) cites estimates by Nagy, Herman, and Anderson that students will learn between 1,500 and 8,250 new words each year from reading (see Nagy, Herman, & Anderson, 1985, p. 250). Yet the same researchers later estimated that students will learn between 800 and 1,200 words per year from reading (see Nagy, Anderson, & Herman, 1987, p. 262). Graves (1986) explains these disparate estimates as follows: "It is important to note that in addition to being hugely discrepant, both estimates are based on a great deal of extrapolation" (p. 70). There is a substantial difference in the assertion that students learn 800 words per year from reading and the assertion that students learn 8,250 words per year. The larger estimate implies that students learn about 22.6 words per day—a feat that seems impossible under any circumstances.

Estimates of the number of words that students learn from reading also suffer because they do not take into enough account how infrequently many of the words actually appear in text. Many of the words students must know to do well in school occur so infrequently that students will have little chance of learning them through reading. To illustrate, consider Figure 4.2, which is based on Nagy and Anderson's (1984) study. Also keep in mind Nagy and Anderson's estimate that the average student will read about one million words of text per year. According to Beck, McKeown, and Kucan (2002), this estimate has been a benchmark for most discussions involving volume of reading. Figure 4.2 paints a dim picture for the potential of reading alone to help students learn the 88,500 words that appear in school-related reading material in grades 3 through 9. Figure 4.2 indicates that students will see 6,700 (or 7.57 percent) of these words one or more times in a year of reading. We can assume that over the seven years spanning grades 3 through 9, the average student will see these words in context multiple times—nine or more times, in fact, from their reading alone. Certainly reading will help, if not ensure, that students will learn these words. However, the next 8,650 (or 9.77 percent) of the 88,500 words appear only three times in 10 years of average student reading. This implies that over the seven years spanning grades 3 through 9, the average student will be exposed to these 8,650 words a little less than three times. Thus, over seven years of reading, average students will encounter about 15,350 words more than once, but more than half of these words will appear only about once every three years. Average readers will have little if any chance of ever encountering the remaining 73,150 (or 82.66 percent) of the

---

FIGURE 4.2
Frequency of Word Occurrence in Texts

6,700 words (7.57%) will be encountered 1 time or more in 1 year of reading.
8,650 words (9.77%) will be encountered up to 3 times in 10 years of reading.
6,350 words (7.18%) will be encountered up to 3 times in 100 years of reading.
24,600 words (27.80%) will be encountered 1 time in 1,000 years of reading.
42,200 words (47.68%) will be encountered up to 3 times in 100,000 or more years of reading.

Source: Based on data in Nagy & Anderson, 1984

words in their reading. These extrapolations severely undermine the logic of wide reading as the sole source of vocabulary development.

Finally, estimates of the impact of reading on vocabulary development do not take into account the research indicating how difficult it is for students to learn words through context alone. In fact, Beck and McKeown (1991) argue that "research spanning several decades has failed to uncover evidence that word meanings are routinely acquired from context" (p. 799). To illustrate, the study by Jenkins, Stein, and Wysocki (1984) demonstrated that to learn a word requires anywhere from 6 to 10 exposures to the word in context. They explain:

> Although the present findings show that fifth graders can learn word meanings incidentally during reading, this learning apparently does not come easily or in large quantities . . . for educators interested in building vocabulary, prescribing large doses of reading may not be the most efficient means of reaching this goal; heavy exposure to words in contexts may be required, and in many cases specific contexts may not be sufficiently rich to allow readers even to derive word meaning, not to mention learn them. (p. 782)

Additionally, Swanborn and de Glopper (1999) report that the chances of learning a word from context are moderated by a student's ability level and grade level, and the density of the text. As shown in Figure 4.3, a high-ability student has a 19 percent chance of learning a new word in context, whereas a low-ability student has

FIGURE 4.3 Chances of Learning New Words in Context		
Moderator	**Level of Moderator**	**Chances of Learning Word**
Ability	Low	8%
	Medium	12%
	High	19%
Grade Level	Grade 4	8%
	Grade 11	33%
Text Density	1 new word for every 10 words	7%
	1 new word for every 75 words	14%
	1 new word for every 150 words	30%

Source: Based on information in Swanborn & de Glopper, 1999

an 8 percent chance. Stated in terms of the argument of this book, this is tantamount to saying that students who have a large store of academic background knowledge have a much greater chance of learning a new word in context than students whose academic background knowledge is sparse.

Figure 4.3 also reports that 11th graders—older students—have a much better chance of learning a new word in context than 4th graders—younger students. This conclusion makes intuitive sense from the perspective of academic background knowledge. As students get older, they develop more background knowledge, which makes it easier for them to learn words in context.

Finally, Figure 4.3 demonstrates that the density of the text influences the chances of a student learning a new word from context. Low-density texts (those with 1 new word for every 150 words) provide a 30 percent chance that students will learn new words from context, whereas high-density texts (those with 1 new word for every 10 words) provide a 7 percent chance of learning new words from context.

Direct Vocabulary Instruction Works

Although the inherent weakness in the argument for wide reading indirectly supports the argument for direct vocabulary instruction, the most powerful argument for such instruction is much more straightforward. Simply stated, direct instruction in vocabulary works. This was demonstrated in the meta-analysis by Stahl and Fairbanks (1986). Figure 4.4 reports the results of that meta-analysis in terms of effect sizes. See Technical Note 5 on p. 131 for a more technical explanation of an effect size. Briefly, Figure 4.4 depicts the impact of two types of direct vocabulary instruction. One is simply referred to as direct vocabulary instruction and has an effect size of .32. This applies to the "typical" direct vocabulary instruction program that teaches about 10 to 12 words per week, with words selected from high-frequency word lists (I discuss these in depth later in this chapter). Now let's consider two students with equal levels of academic background knowledge and reading ability. Student A is in a vocabulary program that teaches 10 to 12 new words per week. Student B does not receive this instruction. Now assume that students A and B take a test on the information they have read and that student B scores at the 50th percentile relative to other students in the class. All else being equal, Student A will score at the 62nd percentile on the same test simply because she has received direct vocabulary instruction.

The effect size of .97 for direct vocabulary instruction that targets academic terms that students will encounter in their reading material (the second approach in Figure 4.4) is even more impressive. Specifically, it indicates that students'

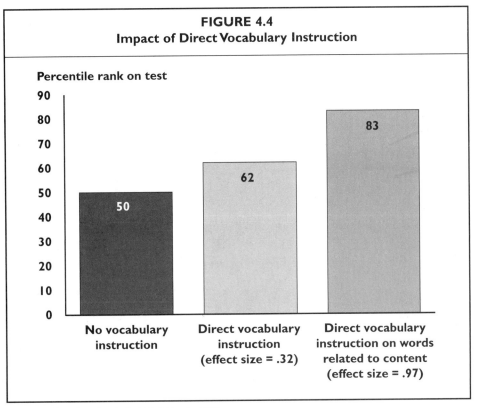

FIGURE 4.4
Impact of Direct Vocabulary Instruction

Percentile rank on test

Source: Based on data in Stahl & Fairbanks, 1986

comprehension will increase by 33 percentile points when vocabulary instruction focuses on specific words important to the content they are reading as opposed to words from high-frequency lists. To illustrate, again consider Students A and B, who have been asked to read and understand new content. Student B, who has not received systematic vocabulary instruction, scores at the 50th percentile. Student A, who has received such instruction, scores at the 83rd percentile.

In summary, the case for direct vocabulary instruction is strong. From a number of perspectives, the research indicates that wide reading probably is not sufficient in itself to ensure that students will develop the necessary vocabulary and consequently the necessary academic background knowledge to do well in school. In contrast, direct vocabulary instruction has an impressive track record of improving students' background knowledge and the comprehension of academic content. What, then, are the characteristics of an effective approach to direct vocabulary instruction?

Characteristics of Effective Direct Vocabulary Instruction

As the previous discussion illustrates, direct instruction in vocabulary terms makes good sense based on the existing research, particularly if those terms are important to academic subject areas. Research also provides strong guidelines as to the nature of effective vocabulary instruction. Here we consider eight research-based characteristics of effective vocabulary instruction.

Characteristic 1: Effective vocabulary instruction does not rely on definitions. One of the most common ways a new vocabulary term is presented to students is in conjunction with a definition. Teachers provide students with a definition outright or ask them to look up the definition in a standard dictionary, write the definition, and then use the new word in a sentence to demonstrate understanding. When we consider the characteristics of most dictionary definitions, however, this practice seems highly questionable. Stahl (1999) explains:

> Definitions, in fact, are conventions we use to talk about words. There is a form for a definition, dating back to Aristotle, in which the definition first identifies which class (*genus*) the word belongs to, and then how that word differs from other members of its class (*differentia*). For example, *The Random House Dictionary* (1978) defines *fissure* as "a narrow opening" [the class] produced by cleavage [the differentiation]. (p.17)

Beck, McKeown, and Kucan (2002, p. 33) further explain why dictionary definitions are not effective instructional devices:

> To understand why dictionary definitions are so often unhelpful, it can be useful to know a bit about how definitions end up in the form they do. Formalized definitional practice can be traced to the time of Samuel Johnson's mid-18th-century *Dictionary of the English Language*. The traditional form of definitions is based on describing a word by first identifying the class to which something belongs and then indicating how it differs from other members of the class. A classic example is *bachelor* defined as "a *man* who is *unmarried*."
>
> The most overriding consideration for definitional format, however, is that definitions in dictionaries must be concise because of space restrictions. Lexicographers, those who develop dictionaries, have called this constraint "horrendous." Indeed, one lexicographer made the point that "almost every defining characteristic common to dictionaries can be traced to the need to conserve space" (Landau, 1984, p. 140), and another has said that dictionary definitions have led to "some remarkable convolutions in dictionary prose style." (Hanks, 1987, p. 120)

Supporting this conclusion, Snow (1990) found that students' ability to construct a definition was related more to their familiarity with the structure of definitions than it was to their comprehension ability.

Beck, McKeown, and Kucan (2002) pose a viable alternative to presenting students with definitions. They explain that when people first learn words, they understand them more as *descriptions* of words as opposed to definitions. They recommend that words' meanings be presented to students in everyday language. I have organized several examples presented by Beck, McKeown, and Kucan in Figure 4.5. As the figure shows, descriptions present information about words in the way someone might respond to a friend when asked about the meaning of a word. At least one dictionary takes this kind of approach to word meanings: the COBUILD English Language Dictionary (Collins, 1987). For example, it describes *lollop* in the following way: "When an animal or a person lollops along, they run awkwardly and not very fast" (see Stahl, 1999, p. 18). Some researchers assert that conventional dictionaries may be more useful after students have established a basic understanding of the meaning of a word provided by a descriptive approach (Nist & Olejnik, 1995).

Characteristic 2: Students must represent their knowledge of words in linguistic and nonlinguistic ways. In Chapter 2, I discussed the importance of processing information in linguistic and nonlinguistic forms in the context of the first principle of background knowledge. Specifically, the dual coding theory (DCT) explains that for information to be anchored in permanent memory, it must have linguistic (language-based) and nonlinguistic (imagery-based)

Word Meaning Presented	
Word	**Definition**
Covert	Kept from sight; secret; hi
Disrupt	Break up; split
Illusion	Appearance or feeling th misleads because it is not
Improvise	To make, invent, or arran whatever is on hand
Morbid	Not healthy or normal

Source: Based on information in Beck, McKeo

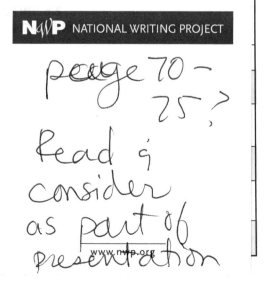

NWP NATIONAL WRITING PROJECT

www.nwp.org

representations. In Chapter 3, this principle was apparent in the recommendation that students should represent the information they have read on their topics for SSR in linguistic and nonlinguistic forms (see Step 4 in Chapter 3, p. 54). This recommendation also holds true for the direct teaching of vocabulary. Specifically, the meta-analysis by Stahl and Fairbanks (1986) demonstrated the effectiveness of both language-based strategies, such as writing a description of vocabulary words, and nonlinguistically based strategies, such as using a graphic organizer to represent the meaning of a word.

In a more focused meta-analysis, Powell (1980) reported that instructional techniques involving nonlinguistically based strategies had an average effect size of 1.00, indicating that these strategies produce a gain of 34 percentile points gain in vocabulary learning. (See Technical Note 5 on p. 131 for a discussion of effect sizes.) Additionally, Powell reported the average effect sizes of studies that contrasted linguistically based techniques with nonlinguistically based techniques. As shown in Figure 4.6, nonlinguistically based techniques produced vocabulary gains that were 37 percentile points higher than those produced by having students review definitions, and 21 percentile points higher than those produced by having students generate sentences that demonstrated an understanding of vocabulary words. The clear implication from Stahl and Fairbanks (1986) and from Powell's (1980) meta-analyses is that both linguistic and nonlinguistic techniques are useful in direct vocabulary instruction, and teachers should highlight nonlinguistic techniques.

In terms of specific techniques for vocabulary instruction, those discussed in Chapter 3 work well. That is, students can be asked to represent words they are learning using graphic representations, pictures, and pictographs. In addition,

! See Voc for MS Student, !

FIGURE 4.6
Effects of Linguistically Versus Nonlinguistically Based Techniques

Technique Compared with Nonlinguistically Based Techniques	Number of Studies	Effect Size	Percentile Gain for Nonlinguistically Based Techniques
Repeating the definition of words	6	1.15	37
Generating sentences using words	4	.56	21

Source: Based on information in Powell, 1980

[handwritten: act out word meanings]

some researchers and theorists suggest that students should be encouraged to create mental pictures of new words and even act out their meanings (see Marzano, Pickering, & Pollock, 2001; Stahl, 1999).

Characteristic 3: Effective vocabulary instruction involves the gradual shaping of word meanings through multiple exposures. The discussion of the fourth principle in Chapter 2 established the fact that knowledge is useful even if it is known at surface levels only. This phenomenon also applies to vocabulary knowledge. Commenting on a study by Dorso and Shore (1991), Stahl (1999) explains:

> One does not always need to know a word fully in order to understand it in context or even to answer a test item correctly. Adults possess a surprising amount of information about both partially known and reportedly unknown words. Even when people would report never having seen a word, they could choose a sentence in which the word was used correctly at a level above chance or discriminate between a correct synonym and an incorrect one. (Stahl, 1999)

[handwritten: You don't need to know the word to know how to use it!]

Vocabulary knowledge also appears to deepen over time. Speaking of a study by Schwanenflugel, Stahl, and McFalls (1997), Stahl (1999) explains: "Thus, vocabulary knowledge seems to grow gradually, moving from the first meaningful exposure to a word to a full and flexible knowledge" (p. 16). Indeed, Sticht, Hofstetter, and Hofstetter (1997) reached the same conclusion. As described in Chapter 1, they examined the vocabulary knowledge of 538 randomly selected adults by giving them a test. They divided their subjects into five levels of vocabulary knowledge. They found that the older the subjects, the more words they knew. For example, subjects 16 to 18 knew no words on their test. Subjects 19 to 24 knew 18 percent of the words. Subjects 25 to 39 knew 34 percent, and subjects 40 to 54 knew 60 percent of the words.

The dynamics involved in the gradual development of words is partially explained by Carey's (1978) distinction between "fast mapping" and "extended mapping." According to Carey, students are quite capable of obtaining an idea of a word's meaning with minimal (e.g., one) exposure to a word. This is called "fast mapping." To understand the word at deeper levels, however, students require repeated and varied exposure to words, during which they revise their initial understandings. Such exposure is referred to as "extended mapping." Without experiences that allow for extended mapping, word knowledge remains superficial but useful. Research by Dolch and Leads (1953) supports this notion by indicating that even adults have a highly superficial understanding of some fairly common

[handwritten: even 1 exposure is helpful!]

words, presumably because of limited exposure to them. This research points to the need for multiple exposures to the words targeted for direct vocabulary. It also correlates well with the discussion of the second principle in Chapter 2, indicating that multiple exposures to information are necessary to anchor that information in permanent memory. The research on vocabulary instruction mirrors this principle. Students must process words multiple times (Graves, 1986; Jenkins, Stein, & Wysocki, 1984).

varied interaction

During these repeated exposures, learning is greatly enhanced if students interact with vocabulary in a variety of ways (Beck, McKeown, & Kucan, 2002; Marzano & Marzano, 1988; Stahl, 1999). Thus, teachers should vary the type of interactions students have with vocabulary terms. One obvious technique is to use both linguistic and nonlinguistic representations. Some activities should involve writing; some should involve constructing graphic representations; others should involve drawing pictures.

A second way to vary how students interact with vocabulary words is to use the various forms of identifying similarities and differences. Research indicates that this activity is one of the most basic cognitive acts and deepens understanding of the items involved (Smith & Medin, 1981; Gentner & Markman, 1994; Markman & Genter, 1993a, 1993b; Medin, Goldstone, & Markman, 1995). Marzano, Pickering, and Pollock (2001) have identified four types of instructional activities that require students to identify similarities and differences: comparing, classifying, creating metaphors, and creating analogies.

W4HSS!

Marzano, Pickering, and Pollock define *comparing* as the process of identifying similarities and differences among or between things or ideas. (Technically speaking, *comparing* refers to identifying similarities, and *contrasting* refers to identifying differences. However, many educators use the term *comparing* to refer to both.) Several studies have demonstrated the instructional effectiveness of asking students to compare items (Chen, 1996, 1999; Chen, Yanowitz, & Daehler, 1996; Flick, 1992; Ross, 1987; Solomon, 1995). In the context of this discussion, comparison activities are those in which the teacher asks students to identify how two terms are similar and different. For example, in the context of vocabulary instruction, a science teacher might ask students to identify how *meiosis* and *mitosis* are similar and different.

classifying!

Classifying is the process of grouping things that are alike into categories based on their characteristics (Marzano, Pickering, & Pollock, 2001). To illustrate, assume that an elementary art teacher has presented the following terms to students: *paint, overlapping, adding in sculpture, clay, shading, subtracting in sculpture, charcoal, varying size, casting jewelry, pencil, varying color, constructing jewelry, wood, collage, mixing color, perspective, stippling, glaze.* The teacher might ask students to sort the terms into the following categories: art materials, art techniques, and art processes. Done correctly, the process would yield the following:

- Art materials: *paint, clay, charcoal, pencil, wood*
- Art techniques: *overlapping, shading, varying size, varying color, collage, perspective, stippling, glaze*
- Art processes: *adding in sculpture, subtracting in sculpture, casting jewelry, constructing jewelry, mixing color*

Research indicates that classifying activities such as this not only help students better understand the content that is classified, but also help them see the content in different ways (Chi, Feltovich, & Glaser, 1981; English, 1997; Newby, Ertmer, & Stepich, 1995; Ripoll, 1999).

Creating metaphors is the process of identifying a general or basic pattern that connects information that is not related at a surface or literal level (Marzano, Pickering, & Pollock, 2001). An example of a metaphor is the statement "Love is a rose." On the surface, *love* and *rose* do not appear related—one term stands for an emotion and the other for a flower. Some similarities, however, link the two things at an abstract level. Both are attractive or alluring; both can result in pain (i.e., if you grab a rose you might be hurt by the thorns; if you hold too tightly to love, it might be extinguished). Research indicates that metaphor activities can help students better understand the abstract features of information (Chen, 1999; Cole & McLeod, 1999; Dagher, 1995; Gottfried, 1998; Mason, 1994, 1995; Mason & Sorzio, 1996). In terms of vocabulary instruction, a teacher might present students with metaphors or ask them to create their own metaphors. For example, a computer technology teacher might first present students with the following metaphors involving the term *Internet* and ask students to explain each:

- The Internet is an information superhighway.
- The Internet is a giant flea market.
- The Internet is a coffee shop.

Next, the teacher might ask students to create and explain their own metaphors for the Internet.

Creating analogies is the process of identifying the relationship between two sets of items—in other words, identifying relationships between relationships (Marzano, Pickering, & Pollock, 2001). Analogies have the following form: A is to

B as C is to D. In the context of vocabulary instruction, a teacher might present students with analogies like the following and ask them to explain the relationships:

- Oxygen is to humans as carbon dioxide is to plants.
- Nucleus is to atom as core is to earthquake.
- Newton is to force and motion as Bernouli is to air pressure.

At a more advanced level, the teacher might provide students with an incomplete analogy and ask students to fill in the missing parts:

- Oxygen is to humans as _____ is to _____.
- Nucleus is to atom as _____ is to _____.
- Newton is to force and motion as _____ is to _____.

Research indicates that analogical thinking is perhaps the most complex activity involving similarities and differences and requires in-depth analysis of the content (Alexander, 1984; Lee, n.d.; Ratterman & Gentner, 1998; Sternberg, 1977, 1978, 1979).

In summary, knowledge of a given vocabulary term deepens over time if a student encounters the term multiple times. During each new encounter, students revise their understanding of the term. Asking students to represent information about vocabulary in linguistic and nonlinguistic ways and engaging them in activities involving similarities and differences are highly useful exercises.

Characteristic 4: Teaching word parts enhances students' understanding of terms. Teaching of roots and affixes has traditionally been a part of regular vocabulary instruction. The logic behind this instructional activity is that knowledge of roots and affixes enables students to determine the meaning of unknown words. Commenting on the work of Dale and O'Rourke (1986), Stahl (1999) explains:

> While words like *geologist*, *interdependent*, and *substandard* can often be figured out from context, decomposing such words into known parts like *geo-*, *logist, inter-, depend*, etc., not only makes the words themselves more memorable, but, in combination with sentence context, may be a useful strategy in determining the meaning of unknown words. (p. 44)

Adams (1990) also attests to the logic of teaching word parts, noting that it is important "to teach [students], for example, that such words as *adduce, educe, induce, produce, reduce,* and *seduce* are similarly spelled because they share a common meaning element: *duce*, 'to lead'" (p. 151). However, she adds the following cautionary note: "Although teaching older readers about roots and suffixes of morphologically complex words may be a worthwhile challenge, teaching beginning or less skilled readers about them may be a mistake" (p. 152).

Affixes include prefixes and suffixes. Prefixes commonly augment the meaning of the words to which they are attached. Suffixes commonly change the part of speech of the words to which they are attached. Some vocabulary researchers and theorists argue against teaching long lists of affixes. Indeed, one of the most comprehensive sources of lists of prefixes and suffixes is *The New Reading Teacher's Book of Lists* (Fry, Fountoukidis, & Polk, 1985). It identifies more than 40 prefixes that indicate where something is (e.g., *in-*, *intra-*, *off-*).

Fortunately, studies have identified those affixes that occur most frequently in the English language. Specifically, White, Sowell, and Yanagihara (1989) identified the most common prefixes based on a study of words in *The American Heritage Word Frequency Book* (Carroll, Davies, & Richmond, 1971). As described by White and colleagues:

> What is striking about these data is that a handful of prefixes account for a large percentage of the prefixed words. The prefix *un-* alone accounts for 26% of the total. More than half (51%) of the total is explained by the top three prefixes, *un-, re-,* and *in-* "not". And with just four prefixes, *un, re, in-* "not", and *dis-*, one could cover approximately three-fifths of the prefixed words (58%). (pp. 302–303)

They recommend a sequence of six lessons. In the first lesson, the teacher explicitly defines and teaches the concept of a prefix by presenting examples and nonexamples. The goal of this first lesson is for students to understand the difference between genuine prefixed words like *unkind* and *refill* as opposed to "tricksters" like *uncle* and *reason*. In the second lesson, the teacher explains and exemplifies the negative meanings of the prefixes *un-* and *dis-*. The third lesson addresses the negative meanings of *in-, im-, ir-,* and *non-*. In the fourth lesson, the teacher explains and exemplifies the two meanings of *re-* ("again" and "back"). The fifth lesson addresses the less common meaning of *un-* and *dis-* ("do the opposite") and the less common meanings of *in-* and *im-* ("in or into"). Finally, in the sixth lesson the teacher explains and exemplifies the meanings of *en-, em-, over-,* and *mis-*.

White, Sowell, and Yanagihara's study (1989) also identified the most common suffixes. About their findings on suffixes, the researchers note:

> It is plain . . . that the distribution of suffixes, too, is not uniform. The first 10 suffixes listed comprise 85% of the sample. Plural and/or third person singular *-s/-es* alone account for about a third (31%) of the sample. Three inflectional suffixes, *-s/-es, -ed,* and *-ing,* account for 65%. In light of this, middle elementary teachers would do well to concentrate on *-s/-es, -ed,* and *-ing.* (p. 303)

Again, they recommend a series of lessons. In the first lesson, the teacher explains and exemplifies the concept of a suffix using examples and nonexamples. The next two lessons present suffixed words that show no spelling change from the base words: *blows, boxes, talking, faster, lasted, sweetly, comical, rainy*. Next, the teacher presents one or more lessons illustrating each of the three major kinds of spelling changes that occur with suffixes: (1) consonant blending (*thinner, swimming, begged, funny*); (2) *y* to *i* (*worried, flies, busily, reliable, loneliness*); and (3) deleted silent *e* (*baking, saved, rider, believable, refusal, breezy*). Finally, a number of lessons provide examples of three inflectional endings (*-s/-es, -ed, -ing*), and the following derivational suffixes: *-ly, -er, -ion, -able, -al, -y, -ness*.

Along with teaching affixes, vocabulary instruction commonly teaches root words. Again, a problem with roots is that they are so numerous that instruction cannot cover all of them. Unfortunately, no usable study has identified the most frequent or the most useful roots. Figure 4.7 identifies some common Greek and Latin roots.

In summary, teaching affixes and roots, when done judiciously, can be a useful aspect of direct vocabulary instruction. To this end, research has identified those affixes that are used most frequently.

Characteristic 5: Different types of words require different types of instruction. It seems logical that instruction should differ somewhat for vocabulary terms that have different syntactic functions. For example, Stahl (1999) distinguishes between nouns and verbs. He notes the importance of considering the type of word that is being addressed on grammatical grounds only: "Although we tend to talk about vocabulary as separate from grammar, they are, of course, connected. *Give*, for example, is as verb. In language, verbs function differently from nouns and modifiers (adjectives and adverbs)" (p. 20).

Stahl explains that each verb implies a relationship with one or more nouns. For example, the verb *jog* implies that someone is performing the action. The verb *give* implies that someone is willingly transferring possession to someone else. As Stahl (1999) notes: "Each verb implies a frame that needs to be filled with nouns or noun phrases" (p. 20). To facilitate learning verbs, Stahl recommends using frames like the following for the verb *pacify:*

_____pacified _____
who   whom

Stahl breaks nouns into two basic categories: concrete (e.g., *lever*) and abstract (e.g., *parsimony*). He notes that concrete nouns can usually be described. Thus a

FIGURE 4.7
Common Greek and Latin Roots

Greek Root	Meaning	Examples
ast	star	astronomy, disaster
cycl	circle, ring	cyclone, cycle
gram	letter, written	telegram, diagram
graph	write	telegraph, autograph
meter	measure	thermometer, centimeter
phon	sound	symphony, telephone
photo	light	photograph, photosynthesis
scop	see	microscope, periscope
therm	heat	thermometer, thermal

Latin Root	Meaning	Examples
act	do	react, transact
ang	bend	angle, angular
aud	hear	audience, audible
credit	believe	discredit, incredible
dict	speak	contradict, dictate
duc, duct	lead	aqueduct, educate
fac	make	factory, manufacture
loc	place	location, allocate
man	hand	manuscript, manipulate
migr	move	immigrant, migratory
miss	send	dismiss, missionary
mob	move	automobile, mobile
mot	move	motion, motor
ped	foot	pedal, pedestrian
pop	people	population, popular
port	carry	import, portable
rupt	break	erupt, rupture
sign	mark	signature, signal
spec	see	inspect, spectator
tract	pull, drag	tractor, attraction
urb	city	urban, suburb
vac	empty	vacant, vacuum
vid	see	video, evidence
volv	roll	revolver, revolution

teacher might initially give the following description for the concrete noun *inver-tebrates:* "They are any type of animal without a backbone, like a worm or slug. Even insects like ants, bees, and spiders are invertebrates. They don't have back-bones." Abstract nouns must be exemplified. Thus a teacher might provide stu-dents with the following example of *parsimony.* "I was practicing parsimony when I described the entire movie in a few sentences."

Whereas Stahl has identified two basic categories (nouns and verbs), others have developed more extensive categorization schemes. For example, Marzano and Marzano (1988) identified four categories: object terms, action terms, event terms, and state terms. Perhaps the most ambitious categorization scheme was undertaken by a team of MIT researchers (see Miller, Beckwith, Fellbaum, Gross, & Miller, 1993; Miller, 1993; Fellbaum, Gross, & Miller, 1993; Fellbaum, 1993; Beckwith, Miller, & Tengi, 1993). Consider these illustrative categories from their combined work:

> *Noun Categories:* natural objects, natural phenomena, persons, plants, quantities/ amounts, processes, relationships, shape, state or condition, substance, time.

> *Verb Categories:* causation, bodily function and care, change, communication, compe-tition, consumption, contact, cognition, creation, motion, emotion, states of being, perception, possession, social interaction.

Categories such as these are informative but not inherently useful as the framework for vocabulary instruction simply because they were not designed for such purposes. Rather, they are intended as systems that facilitate computer pro-cessing of natural language, or "artificial intelligence." They are too detailed and complex for straightforward use in vocabulary development. However, the work in artificial intelligence can inform the further development of categories useful for vocabulary instruction. To this end, I have combined work from artificial intelli-gence with that from vocabulary development (Marzano & Marzano, 1988; Stahl, 1999) to create the categories depicted in Figure 4.8. Note that the categories dis-tinguish between general and specific terms. As discussed in Chapter 2, to develop academic background knowledge, discussion should focus on both proper and common nouns. Also note that the right-hand column of Figure 4.8 is entitled "Semantic Features." In simple terms, psychologists explain that semantic features are the basis of how we know words (Katz & Fodor, 1963). That is, we understand words in terms of the semantic features they do or do not possess.

Figure 4.9, p. 85, shows how semantic features work. The words in set A of Figure 4.9 all represent things that are human and two legged. The words in B1 and B2 are differentiated because all B1 words contain the added semantic feature

	FIGURE 4.8
	Categories and Semantic Features of Words
Category	**Semantic Features**
Types of people (general)	1. The type of person performs specific actions (e.g., firefighter). 2. Specific requirements are necessary to become the type of person (e.g., doctor). 3. The type of person has a specific set of physical or psychological characteristics (e.g., basketball player, psychologist).
Specific people	The characteristics above will apply, plus the following: 4. The person is associated with a specific time period (e.g., George Washington). 5. The person is associated with a specific place (e.g., Saddam Hussein). 6. The person is associated with a specific event (e.g., Lee Harvey Oswald). 7. The person is associated with a specific accomplishment (e.g., Babe Ruth).
Natural objects and places (general)	1. The object or place is associated with a specific setting (e.g., beach). 2. The object or place is associated with specific physical characteristics (e.g., granite, mountain range). 3. The object or place is developed or formed in a specific way (e.g., tidal basin). 4. The object or place is associated with specific uses (e.g., lumber).
Natural objects and places (specific)	The characteristics above will apply, plus the following: 5. The object or place is associated with specific events (e.g., Mt. St. Helens). 6. The object or place is associated with specific people (e.g., Little Bighorn). 7. The object or place is associated with a specific time (e.g., the land bridge connecting Alaska and Siberia). 8. The object or place is associated with a specific location (e.g., the Amazon).
Man-made objects and places (general)	1. The object or place is associated with a specific setting (e.g., coastal city). 2. The object or place is associated with specific physical characteristics (e.g., wheel). 3. The object or place is developed or built in a specific way (e.g., railroad). 4. The object or place is associated with specific uses (e.g., automobile).

FIGURE 4.8
(continued)

Category	Semantic Features
Man-made objects and places (specific)	The characteristics above will apply, plus the following: 5. The object or place is associated with specific events (e.g., New York City). 6. The object or place is associated with specific people (e.g., Versailles). 7. The object or place is associated with a specific time (e.g., the Parthenon). 8. The object or place is associated with a specific location (e.g., Stonehenge).
Man-made events (general)	1. The event is associated with specific types of people (e.g., football game). 2. The event is associated with a specific process or specific actions (e.g., party). 3. The event is associated with specific equipment, material, resources, or context (e.g., polo match). 4. The event is associated with a specific setting (e.g., picnic). 5. The event is associated with specific causes and consequences (e.g., graduation).
Man-made events (specific)	The characteristics above will apply, plus the following: 6. The event is associated with specific people (e.g., Holocaust). 7. The event is associated with a specific time (e.g., Christmas). 8. The event is associated with a specific place (e.g., 9/11/01). 9. The event is associated with a specific cause or outcome (e.g., World War II).
Natural phenomena (general)	1. The phenomenon is associated with a specific process (e.g., volcanic eruption). 2. The phenomenon is associated with specific causes and consequences (e.g., tornado). 3. The phenomenon is associated with a specific setting (e.g., tidal wave).
Natural phenomena (specific)	The characteristics above will apply, plus the following: 4. The phenomenon is associated with a specific place (e.g., Alaskan earthquake of 1964). 5. The phenomenon is associated with a specific time (e.g., ice age).

	FIGURE 4.8 (continued)	
Category	**Semantic Features**	
Intellectual, artistic, or cognitive products (general)	1. The product is associated with a specific process (e.g., a painting). 2. The product is associated with a specific purpose or use (e.g., a letter). 3. The product is associated with specific types of people (e.g., opera). 4. The product is associated with specific equipment (e.g., sculpture).	
Intellectual, artistic, or cognitive products (specific)	The characteristics above will apply, plus the following: 5. The product is associated with a specific person (e.g., the Mona Lisa). 6. The product is associated with a specific time or event (e.g., Rosetta Stone). 7. The product is associated with a specific cause or consequence (e.g., U.S. Constitution). 8. The product is associated with a specific place (e.g., ceiling of the Sistine Chapel).	
Physical actions (general)	1. The physical action is associated with a specific process (e.g., running). 2. The physical action is associated with specific types of people (e.g., mountain climbing). 3. The physical action is associated with a specific location (e.g., fishing). 4. The physical action is associated with a specific purpose (e.g., weight lifting). 5. The physical action is associated with a specific cause or consequence (e.g., fighting).	
Mental actions (general)	1. The mental action is associated with a specific process (e.g., experimenting). 2. The mental action is associated with specific types of people (e.g., arbitration). 3. The mental action is associated with a specific location (e.g., legal defense). 4. The mental action is associated with a specific cause or consequence (e.g., problem solving).	
Social/societal groups, institutions, or organizations (general)	1. The institution or organization is associated with a specific purpose (e.g., posse). 2. The institution or organization is associated with specific types of people (e.g., governing board). 3. The institution or organization is associated with a specific setting (e.g., jury).	

FIGURE 4.8 (continued)	
Category	**Semantic Features**
Social/societal groups, institutions, or organizations (specific)	The characteristics above will apply, plus the following: 4. The institution or organization is associated with a specific location (e.g., U.S. Congress). 5. The institution or organization is associated with a specific time (e.g., KKK). 6. The institution or organization is associated with a specific event (e.g., Chicago Seven).
Shapes/ direction/ position	1. The shape/direction/position has distinguishing physical features (e.g., triangle). 2. The shape/direction/position is associated with specific uses (e.g., arch). 3. The shape/direction/position is associated with specific reference points (e.g., south).
Quantities/ amounts/ measurements	1. The quantity, amount, or measurement has a specific relationship with other quantities, amounts, or measurements (e.g., one million). 2. The quantity, amount, or measurement has a specific referent (e.g., inches).

"male"; all B2 words have the semantic feature "female." Words in set C do not share a male-female distinction, but they have a common semantic feature that might be called "siblings." Semantic-feature theory suggests that for each term we know, we associate a number of semantic features, as these examples illustrate:

- cow [animal] [concrete] [four legged] [milk producing]
- girl [animal] [concrete] [two legged] [human] [female]
- desk [not animal] [concrete] [four legged]

In essence, the list in Figure 4.8 is a set of very general semantic features. It is designed to provide guidance regarding the critical semantic features for words that are the target of direct vocabulary instruction. Research indicates that instructional activities focusing on key semantic features positively affect student learning of vocabulary terms (Johnson, Toms-Bronowski, & Pittleman, 1982; Anders, Bos, & Filip, 1984). To illustrate, assume that the term *port city* is the focus of instruction. Using Figure 4.8, it would most likely be classified as a general (as

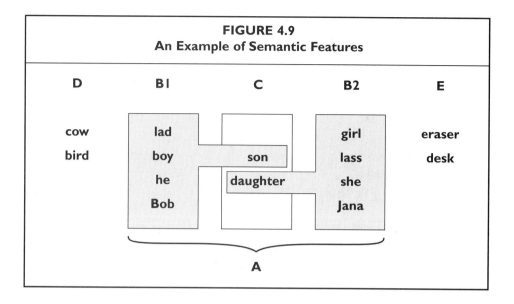

FIGURE 4.9
An Example of Semantic Features

D	B1	C	B2	E
cow	lad		girl	eraser
bird	boy	son	lass	desk
	he	daughter	she	
	Bob		Jana	

A

opposed to specific) man-made object or place. As identified in Figure 4.8, the critical features of this type of term include the following:

- Its typical setting
- Its specific physical characteristics
- How it is developed or built
- Its typical uses

Teachers can use the information in Figure 4.8 in several ways. For example, it can help them determine which characteristics they might emphasize in an initial description of the word presented to students. In this case, the characteristics identified in Figure 4.8 would cue a teacher to emphasize the following:

- The setting of a port city is usually near an ocean with easy access to open waters.
- Typical physical characteristics of a port city are that it has large docks and equipment for unloading ships, and it is close to railroads so that cargo can be transported inland.
- Port cities usually develop because early settlers coming from the ocean landed at that location and found it highly useful in terms of receiving new people and supplies.
- Typical use of a port city is that it is a center for trade, commerce, and the mixing of many cultures.

Armed with this information about the important semantic features of *port city*, the teacher would construct a description or provide examples that contain all the key features.

Figure 4.8, p. 81, can also help with an activity that Johnson and Pearson (1984) have developed, "attribute comparison," in which students compare two or more terms on selected attributes or semantic features. For example, assume that a teacher asked students to compare attributes for the terms *port city* and *industrial city*. The teacher would first have students identify the specifics of port cities and industrial cities using the semantic features selected from Figure 4.8 (i.e., typical setting, physical characteristics, how developed, typical uses). Next, students would be asked to compare how these terms are similar and different in terms of these semantic features.

One qualifying note should be attached to the use of Figure 4.8. It is not an exhaustive list of categories for organizing vocabulary terms, but it should provide a good starting place for teachers. Also, many terms can be associated with more than one category. With these qualifications, Figure 4.8 serves as a tool for enhancing vocabulary instruction.

Characteristic 6: Students should discuss the terms they are learning. I have already addressed the importance of discussion in conjunction with SSR. Among its many benefits, discussion helps students encode information in their own words, helps them view things from different perspectives, and allows for self-expression. These virtues also hold true for vocabulary instruction. As students discuss new terms, they gain deeper understanding and increase the probability that they will store the words in permanent memory. Research supports these benefits. Stahl and Clark (1987) found that students who knew they were not going to be called on during vocabulary instruction recalled fewer words than students who knew they might be called on in class. Fisher, Blachowicz, Costa, and Pozzi (1992) found that asking students to discuss the words they were learning positively affected the amount of time students spent studying words as well as the strategies they used to determine and verify the meaning of words. Finally, discussion about words being learned is an important aspect of the Vocabulary Self-Collection Strategy, or VSS (Haggard, 1982; Ruddell, 1993). VSS is a program that emphasizes student choice regarding the words they study and systematic discussion of those words. As reported by Ruddell, studies of VSS versus traditional approaches with high school students indicate that the VSS condition "increased collaborative time in the classroom and that students took ownership and enjoyed being in a position of self-determination in the VSS condition. . . . Students in the

VSS condition scored higher on short-term tests administered at the end of . . . the experimental treatment" (p. 436).

Although interaction about words will typically occur during the natural course of instruction, teachers should occasionally organize students into groups for the specific purpose of discussing what they have learned about vocabulary terms.

Characteristic 7: Students should play with words. One powerful instructional technique that schools typically underuse is games. Covington (1992) summarizes much of the research on game theory and its use in the classroom. Malone (1981a, 1981b) explains that games have at least three distinguishing characteristics. First, they present manageable challenges for students. As Covington (1992) explains, games provide tasks that "challenge the individual's present capacity, yet permit some control over the level of challenge faced" (p. 160). Second, games arouse curiosity. They do this by "providing sufficient complexity so that outcomes are not always certain" (Covington, 1992, p. 160). Finally, games involve some degree of fantasy arousal. Again, Covington explains that fantasy arousal is not "merely unbridled wish fulfillment or fairy tales, but rather the creation of imaginary circumstances that permit the free and unfettered use of one's growing abilities" (p. 160).

Several sources describe how to use games and gamelike activity to help stimulate students' thinking about vocabulary. Johnson, von Hoff Johnson, and Schlichting (2004) discuss *logology*—word and language play—and identify a number of ways word play can be integrated into vocabulary instruction. In their book *Literacy Plus: Games for Vocabulary and Spelling,* Marzano and Christensen (1992) describe in depth how teachers might use games in vocabulary instruction. They note:

> Vocabulary learning need not be a drudgery for students. Rather, activities should be designed to create an awareness and appreciation of words and to stimulate word fluency through experiences that are meaningful and enjoyable. The purpose of this collection of games is to help teachers and students achieve this goal. (p. i)

Their book lists 15 games that can be used as "sponge activities" to enhance vocabulary development. As the name implies, a sponge activity is intended to "soak up" the "dead time" that frequently occurs in classes. For example, a teacher might use sponge activities during the last few minutes of class, when instructional activities have wound down. Sponge activities might be used at the beginning of class to generate students' enthusiasm and excitement. When students are playing vocabulary games, they are having fun and experiencing vocabulary terms in a new context and seeing them from different perspectives.

Characteristic 8: Instruction should focus on terms that have a high probability of enhancing academic success. As we have seen, one of the primary arguments against the direct teaching of vocabulary is that important terms are too numerous to teach. But we have also seen that this argument is a bit of a "straw man" for a number of reasons. Estimates of the number of words students should know vary greatly, and not all words students might encounter are critical to know. It is my firm belief that if some basic distinctions could be made between words that are critical to students' academic success and those that are not, a viable and straightforward approach to direct vocabulary instruction could be devised. The issue, then, is identifying a listing of vocabulary terms critical to academic success.

Beck and McKeown (1985) suggest that vocabulary be thought of in three tiers. As described by Beck, McKeown, and Kucan (2002), the first tier consists of the most basic words, such as *clock, baby, happy, walk,* and the like. Beck and colleagues (2002) explain: "Words in this tier rarely require instructional attention to their meanings in school" (p. 8). Virtually all of the words in this tier are found in the first category in Figure 4.2 (p. 66). Students will encounter them frequently during reading. Thus, it makes sense to rely on wide reading for the learning of these words. Specifically, if a school implements the SSR process described in Chapter 3, we might assume that for the most part, students will learn these first-tier words through context. Unfortunately, these are the very words that are commonly the focus of instruction at the lower grades. Adams (1990) reports that "it seems that the majority of the words listed for instruction by the basals are already familiar to most children" (p. 148). To illustrate, a study by Roser and Jule (1982) of 3rd, 4th, and 5th grade students found that students already knew 72 percent of the words listed in the basal as appropriate targets for vocabulary instruction. Even students in the lowest reading group knew 48 percent of the words.

Tier-two words, according to Beck, McKeown, and Kucan (2002) are those that appear infrequently enough that the chance of learning them in context is slim. Tier-three words are those that are specific to subject areas. Beck, McKeown, and Kucan (2002) focus on tier-two words as the appropriate target of vocabulary instruction. I believe that this is a mistake for two reasons.

First, although the criterion commonly used to order words is how frequently they appear in written text, studies indicate that word frequency is not a reliable indicator of a word's importance. To illustrate, Breland, Jones, and Jenkins (1994) analyzed the research on the various word-frequency lists over the decades. They note that the assumption that the frequency of a word is a good indicator of how difficult it is to learn is highly questionable: "Word frequency can only be an approximation of word difficulty" (p. 3).

To illustrate, consider the following examples from the *American Heritage Word Frequency Book* (Carroll, Davies, & Richman, 1971). According to this source, words that appear once in every one million words of running text include *diatoms, tinder, fortnight, skinks, pupa, slunk, rheumatic, sheaves, ramparts, alight, fiords, wooly, spectra,* and *ere*. Words that appear once in every one hundred million words of running text include *amnesty, assimilate, busybody, cheeseburger, contemporary, flex, fluent, furor, jellybean, liturgy, mediate, persecute, poolside, raccoon, rambunctious, shamrock,* and *stenographer*. There is something intuitively wrong about the two lists of words. A typical student is certainly more likely to know the words *busybody, cheeseburger,* and *contemporary* than the words *diatoms, fortnight,* and *skinks*. Yet the latter are 100 times more frequent in text, at least according to one frequency list. In short, word frequency is not the guide we need to identify the target words for direct vocabulary instruction.

The second problem with the suggestion that tier-two words should be the target of vocabulary instruction is that there typically is no distinction between words that are important to specific subject areas and words that are more general in their use. Recall the discussion in Chapter 2 regarding the specific nature of academic background knowledge. A knowledge of general terms (e.g., tier-two words as described by Beck, McKeown, and Kucan, 2002) might do little to help students develop the academic background knowledge that will help them succeed in mathematics, science, and history. Also recall the findings of Stahl and Fairbanks (1986) that instruction in general vocabulary drawn from word-frequency lists is associated with a gain of 12 percentile points in comprehension, but instruction in words that are specific to the content being taught is associated with a gain of 33 percentile points.

If the goal of direct vocabulary instruction is to enhance academic background knowledge, then what is clearly needed is a list of subject-specific terms. Indeed, one of the contributions of this book to the field of vocabulary instruction is a list of 7,923 terms critical to success in 11 academic subject areas. How this list was constructed and its use are described in depth in Chapters 6 and 7.

Summary

A strong rationale supports the use of direct vocabulary instruction as a means to enhance academic background knowledge. That rationale encompasses erroneous assumptions about the adequacy of wide reading as a means to enhance academic background knowledge as well as the impressive track record of direct vocabulary instruction. This strong basis of support suggests that effective vocabulary instruction involves

- Descriptions as opposed to definitions
- Use of linguistic and nonlinguistic representations
- Gradual shaping of word meanings
- Teaching and using word parts
- Different types of instruction for different types of words
- Students interacting about the words they are learning
- Use of games
- Focus on terms important to academic subjects

5

Six Steps to Effective
Vocabulary Instruction

Chapter 4 focused on eight characteristics of effective vocabulary instruction. In this chapter we consider how to apply those eight characteristics in a program to enhance academic background knowledge.

Assuming that a comprehensive list of critical academic terms has been identified (chapters 6 and 7 deal with this issue), I recommend a six-step approach to direct vocabulary instruction. Regular classroom instruction provides the context for these steps. That is, mathematics teachers teach selected mathematics terms in mathematics class; science teachers teach science terms in science class. Although this is no different from what many teachers do now, what *is* different is that all teachers use the same six-step process. Additionally, the students record the terms in their academic notebooks—the same notebooks described in Chapter 3 as the repository for students' reflections during SSR. Those notebooks also have sections for subject matter vocabulary taught using the following six-step process.

Step 1: The Teacher Provides a Description, Explanation, or Example of the New Term

During the first step, the teacher explains the target word. As we have seen, definitions do not appear to be useful instructional tools, particularly in the initial stages of learning a word. However, conversational descriptions, explanations, and examples are very useful to students when first learning a term. Ideally, the semantic features listed in Figure 4.8 (pp. 81–84) would guide the choice of information presented in these descriptions, explanations, and examples. That is, for each term the teacher would identify the critical features that form the basis of the descriptions. Although the teacher's description might be informal, it should contain all the elements considered important to an accurate understanding of the word.

❖ Elementary School

Mrs. Haystead is teaching vocabulary terms for her unit on explorers and inventors. She realizes that her 3rd grade students at Stevens Elementary have probably heard the term *discovery* before, but it is a concept critical to the unit, and she wants the students to think about it in depth. To help her identify the important characteristics of this term, she thinks about its critical semantic features. She consults a chart that lists possible important characteristics for different types of terms (see Figure 4.8, pp. 81–84). Looking at the chart, she decides that discovery is best thought of as a general type of "man-made event." She looks at the semantic features associated with this type of term and decides that the following three seem important to what students should know about a discovery:

- It is associated with specific types of people.
- It is associated with a specific process or specific actions.
- It is associated with specific causes and consequences.

In terms of specific types of people, Mrs. Haystead wants students to know that discoveries are commonly associated with people who are daring and do things that others probably wouldn't do. Many times they have to demonstrate great courage and bravery. In terms of a specific process or action, she concludes that discovery does not involve a specific process, but actions commonly associated with discoveries include these:

- A person has an idea about doing something that hasn't been done before.
- The person tries different ways to accomplish the goal.
- The person encounters obstacles and sometimes fails before finally succeeding.
- Sometimes the person's accomplishment is not immediately recognized.

Relative to specific causes and consequences, Mrs. Haystead thinks students should have some awareness that discoveries commonly result from a need in society. With these characteristics identified, Mrs. Haystead thinks of two examples she will provide for a discovery—Thomas Edison's discovery of the light bulb and Christopher Columbus's so-called discovery of the New World.

When she presents the term to students, she explains: "One of the important words in this unit is *discovery*." She then writes the word on the white board. "You've probably heard the word before. We are going to study different types of discoveries."

She then tells the students the stories of Thomas Edison and Christopher Columbus, making sure to emphasize the characteristics she has identified. As she mentions these characteristics, she writes them on the board. For example, when she tells students about Edison's experience with the light bulb, she describes in detail how many trials he went through before he succeeded and writes on the board: Edison had hundreds of failures before he finally succeeded.

By the time she has told both stories she has listed all the characteristics she has identified as important.

❖ Middle School and Junior High School

At Prairie Ridge Middle School, Mr. Johnson is considering the vocabulary terms he wants to emphasize in his unit on mathematical problem solving. One of the important and more difficult terms is *deductive reasoning*. He concludes that it is perhaps best thought of as a mental process. When he examines the possible semantic features (see Figure 4.8, pp. 81–84) for mental processes, he decides that it would be useful to focus on these:

- The process or steps involved in deductive reasoning.
- The fact that deductive reasoning is commonly done for a specific purpose.

The process he wants to emphasize is that deductive reasoning starts with what is known to be true and then proceeds to identifying what must be true but is not stated. The purpose he wants to emphasize is that deductive reasoning is usually done to prove something.

To introduce students to the term, Mr. Johnson finds a clip from one of his favorite Sherlock Holmes movies. Before showing the clip, he writes the words *deductive reasoning* on the board and explains that Sherlock Holmes is a famous fictional detective known for his skill at deductive reasoning.

In the clip he has selected, Sherlock Holmes reviews all the facts that have been collected about a murder and demonstrates that the murderer had to be a woman, not a man as everyone had initially assumed. After the clip, Mr. Johnson discusses with students the process Sherlock Holmes used. As students mention the key semantic features, Mr. Johnson writes them on the board.

❖ High School

Mr. Brooke is teaching a unit on Greek mythology in his freshman English class at O'Dea High School. His main learning goals for the unit center around the specific gods and goddesses the ancient Greeks believed in and how those beliefs affected their lives. Mr. Brooke wants students to have some background information. For one thing, he wants them to understand *The Iliad* and *The Odyssey* and how they influenced beliefs about various gods and goddesses. Students won't actually read these works, but they will be considered important background information. Mr. Brooke, therefore, chooses to address them as vocabulary terms. He consults a semantic feature chart (see Figure 4.8, pp. 81–84) and concludes that for his purposes, the terms are best thought of as specific types of intellectual or artistic products. The characteristics he wants students to understand are these:

- The poems are associated with a specific purpose.
- The poems are associated with a specific person.
- The poems are associated with a specific time or event.
- The poems are associated with a specific place.

Mr. Brooke wants students to know that the purpose of the poems was to provide Greeks of the 8th and 7th century B.C. with information about the fictional adventures of Odysseus and, probably more important, about the gods and goddesses of their society. Additionally, Mr. Brooke wants students to know that the poems are associated with a specific person, Homer, despite the fact that many scholars believe that the poems were probably written by several people and that Homer might not even have been a real person. The specific time the poems were written is the late 8th and early 7th century B.C.; however, the events of the poems take place sometime around the 12th century B.C. Finally, the poems detail events that took place in a specific place, the area around what is now modern Greece and the Aegean Sea.

With these features identified, Mr. Brooke has a strong focus for the terms *Iliad* and *Odyssey*. When he presents these terms to the students, he hands out a brief paragraph describing the important features. He asks students to read the paragraph and invites their questions and comments. As he answers their questions and reacts to their comments, he fills in some details about *The Iliad* and *The Odyssey* not contained in the paragraph.

Step 2: Students Restate the Explanation of the New Term in Their Own Words

As Stahl (1999) notes, "the goal of vocabulary learning is to have students store the meanings of the words in their long-term memory . . ." (p. 14). The discussion in Chapter 2 regarding the role of working memory tells us that students must process information actively and repeatedly for this to occur. This step begins that process. In Step 2, students are asked to restate *in their own words* what the teacher has presented about a new vocabulary term. It is important that students not simply copy the teacher's explanation of a term. Rather, students should construct their own explanations based on what the teacher has presented. Additionally, combining this step with the use of the academic notebook creates a vehicle for the multiple exposures and the gradual "shaping" of understanding of terms so vital to vocabulary development.

The academic notebook was introduced in Chapter 3 in conjunction with SSR and discussed briefly at the beginning of this chapter. Students should have a section of their notebooks dedicated to their SSR topic. That section would contain their written responses and their representations of the information about their topics. Their notebooks should also have sections devoted to their academic subject areas. Thus, a middle school student with classes in mathematics, science, social studies, and language arts would have notebook sections for each of these subject areas. As the various teachers present new terms, the student records them in the appropriate section in the notebook. The notebook pages can be formatted so that each page has three columns with the following headings: My Description, Representation, and New Insight. This step in the vocabulary development process addresses the first column of the notebook. As indicated by its heading, in this column students record their understanding of what the teacher has presented.

❖ Elementary School

After relating the stories about Thomas Edison and Christopher Columbus and recording the important characteristics on the white board, Mrs. Haystead instructs students to write their own descriptions of the term *discovery*. Aida opens her academic notebook to the section dedicated to social studies. The first section of the notebook contains her reactions to her PRRT reading. She has also divided the notebook into sections for each subject area. These sections contain the vocabulary terms for those subjects and anything else about the subject students wish to record. Aida likes the academic notebook because it contains the important information about all the classes she is taking as well as what she has learned from PRRT. Everything is right there in one notebook.

Now she has been presented with a new vocabulary term—*discovery*. She understood what a discovery is before Mrs. Haystead provided the examples, but now she has some new ideas, and it's clear that Mrs. Haystead considers this important. After the term *discover*, Aida writes the following:

> People who make discoveries work very hard and a lot of times they don't get rewarded very much for what they did.

❖ Middle School and Junior High School

While Mr. Johnson has been providing students with the information about deductive reasoning, students have had their academic notebooks open to the mathematics section, which is right after the section dedicated to SRL—Silent Reading and Learning. When Mr. Johnson wrote the term *deductive reasoning* on the board, Andre wasn't sure what it meant. He had heard the term before but never thought much about it. However, after watching the movie clip about Sherlock Holmes and listening to the brief discussion, he thinks he has a good idea. He writes the following description in the first column of his notebook after the term:

> Sometimes you can show that something must have happened because some other things happened before it. You can prove things using deductive reasoning.

❖ High School

Henry reads the paragraph about *The Iliad* and *The Odyssey* that Mr. Brooke handed out. It gives him some idea about what they are, but the discussion provides more information. Next to the terms Iliad and Odyssey in his academic notebook, he writes the following:

> These were two stories that the Greeks used to teach people about all the different gods and goddesses. The stories weren't really true but they were a big part of their culture. They liked telling it to their children.

Henry likes the way Mr. Brooke approaches vocabulary. There are no definitions to look up or memorize. As long as you have a general idea of what the word means, Mr. Brooke is satisfied. Henry also likes the idea of the academic notebook. He was not sure about it at first—a single three-ring binder with sections for all his courses, and a section for what he writes during MTP period. After a while, though, he began to see how useful the academic notebook was—everything stored in one place. It wasn't long before the teachers in different courses started referring to the vocabulary terms from other subject areas. For example, just the other day in math class, Mr. Clarke asked students to identify how some of the terms he had taught were similar to and different from one or more terms from another subject area.

Step 3: Students Create a Nonlinguistic Representation of the Term

The discussions in chapters 2 and 4 illuminated the importance of students representing information nonlinguistically. For vocabulary development, this step is best done immediately after students have generated their own linguistic description of the term. In other words, Steps 1 through 3 follow a related instructional sequence: the teacher presents the new term along with a description; students then create their own linguistic descriptions of the term. After approaching the term linguistically, students create a nonlinguistic representation of it. These representations can be in the form of graphic organizers, pictures, or pictographs, as described in Chapter 4.

❖ Elementary School

After she has given students some time to write their descriptions of the term *discovery*, Mrs. Haystead tells them that she would like them to represent what they have written using a picture or symbols. Aida thinks for a while and comes up with the idea of using horses to remind her of the meaning of the term *discovery* because horses are her topic for PRRT. She reasons that someone must have invented a saddle, so that person must have made a discovery. The thought intrigues her, and she even tells herself that next time they have PRRT she is going to try to find out when the first saddles were used. She guesses that it had to be a long time ago. She knows that the Romans lived a long time ago and made a great many discoveries, so she draws a picture of what she imagines to be a Roman putting a saddle on a horse. She knows that Mrs. Haystead might ask her to explain what her picture of the horse and saddle has to do with the term *discovery*, but she is confident that she can make the connection.

❖ Middle School and Junior High School

After he writes his description of *deductive reasoning*, Andre immediately turns his attention to creating a nonlinguistic representation of the term. Mr. Johnson has taken a fair amount of time explaining the various types of nonlinguistic representations students can use and why these representations are important. But this term proves to be a real challenge. At first, he thinks about drawing a picture of Sherlock Holmes, but he's not sure that will help him remember what deductive reasoning means. He thinks, "There has to be a way to show how one idea leads to another." After a while, he comes up with the diagram depicted in Figure 5.1. Andre knows that as long as his representation means something to him and he can explain it, Mr. Johnson will accept it. When he is done with his representation, Andre feels satisfied because he thinks it captures the meaning of deductive reasoning pretty well.

❖ High School

Mr. Brooke has explained the importance of nonlinguistic representations to his students, and they are all familiar with graphic organizers, pictographs, and pictures. For the terms *Iliad* and *Odyssey*, Henry thinks that a simple graphic organizer is appropriate. He creates the representation depicted in Figure 5.2, p. 99. Even though his graphic representation is a bit sparse, Henry knows that he will be able to add information over time.

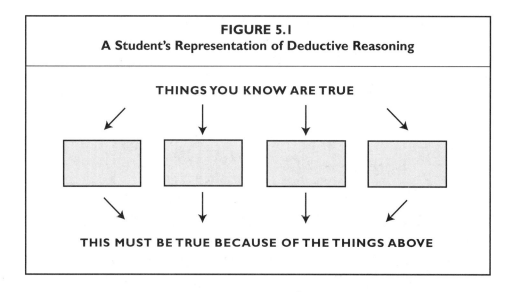

FIGURE 5.1
A Student's Representation of Deductive Reasoning

Step 4: Students Periodically Do Activities That Help Them Add to Their Knowledge of Vocabulary Terms

To ensure multiple exposures to terms, students should take part in activities that allow them to interact with vocabulary terms in a variety of ways. Chapter 4 described a number of these activities:

- Comparing terms
- Classifying terms
- Generating metaphors using terms
- Generating analogies using terms
- Revising initial descriptions or nonlinguistic representations of terms
- Using understanding of roots and affixes to deepen knowledge of terms

A critical point to remember is that after these activities, students go back to their academic notebooks and record new insights. New Insights is the third column in the academic notebook.

❖ Elementary School

About once every two weeks, Mrs. Haystead goes over the terms she has taught in various subject areas. She does this by providing structured review activities that make her students think more deeply about the vocabulary words. Recently she has spent some time teaching her students about various prefixes, suffixes, and root words. Today Mrs. Haystead reviews the meaning of the prefixes *un-, im-, ir-, non-* and *re-*. She

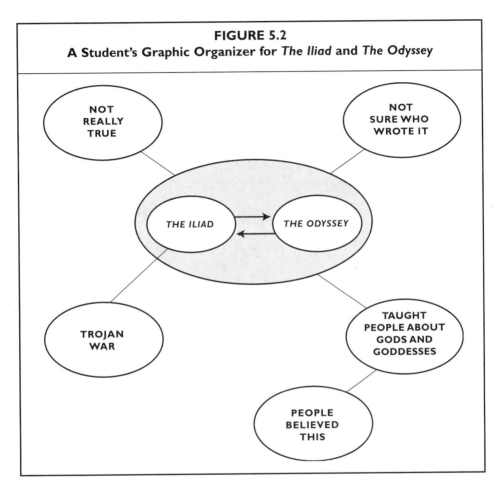

FIGURE 5.2
A Student's Graphic Organizer for *The Iliad* and *The Odyssey*

then gives the following directions to the class: "Pick one or more words from the vocabulary in your academic notebooks and create new words using these prefixes. Make sure you can explain the meanings of your new words."

Aida looks through her notebook and stops when she gets to the word *discovery*. She knows what it means, as well as the meaning of the prefix *re-*. She thinks, "If a discovery is finding something new, then a rediscovery is when someone discovers something that was already discovered a long time ago but then people forgot about it."

She usually enjoys these types of activities because they make her think, and they are fun. She knows Mrs. Haystead will soon have students break into small groups and share their newly created words. After these discussions, Mrs. Haystead gives them time to record new insights they might have in the third column of the vocabulary pages of their notebooks.

❖ Middle School and Junior High School

Today, instead of teaching new mathematics terms, Mr. Johnson provides students with a few analogies he has created, for example: The mean is to the average as the mode is to _____. He has explained analogies to students and emphasized the importance of seeing the common relationships between pairs of items. Students generally enjoy these activities because they offer a break from routine and are challenging but not frustrating. When students have completed the analogies he has provided, he directs them to create their own.

Andre looks over the mathematics vocabulary in his academic notebook. He finds the terms *deductive reasoning* and *inductive reasoning*. At first these terms gave him some trouble, but now he thinks he understands the difference. After a little thought, he creates the following analogy: "Deductive reasoning is to inductive reasoning as multiplication is to guessing who will win the Super Bowl." When Mr. Johnson asks Andre to present his analogy and explain it, Andre notes that with multiplication, the answer you get is absolutely right as long as you multiply correctly. That's the way deductive reasoning is. But you can never be sure about who will win the Super Bowl. That's the way inductive reasoning is. Simple and straightforward, Andre's analogy helps some other students better understand the distinction between the two terms.

❖ High School

Sometimes, instead of presenting new vocabulary terms, Mr. Brooke gives students time to review the vocabulary in their academic notebooks. His charge to them is this: "See if there is anything you would like to add to what you have recorded for a particular vocabulary term and if there is anything you would like to change or delete." On this particular day Henry focuses on the terms *Iliad* and *Odyssey*. As the unit has progressed, these poems have come up a few times, and each time Henry has become a little clearer about them and their role in Greek culture. He found out that the Greeks really believed that the age in which the stories are set was a time when gods and goddesses roamed the earth. He also discovered that the stories took place during the Bronze Age, but they make many references to iron tools and weapons. This means that they were historically inaccurate, but the Greeks didn't seem to care. Finally, Andre realized that the Trojan War, which was central to much of the action in the stories, was the subject of debate. For years scholars believed that the war and the city of Troy were entirely a creation of the Greek imagination, but then a 19th century archeologist found ruins that some now believe to be the site of the historical city. He adds this information about *The Iliad* and *The Odyssey* to the third column of the vocabulary section in his notebook.

Step 5: Periodically Students Are Asked to Discuss the Terms with One Another

As explained in Chapter 4, just as student interaction plays a key role in SSR, so too does it play a role in the development of academic vocabulary. Consequently, teachers should periodically organize students into groups and ask them to discuss the terms in the vocabulary sections of their notebooks. Again, this would occur as part of regular subject matter instruction. To stimulate discussion, the teacher might pose questions each group will address. These questions might simply direct students to terms they find interesting, or they might ask students to identify issues and questions they have about specific terms.

❖ Elementary School

Mrs. Haystead likes her students to spend some time discussing the terms in their academic notebooks. To facilitate this she sometimes asks them to identify the "most interesting" word in their notebooks or their "favorite" word. One by one, students stand up and present the term they have selected and explain why it is their most interesting or favorite word. Other students can ask them questions or add information. After each presentation the students add information to their academic notebooks based on what they have learned from the presentation.

❖ Middle School and Junior High School

Occasionally Mr. Johnson organizes students into groups of three. Each student identifies those terms that he is having difficulty with. The other two students provide information based on what they have written about the term in question or the way they have represented it nonlinguistically in their academic notebooks. If a group of students is having trouble with a given vocabulary term, they consult another team for help. Mr. Johnson is pleased and somewhat surprised at how this activity clears up misconceptions about terms and deepens students' understanding despite the fact that the activity is highly undirected.

❖ High School

To stimulate students' thinking about the vocabulary he has taught, Mr. Brooke occasionally organizes students in pairs and gives them a list of two or three of the most difficult terms that have been addressed. The task for each pair is to compare the information they have recorded and represented nonlinguistically. For each of the terms on the list, pairs of students identify what's true, what's false, what's new, and what's confusing. "What's true" is information that both students agree is accurate about the term or phrase. "What's false" is information both students agree is incorrect in one or both of the students' notebooks. "What's new" is information neither student has in their notebooks but both agree should be there. "What's confusing" is information that students in a pair cannot agree on. As each pair shares their conclusions, other students discuss what they have concluded about the target terms.

Step 6: Periodically Students Are Involved in Games That Allow Them to Play with the Terms

In Chapter 4, I discussed the importance of games as a tool for vocabulary development. Students can play with new vocabulary terms in many ways. Johnson, von Hoff Johnson, and Schlichting (2004) identify eight categories of word play. Marzano and Christensen (1992) describe 15 types of vocabulary games suitable for the classroom. As discussed previously, teachers can use games as sponge activities to stimulate interest and enthusiasm about vocabulary as well as provide multiple exposures to terms.

❖ Elementary School

Mrs. Haystead occasionally has students play games using the terms in their academic notebooks. Because she has all of the students for most of the day, she introduces new terms for a variety of subject areas. She uses games throughout the day to provide breaks in the routine and to help students make connections between terms from different subject areas. For this particular game, she has organized students into teams of five. She has tried to match up students strong in vocabulary with students who are not so strong to make sure that teams are fairly equal. She calls on a team to come to the front of the class. One member is selected to perform a pantomime for a vocabulary term provided by Mrs. Haystead. The remaining team members have three minutes to determine the word. If they guess correctly, the pantomimist gets another word. The team wins points based on the number of words they correctly guess in three minutes. The games last for two weeks, which provides enough time for each team to be at the front of the class twice. At the end of the two weeks, the team with the most points is recognized and rewarded. However, all students have participated in a review of words from different subject areas in their academic notebooks and Mrs. Haystead believes that everybody has won.

❖ Middle School and Junior High School

Mr. Johnson is using a variation of the popular game Pictionary to provide students with a review of important mathematics terms he has presented over the last few weeks. He assigns each student a word from the list of mathematics terms in their academic notebooks. He tries to match the complexity of the terms with students' levels of understanding of those terms. During the next two weeks, he calls on each student to present their word using the Pictionary format. A student gets 5 points if other students in the class guess the word within 2 minutes. Additionally, students receive 2 points for each word they correctly identify. The game goes on for two weeks, and students seem to enjoy it. At the end of the two weeks, the winner is declared, but all students agree that they understand the mathematics vocabulary terms better as a result of this adaptation of Pictionary.

❖ High School

Mr. Brooke has developed a variation of a popular television game show to help students review the words in the language arts section of their academic notebooks. He organizes the class into two teams. Each day he randomly selects one member of each team to come to the front of the class. Mr. Brooke hands each of the two students an envelope with five terms he has selected. One team is chosen to go first, and the representative has two minutes to provide clues for the words on the list. If the representative is having trouble with a word, he can skip it and go on to the next word. The team gets a point for each word identified within a two-minute limit. The next team then has a two-minute turn. The game continues over the next few weeks until each member of each team has had a turn in the front of the room. The team with the most points is acknowledged and rewarded.

Summary

The eight characteristics described in Chapter 4 form the basis for a six-step process for direct vocabulary instruction. The process involves the teacher describing vocabulary terms; students constructing their own descriptions of terms; students constructing nonlinguistic representations; the teacher providing opportunities for students to review and add to their knowledge of the terms; students interacting about the terms; and students playing games involving vocabulary terms. This process, combined with the approach to SSR described in Chapter 3, constitutes a powerful way to enhance academic background knowledge.

6

Defining an Academic Vocabulary

One of the characteristics of effective vocabulary instruction as described in Chapter 4 is a focus on terms that are important to the content presented in school. By definition, this is a critical aspect of any program that seeks to develop academic background knowledge through direct vocabulary instruction. If we select terms that do not relate to specific academic subjects as the target for instruction, we cannot expect much of an effect on academic background.

As noted in Chapter 4, terms taken from lists of high-frequency words are probably not the best source of target words for direct instruction. How frequently words appear tells us little about their difficulty and nothing about their relevance to specific subject areas. This chapter describes the process that was used to identify the subject area terms in the Appendix and contrasts them with those from previous efforts.

Another Look at Frequency Lists

Although Chapter 4 briefly discussed the problem with word-frequency lists, a more in-depth analysis is appropriate for one popular list that does attempt to identify subject-specific words—a positive feature not characteristic of the other commonly used lists. That list is *Basic Elementary Reading Vocabularies* (Harris & Jacobson, 1972). As its title implies, the list identifies basic vocabulary terms through grade 6. For each grade level, it provides a "core" list of words and an "additional" list. The core words appear in the majority of the basal readers that were analyzed in the study. Words on the additional list appear in some, but not a majority, of the basal readers that were analyzed. Finally, the lists include words specific to social studies, science, mathematics, and English—another feature that distinguishes the Harris and Jacobson word-frequency list from other similar efforts. In all, the Harris and Jacobson list contains 5,167 words in the core lists, 1,699 words in the additional lists, and 805 words in the subject-specific lists.

To get a sense of the words identified in the Harris and Jacobson list, consider these examples from the core 6th grade list:

aircraft	dungeon	gantry
athlete	ebb	photograph
bluster	estimate	pill
catsup	footstep	seethe
cell	fro	seventeen

Here we see notable disparity in the terms that are identified as appropriate for 6th grade vocabulary instruction. Some of the words—*aircraft, athlete, catsup, cell, dungeon, estimate, photograph, pill,* and *seventeen*—appear too familiar to be on a 6th grade vocabulary list. Other words—*bluster, ebb, gantry, fro,* and *seethe*—appear to be too obscure to be the focus of 6th grade vocabulary instruction. Although learning these words would be good for students, given the limited time for vocabulary instruction, we may well wonder if these words provide the most benefit for the cost in time and energy that will be required to teach them.

The "additional list" for 6th grade prompts even more confusion. These words are defined as being appropriate for vocabulary instruction at a given grade level but are considered to be of such low frequency that they should be addressed only after the words in the core lists have been taught. The additional list for 6th grade includes the following words: *cavity, custard, funeral, nineteenth,* and *summary.* Again, this conflicts with intuition about the importance of words. Isn't it more important for 6th grade students to understand *cavity, custard, funeral, nineteenth,* and *summary* (all of which are on the additional list) than it is for them to understand *bluster, ebb, gantry, fro,* and *seethe* (all of which are on the core list)?

Finally, although Harris and Jacobson include subject-specific vocabulary for mathematics, social studies, science, and English, these lists are sometimes sparse and inconsistent. For example, only 86 words are listed for mathematics, and 359 words are listed for science. The word *estimate* is on the core list but not on the mathematics list, whereas *closure* is on the mathematics list but would seem more appropriate on the core list. Similarly, *cell* is on the core list but not on the science list, whereas *corkscrew* is on the science list but not on the core list.

In summary, even though word-frequency lists have historically been the source for vocabulary instruction, they are plagued by inconsistencies and incongruities. These deficiencies are most likely a function of the manner in which such lists are constructed. To illustrate, consider Figure 6.1, which identifies some of the defining features of five major word-frequency lists. The critical piece of information in Figure 6.1 is that all the lists are based on an analysis of "running text." The Thorndike and Lorge (1944) list used 18 million words of running text, the Kucera and Francis (1967) list used 1 million words of running text. This means that the list designers analyzed sentences from textbooks, novels, and other works students typically read, keeping track of the frequency of the words in those sentences. This is a daunting task that is typically carried out by computer analysis, however, such analysis does not allow for any judgment as to the importance of words—frequency is the sole criterion. Herein lies the major weakness of word-frequency lists.

Depending on the type of material fed into the computer, results vary considerably. Consider the following contrived but informative example. Assuming that a novel consists of about 100,000 words of running text, 10 novels will represent

FIGURE 6.1
Major Word Frequency Lists

Source	Characteristics
Thorndike and Lorge (1944), *The Teacher's Word Book of 30,000 Words*	• Source: 18 million words of running text collected in the 1920s and 1930s from elementary, secondary, and adult reading materials • Number of words: 30,000
Kucera and Francis (1967), *Computational Analysis of Present-Day American English*	• Source: 1 million words of running text from adult reading material • Number of words: 50,000 words
Carroll, Davies, & Richman (1971), *The American Heritage Word Frequency Book*	• Source: 5 million words of running text in educational materials for grades 3 through 9 • Number of words: 86,741
Harris & Jacobson (1972), *Basic Elementary Reading Vocabularies*	• Source: 4.5 million words of running text in 127 elementary school textbooks • Number of words: 7,613 words
Breland, Jones, & Jenkins (1994), *The College Board Vocabulary Study**	• Source: 14 million words of running text in materials read by high school and college students • Number of words: not reported

*This is a report on the development of the College Board study. The actual list is not available.

a million words. If those novels are about the Wild West, then words such as *stage-coach* and *corral* will have high frequencies. If those novels are about skin diving, then words such as *tide, boat, fins,* and *goggles* will have high frequencies. With this said, it is important to note that all the lists profiled in Figure 6.1 made a concentrated effort to analyze a representative sample of the materials that students read. However, the contrived examples demonstrate the continuing problem. Without expert judgment as to what is important, word frequency is simply not a strong enough criterion. Indeed, research has shown that individuals knowledgeable in a given subject area can accurately estimate the difficulty of terms (Breland, Jones, & Jenkins, 1994; Shapiro, 1969). Fortunately, in the last decade the "standards movement" has produced documents that used expert judgment as to the important terms in specific subject areas.

The Standards Movement

Arguably, the standards movement has been one of the most significant educational reforms of the last half of the 20th century and will continue its influence well into the 21st century. Glaser and Linn (1993) explain:

> In the recounting of our nation's drive toward educational reform, the last decade of this century will undoubtedly be identified as the time when a concentrated press for national educational standards emerged. The press for standards was evidenced by the efforts of federal and state legislators, presidential and gubernatorial candidates, teachers and subject-matter specialists, councils, governmental agencies, and private foundations. (p. xiii)

Many educators point to the report *A Nation at Risk* (National Commission on Excellence in Education [NCEE], 1983), commissioned during the Reagan administration as a comprehensive study of the health of the U.S. educational system, as the beginning of the modern standards movement. The report painted a sobering picture of the health of the nation's K–12 education system. It noted that "the educational foundations of our society are presently being eroded by a rising tide of mediocrity that threatens our very future as a nation and as a people. . . . We have, in effect, been committing an act of unthinking, unilateral educational disarmament" (NCEE, 1983, p. 5). Shepard (1993) explains that the publication of *A Nation at Risk* changed the very rhetoric regarding education in that the general public began to associate the security of the country with the well-being of the K–12 education system.

The concerns about the well-being of the educational system prompted President George H. W. Bush to call the nation's governors together at an education summit in Charlottesville, Virginia, in September 1989. Six broad national goals were set and published under the title *The National Education Goals Report: Building a Nation of Learners* (National Education Goals Panel [NEGP], 1991). Two of the six goals dealt directly with the academic achievement of K–12 students:

> Goal 3: By the year 2000, American students will leave grades four, eight, and twelve having demonstrated competency in challenging subject matter including English, mathematics, science, history, and geography; and every school in America will ensure that all students learn to use their minds well, so they may be prepared for responsible citizenship, further learning, and productive employment in our modern economy.

> Goal 4: By the year 2000, U.S. students will be first in the world in science and mathematics achievement. (p. 4)

One of the tacit purposes of the education summit was to inspire educators to identify the important knowledge and skills that students should master by the time they graduate from high school. The National Council of Teachers of Mathematics (NCTM) had already made great strides to this end with the publication of *Curriculum and Evaluation Standards for School Mathematics* in 1989. Since then, standards documents have been identified for a variety of subject areas. Figure 6.2 lists standards documents that were either funded by the U.S. Department of Education or represented themselves as the consensus opinions of experts in their field as articulating what is essential for students to know and be able to do.

Taken as a group, the documents listed in Figure 6.2 represent an unprecedented articulation of the knowledge and skills identified by subject area specialists as important for K–12 education. The efforts taken and the level of agreement reached by subject-matter experts to construct the standards in the various subject areas are truly impressive. To illustrate, consider the efforts of the NCTM. In their original standards document (1989, p. vi–vii), they identify three levels of cooperation in the development and dissemination of their standards: endorsers, supporters, and allies. *Endorsers* are described as organizations that join with NCTM in "promoting the vision of school mathematics described" in the NCTM document. The 15 endorsers include the American Mathematical Society, the Association for Women in Mathematics, and the Council of Presidential Awardees in Mathematics. *Supporters* are defined as those organizations that lend "their support for the quality mathematics curricula and assessment criteria provided by the" NCTM document. The 25 supporters include the American Association of Physics Teachers, the American Chemical Society, and the National Education Association. *Allies* are defined as those organizations that "have agreed to serve as allies in our effort to improve the teaching and learning of mathematics as described in the" NCTM document. The 20 allies include the

FIGURE 6.2
Formally and Informally Recognized Standards Documents

Content Area	Documents
Mathematics	National Council of Teachers of Mathematics. (2000). *Principles and standards for school mathematics.* Reston, VA: Author.
Science	National Research Council. (1996). *National science education standards.* Washington, DC: National Academy Press.
History	National Center for History in the Schools. (1994). *National standards for history for grades K–4: Expanding children's world in time and space.* Los Angeles: Author. National Center for History in the Schools. (1994). *National standards for United States history: Exploring the American experience.* Los Angeles: Author. National Center for History in the Schools. (1994). *National standards for world history: Exploring paths to the present.* Los Angeles: Author. National Center for History in the Schools. (1996). National standards for history: Basic edition. Los Angeles: Author.
Social Studies	National Council for the Social Studies. (1994). *Expectations of excellence: Curriculum standards for social studies.* Washington, DC: Author.
Language Arts	National Council of Teachers of English and the International Reading Association. (1996). *Standards for the English language arts.* Urbana, IL: National Council of Teachers of English.
The Arts	Consortium of National Arts Education Associations. (1994). *National standards for arts education: What every young American should know and be able to do in the arts.* Reston, VA: Music Educators National Conference.
Civics	Center for Civic Education. (1994). *National standards for civics and government.* Calabasas, CA: Author.
Economics	National Council on Economic Education. (1997). *Voluntary national content standards in economics.* New York: Author.
Foreign Language	National Standards in Foreign Language Education Project. (1996). *Standards for foreign language learning: Preparing for the 21st century.* Lawrence, KS: Allen Press.
Geography	Geography Education Standards Project. (1994). *Geography for life: National geography standards.* Washington, DC: National Geographic Research and Exploration.
Health	Joint Committee on National Health Education Standards. (1995). *National health education standards: Achieving health literacy.* Reston, VA: Association for the Advancement of Health Education.
Physical Education	National Association for Sport and Physical Education. (1995). *Moving into the future: National standards for physical education: A guide to content and assessment.* St. Louis: Mosby.
Technology	International Technology Education Association. (2000). *Standards for technology literacy: Content for the study of technology.* Reston, VA: Author.

American Consulting Engineers Council and Institute of Electrical and Electronics Engineers.

In 2000, the NCTM standards document was updated and published under the title *Principles and Standards for School Mathematics* (NCTM, 2000). The same level of rigor was maintained. The updated document lists the following organizations as critical reviewers: American Mathematical Association of Two-Year Colleges, American Mathematical Society, Association of Mathematics Teacher Educators, American Statistical Association, Association for Symbolic Logic, Association of State Supervisors of Mathematics, Association for Women in Mathematics, Benjamin Banneker Association, Institution for Operations Research and the Management Sciences, Institute of Mathematical Statistics, Mathematical Association of America, National Association of Mathematicians, National Council of Supervisors of Mathematics, and Society for Industrial and Applied Mathematics.

The standards documents from the other subject areas sport similarly impressive lists of collaborators and supporters. For example, the national science standards published in the document *National Science Education Standards* and produced by the National Research Council (1996) described the process it used to generate the science standards:

> After the many suggestions for improving the predraft were collated and analyzed, an extensively revised standards document was prepared as a public document. This draft was released for nationwide review in December 1994. More than 40,000 copies of the draft *National Science Education Standards* were distributed to some 18,000 individuals and 250 groups. The comments of the many individuals and groups who reviewed this draft were again collated and analyzed; these were used to prepare the final *National Science Education Standards* that are presented here. (p. 15)

The authors of the national geography standards (Geography Education Standards Project, 1994) describe the process they used in the following way:

> Further input was received from nine public hearings, each held in a different city. In addition to the more than 2,000 persons who were asked to review the standards, project administrators sent drafts for critique to a hundred state social studies and science coordinators, 750 geography teachers, all National Geographic Society Alliance network coordinators, legislative aides to state education committees, governors' aides to education, and stakeholders whose names were provided by the National Parent-Teachers Association, the Association for Supervision and Curriculum Development, state and local boards of education, the Business Roundtable, the American Geographical Society's business members, and teachers' unions. Project members met directors of other standards-writing projects and shared drafts among all the writing groups. Furthermore, the authors maintained close contact with the history and science groups—the disciplines with the strongest curriculum ties to geography. (p. 246)

In short, the national standards documents listed in Figure 6.2 (p. 109) represent an unprecedented level of collaboration and agreement regarding the critical content to be mastered by U.S. students. In addition to national efforts, individual states have developed their own standards documents. To date, 49 states (all except Iowa) have developed documents. Finally, two major synthesis efforts have emerged from Mid-continent Research for Education and Learning (McREL) and the Council for Basic Education (CBE).

The McREL document is entitled *Content Knowledge: A Compendium of Standards and Benchmarks for K–12 Education* (Kendall & Marzano, 2000). It synthesizes more than 100 national and state documents and organizes their content into 14 major categories: mathematics, science, history, English language arts, geography, the arts, civics, economics, foreign language, health, physical education, behavioral studies, technology, and life skills. Within these 14 categories, 256 standards and 4,100 benchmarks are identified.

The CBE document is entitled *Standards for Excellence in Education* (CBE, 1998). It includes a synthesis of 22 national and state documents organized into eight categories: the arts, civics, English language arts, foreign language, geography, history, mathematics, and science. In all, 164 standards and 1,693 benchmarks are identified.

It is clear that U.S. education stands in a unique position. For the first time in its history, consensus standards documents have been constructed across the entire spectrum of content that forms the basis of K–12 education. These documents (and others) were analyzed to identify the terms presented in the Appendix.

How Is This Effort Different from Others?

Before considering the findings from the study that forms the basis of the lists of terms in the Appendix, it is useful to explain how this effort differs or expands upon other efforts. We have already seen that word-frequency lists have severe limitations as a way to identify the vocabulary important to specific academic areas because they rely on frequency of occurrence and ignore expert judgment. One recent effort to identify important content-related vocabulary *did* rely on judgment, however, and as such, it deserves some discussion and a comparison with the list in the Appendix.

Recall from the discussion in Chapter 2 that in 1987 E. D. Hirsch Jr. released a list of 4,546 terms, phrases, and dates that all students should know to be "culturally literate." The first book published by Hirsch, *Cultural Literacy: What Every American Needs to Know,* was immensely popular and has been followed by several other works. *The Dictionary of Cultural Literacy: What Every American Needs to*

Know was published in 1988 (Hirsch, Kett, & Trefil, 1988). It differed from the 1987 book in that it included definitions for each entry. The *Dictionary* was updated and republished in 1993 (Hirsch, Kett, & Trefil, 1993). The *Dictionary* was followed by the *Core Knowledge Sequence,* which was published in 1999 (Core Knowledge Foundation, 1999). The sequence organized the terms into grade levels, thus establishing the list as a curriculum for schools. The sequence was published in a series of books entitled *What Your Kindergartner Needs to Know, What Your First Grader Needs to Know,* and so on, up to grade 6. (See Hirsch, 1991a, 1991b, 1992a, 1992b, 1993a, 1993b, 1997, 1998; Hirsch & Holdren, 1996.) These grade-level publications also organized words by subject area. This alleviated the problem inherent in Hirsch's earlier efforts to identify a generic list of terms that cut across all content areas. In effect, these later works by Hirsch and his colleagues appear quite similar in principle to the subject area lists presented in the Appendix of this book.

How does the list in the Appendix differ from the impressive lists provided by Hirsch and his colleagues? First, as discussed in Chapter 2, my effort is based on a different philosophy of background knowledge. Specifically, whereas Hirsch considers knowledge of his terms as the "glue" that holds U.S. society together, I view knowledge of academic terms as necessary information for success in school only. Although academic knowledge is critically important, it is not, I believe, a necessary condition for successful participation in U.S. society.

Second, I do not necessarily agree with Hirsch's contention that the background knowledge of students in the United States has declined or that educational philosophers and practitioners have wittingly or unwittingly conspired to bring that about. As discussed in Chapter 2, considerable evidence supports the contention that students' background knowledge has actually increased.

Third, and perhaps most important, the list of terms in the Appendix is based on a rigorous analysis of standards documents, whereas the Hirsch listing used a different and (I assert) less valid approach. As stated by Hirsch in his first book, *Cultural Literacy: What Every American Needs to Know* (1987), the initial source of his list of 4,546 terms, phrases, and dates was the composite wisdom of Hirsch and two colleagues: "In 1983, I persuaded two of my colleagues at the University of Virginia, Joseph Kett, chairman of the department of history, and James Trefil, professor of physics, to help me compile such a list" (p. 135). As a check on the initial list, Hirsch had it reviewed by "more than one hundred consultants" (p. 146). However, it is not clear who these consultants were or what process they used to reach agreement on specific terms. As a result, Hirsch's list has been criticized for relying too heavily on personal opinion. For example, researchers House,

Emmer, and Lawrence (1988) from the prestigious UCLA Center for Research on Evaluation, Standards, and Student Testing (CRESST), concluded that Hirsch's 1987 listing of what every American needs to know was "politically conservative in what it includes and excludes" (p. 25). House, Emmer, and Lawrence explain that Hirsch's 1987 list contained "a great many proper names of Anglo American origin, many English literary terms, a surprising number of foreign phrases, many clichés, and only a few historical dates" (p. 13). House, Emmer, and Lawrence also identify many omissions in Hirsch's accounting of what every American should know:

> The list is short on athletics, health, entertainment, social science, and military terms. It systematically omits terms associated with the sixties such as the Age of Aquarius, the Beats, the Chicago Seven, counterculture, Bob Dylan, Allen Ginsberg, Howl, Jack Kerouac, One Dimensional Man, Students for a Democratic Society, We Shall Overcome, and Woodstock. It omits certain political terms such as Amnesty International, ERA, Greenpeace, Haymarket Square massacre, IWW (International Workers of the World), the Internationale, Jack London, nothing to lose but your chains, nuclear winter, and John Reed. It omits certain writers such as Henry Miller, Ezra Pound, Sam Shepard, and John Steinbeck. It omits ethnic terms such as Black Elk Speaks, the blues, Harlem Renaissance, soul (music, food), and omits certain music terms such as the blues, Billie Holiday, punk, reggae, rock and roll, while including Fred Astaire, Ginger Rogers, and the Beatles. It omits social terms such as Margaret Mead, Thorstein Veblen, weltanschauung. It omits health terms such as AIDS, carcinogenic, Lamaze, and stress. (p. 13)

In contrast to Hirsch's reliance on the experiences of three university professors and the reactions of 100 consultants, the basic sources of the terms in the Appendix are the standards documents listed in Figure 6.2, p. 109, and the synthesis documents developed by McREL and CBE. As discussed previously, these documents represent an unprecedented source of consensus about what students should know and be able to do in terms of K–12 academic content. Based on the manner in which the standards documents were constructed, we might conclude that the list of terms in the Appendix of this book has both *face validity* and *content validity*. Face validity is defined as the extent to which the terms represent the important content within a subject area (Kumar, 1996). Because the terms are extracted from the consensus opinions of subject matter specialists, by definition they represent the essential content. Content validity is defined as the extent to which the terms address the entire spectrum of content within a given subject area (Kumar, 1996). Again, because the standards documents from which I derived the terms represent a comprehensive listing of each content area, the terms have content validity.

As mentioned previously, the source documents used for the list of terms and the manner in which those documents were analyzed also separate this effort from the word-frequency lists such as those referenced in Figure 6.1, p. 106. Recall that those lists are based solely on word frequency and that this method can produce inconsistencies and incongruities. The list of terms presented in this book has the advantage of expert judgment because the standards documents from which the terms were extracted grew out of impressive consensus efforts.

Analyzing the Standards Documents

The documents listed in Figure 6.2 (p. 109) formed the basis for *Building Background Knowledge,* although I consulted other supplemental works for some subject areas. (See the Appendix for a discussion of the specific sources used for each subject area.) In addition, I used the synthesis documents by McREL and CBE. I analyzed each of the benchmark statements in these documents using a linguistic approach based on an analysis of propositions. For a technical description of this approach, see Marzano (2002). Briefly, though, consider the following benchmark from the National Council of Teachers of Mathematics standards document (NCTM, 2000), which represents what students should know and be able to do by the end of 5th grade: "Develop fluency in adding, subtracting, multiplying, and dividing whole numbers." This statement contains at least five terms that might be the focus of vocabulary instruction: *adding, subtracting, multiplying, dividing,* and *whole numbers.* Words like these directly extracted from the standards documents were then transformed to a more useful syntactic form for the purposes of vocabulary instruction. For example, *adding* was changed to *addition; subtracting,* to *subtraction.* In some cases, the terms identified in the standards documents led to the identification of related terms important to an understanding of the terms in the standards document. For example, the term *addend* is important to an understanding of the term *addition;* the term *dividend* is important to an understanding of the term *division.* Again, a more detailed description of the process used to analyze the standards document is presented in Marzano (2002). This example, however, demonstrates that the terms in the Appendix were extracted directly from the statements in standards documents and then supplemented to produce the lists of subject matter terms.

Findings from the Study

The analysis of the standards documents produced 7,923 terms across 11 subject areas. The terms in each subject area are organized in four levels, as shown in Figure 6.3, which depicts the general findings from the study. Note that the subjects of history and the arts are subdivided into more discrete topics. History is organized into three categories: general history, U.S. history, and world history. The arts

FIGURE 6.3
Number of Terms Per Level in Each Subject Area

Subject Area	Level 1 (K–2)	Level 2 (3–5)	Level 3 (6–8)	Level 4 (9–12)	Totals
Mathematics	80	190	201	214	685
Science	100	166	225	282	773
English Language Arts	83	245	247	223	798
History					
General History	167	560	319	270	1,311
U.S. History	0	154	123	148	425
World History	0	245	301	297	843
Geography	89	212	258	300	859
Civics	45	145	210	213	613
Economics	29	68	89	155	341
Health	60	68	75	77	280
Physical Education	57	100	50	34	241
The Arts					
Arts General	14	36	30	9	89
Dance	18	24	42	37	121
Music	14	83	67	32	196
Theater	5	14	35	13	67
Visual Arts	3	41	24	8	76
Technology	23	47	56	79	205
TOTALS	**782**	**2,398**	**2,352**	**2,391**	**7,923**

are organized into five categories: arts general, dance, music, theater, and visual arts. The rationale for this subdivision is explained in the Appendix. Also note that no terms were identified at Level 1 (K–2) for U.S. history and world history. Again, the rationale is explained in the Appendix.

One interesting aspect of the findings reported in Figure 6.3 is the highly uneven distribution of terms across subject areas. History, for example, has more terms by far than any other subject area—a total of 2,579 (1,311 from general history, 425 from U.S. history, and 843 from world history). The history terms make up 32.6 percent of all the terms in the Appendix. One reason for the high number of history terms is that the history standards documents are highly specific in terms of identifying individuals, events, and places that students should know. Another reason is that the list includes social studies terms from the document *Expectations of Excellence: Curriculum Standards for Social Studies* (National Council for the Social Studies, 1994). These terms were included because the content specified in the social studies document overlapped conceptually with much of the content identified in the history standards documents. In effect, the category in the Appendix entitled General History includes the terms typically associated with social studies education.

Another interesting aspect of the findings reported in Figure 6.3 is the large number of terms at Level 2, or grades 3 through 5. Specifically, more terms appear at Level 2 (2,398) than at any other level. One might logically expect that Level 4—grades 9 through 12—would have the most terms. The explanation for the high number of terms at Level 2 is most likely that many terms are introduced at Level 2 but then developed in more depth later in the K–12 sequence. For example, the health term *drug abuse* is introduced at Level 2 but then is further developed at Levels 3 and 4 as described by the health standards documents (Joint Committee on National Health Education Standards, 1995). This multilevel approach makes good sense from the perspective of Carey's (1978) notion of vocabulary development. Recall from the discussion in Chapter 4 that Carey proposed a developmental sequence of vocabulary learning that begins with a very general understanding of a term but develops into a detailed, mature understanding of the term, given appropriate time and the requisite number of quality interactions with the term. This approach is also consistent with Taba's (1962) notion of a "spiraling" curriculum, in which concepts are introduced at a surface level in the early grades and then revisited at the higher grade levels, where detail and breadth of understanding are cultivated. Even with these qualifications, however, it is still striking how much new content students are exposed to in grades 3 through 5. Whereas they are exposed to 782 terms in grades K through 2, they are exposed to 2,398 terms in grades 3 through 5. This represents a 300 percent increase in the amount of content students are expected to understand. We might reasonably question the logic of this approach.

The terms in the Appendix are the raw material from which educators can develop a comprehensive program of direct vocabulary instruction. As discussed in Chapter 7, schools and districts must make some decisions about how to design such a program.

Summary

Subject-specific terms are the best target for direct vocabulary instruction. Previous efforts to identify subject-specific vocabulary terms have been inadequate. The standards movement, with its unprecedented emphasis on specifying what students should know and do in the various subject areas, has produced documents that serve as valuable sources for vocabulary terms. An analysis of these documents, and others, produced the lists of 7,923 subject-specific terms in the Appendix.

7

Setting Up a Schoolwide or Districtwide Program

Chapters 1 through 6 have presented the rationale and recommendations for a comprehensive approach to enhancing students' academic background knowledge. I have proposed two basic interventions. The first is a sustained silent reading (SSR) program that focuses on students reading nonfiction and fiction materials in a variety of formats (e.g., books, magazines, information from the Internet) on topics of their choice. Key to the success of this approach is to systematically engage students in sustained reading, reflection, and interaction with other students. I proposed using the academic notebook for students' written reflections regarding their readings. To implement such an intervention, schools must schedule appropriate time for SSR, gather the reading material identified by student interests, and then follow the suggested steps outlined in Chapter 3. Although these steps are not easy tasks, they are relatively straightforward.

The second recommended intervention is a program of direct vocabulary instruction focusing on the terms and phrases that students will encounter in their academic subjects. This intervention also uses the academic notebook. Students record their understandings and representations of the terms presented in their subject area classes in the academic notebook. To help implement a program of direct vocabulary instruction, I have identified 7,923 terms in 11 subject areas; these terms appear in the Appendix. They were extracted from national standards documents and two documents that synthesize the national and state standards documents. Although these terms represent a useful resource, 7,923 terms are still too many to teach directly. Consequently, to implement an effective program of direct vocabulary instruction, a school or district must first identify the terms to target.

Establishing Reasonable Targets

As many researchers and theorists have noted, the number of terms that can be addressed in a program of direct vocabulary instruction is limited (Adams, 1990; Graves, 1986; Nagy & Anderson, 1984; Stahl, 1999). A common assumption is that a program of direct vocabulary instruction will address from 10 to 12 words per week. Assuming that such a program runs for about 32 weeks during the school year, direct instruction can account for about 384 words, at best, under the logic of conventional estimates. These estimates address direct vocabulary instruction in general terms (not subject-specific terms), typically identified from lists of high-frequency words. Also, these programs are usually carried out in language arts, English, or reading classes. What estimates of 10 to 12 words per week fail to acknowledge is that teachers in specific subject area classes also teach vocabulary as part of regular instruction, and these words are taught in addition to the general vocabulary words. Consequently, I contend that schools typically teach more words than previous estimates would indicate, if we look across the spectrum of the multiple subject areas addressed during the entire school day.

An important question related to the purpose of this book is, what is a reasonable number of terms that can be addressed in a school year across all subject areas? In response, Figure 7.1 (p. 122) presents some estimates. The cumulative numbers in Figure 7.1 indicate that 4,096 terms can be taught across the K–10 spectrum, the duration of time I am recommending for SSR and a schoolwide program of direct vocabulary instruction. This is not to say that schools should suspend direct vocabulary instruction at grades 11 and 12. Indeed, such instruction makes sense even in college and graduate courses. As the previous chapters indicate, however, I am recommending that direct vocabulary instruction be addressed schoolwide through grade 10, and that students record vocabulary words from all subject areas in a single academic notebook. If students have a single notebook for all vocabulary terms, teachers in different subject areas can address terms in other subject areas. For example, a mathematics teacher might ask students to make connections between math and science terms recorded in their academic notebooks. Students would thus have the opportunity to make interdisciplinary connections they might otherwise not make.

The estimates in Figure 7.1 provide great hope for direct vocabulary instruction. I assert that they are quite reasonable and even somewhat conservative. Kindergarten has no terms slated for instruction, and 1st grade has only 32, with the numbers increasing gradually to a high of 800 at grades 9 and 10. To gain a perspective on the practical implications of these estimates, consider the column entitled "Number of Words Per Week" while keeping in mind the assertion that typical vocabulary development programs teach from 10 to 12 words per week. According to Figure 7.1, p. 122, this level is not reached until grade 5. From grade 6 on, the 12-word upper limit is exceeded, and by grade 9 it is more than doubled. However, the figure of 25 words per week in 9th and 10th grade is still reasonable. Assuming that the typical 9th or 10th grade student is taking five courses, this implies that one vocabulary term is taught each day in each of the five courses for 32 weeks. If 9th and 10th grade students have been systematically schooled in the process of learning new terms and phrases, one word per day per subject area should not be too labor intensive.

When considering the estimates in Figure 7.1, it is also important to keep in mind that the goal of direct vocabulary instruction is to provide students with a surface-level, not an in-depth, understanding of vocabulary terms. Recall Carey's (1978) concept of "fast mapping." According to this theory, even one direct-instruction exposure to a word might be enough to provide students with the kernel of understanding that will deepen as they encounter it further. Even those vocabulary researchers and theorists who are commonly associated with arguments in favor of wide reading as opposed to direct vocabulary instruction attest to the usefulness of brief instructional encounters with words. For example, citing a personal communication with Isabel Beck as the inspiration for their comments, Nagy and Herman (1987) state:

> Although a strong case can be made for rich, knowledge-based vocabulary instruction, one should not underestimate the possible benefits of less intensive instruction. . . . One should not underestimate the value of any meaningful encounter with a word, even if the information gained from the one encounter is relatively small. (pp. 31–32)

In summary, the target of 4,096 words taught through direct vocabulary instruction in grades kindergarten through 10 is quite reasonable. This number of words, however, is still less than the 7,923 terms in the Appendix. Obviously this situation must be resolved.

Identifying Essential Terms

How does one cull the 4,096 terms that will be the subject of direct instruction from the list of 7,923? A number of aspects of the list in the Appendix make the task easier than expected.

First, the terms in the Appendix span grades kindergarten through 12, and the approach described in this book spans grades kindergarten through 10. Of the 7,923 words identified in the Appendix, 2,391 are at the 9th through 12th grade levels. Thus, at least half of these terms (or about 1,196) would not be included in a K–10 schoolwide program. This reduces the total to 6,727. A district or school, then, need only identify which terms are more appropriate for instruction in grades 11 and 12, presumably in advanced courses, to significantly reduce the number of terms in the Appendix from which to choose.

Second, a school or district may limit the number of subject areas for which vocabulary will be taught as part of the schoolwide or districtwide approach. The Appendix contains terms for 11 subject areas that span the K–12 spectrum; however, an individual student will certainly not encounter 11 subject areas each year. To illustrate, consider a typical 8th grade student who is taking five courses: mathematics, English, science, social studies, and music. The terms taught in the social studies class would be drawn from the General History section, Level 3. The total number of Level 3 terms for general history, mathematics, English, science, and music is 1,059 (319 + 201 + 247 + 225 + 67). However, Level 3 spans three grade levels—6, 7, and 8. Distributing the 1,059 terms evenly across the three years indicates that only 353 terms need be taught in a given year. This is well below the 640 terms slated for instruction in 8th grade and even below the 480 terms for 6th grade (see Figure 7.1).

At the elementary level, it is even less likely that students need terms in all of the 11 subject areas; in fact, one might make a case that vocabulary instruction should focus on only a few subjects. For example, if direct vocabulary instruction in grades 3 through 5 were to focus on mathematics, science, and the English language arts, the total number of terms from the Appendix that apply is 601 (190 + 166 + 245). This total is less than the target number of 606 terms identified in Figure 7.1 for these grade levels.

A third approach to decreasing the number of words that are addressed through direct instruction is to identify those terms that are considered essential versus supplemental. This suggestion has been made by several researchers and theorists (e.g., Wiggins & McTighe, 1998; English, 2000), including myself in the book *What Works in Schools: Translating Research into Action* (Marzano, 2003). There I made the point that the standards movement has created the expectation that U.S. educators will teach more content than is possible within the time available. In fact, assuming a 180-day school year, the standards identified in the national documents involve 71 percent more content than is possible to teach in the instructional time currently available. (For a discussion of this issue, see Marzano, 2003.) A viable option for schools and districts is to decrease the terms that will be addressed by identifying those that are essential for all students to learn regardless of their aspirations after high school. To illustrate how this might

FIGURE 7.1
Estimated Number of Terms That
Can Be Taught at Various Grade Levels

Grade Level	Number of Words Per Week	Total Words in 32 Weeks	Cumulative Total
K	0	0	0
1	1	32	32
2	3	96	128
3	4	128	256
4	5	160	416
5	10	320	736
6	15	480	1,216
7	20	640	1,856
8	20	640	2,496
9	25	800	3,296
10	25	800	4,096

be done, consider a study I conducted on mathematics terms (Marzano, 2002). I gave a list of 741 mathematics terms to 10 mathematics educators to whom I posed this question: Which of these terms are essential for students to know regardless of whether they intend to go to college? Figure 7.2 presents the results of that study. To interpret the figure, consider the first row, which shows that 299 terms were identified by all 10 educators as essential for all high school graduates to know. This number equals 40.4 percent (299 ÷ 741). Row 2 shows that 17 additional math terms were identified by nine educators as essential for high school graduates to know. Combining the results of rows 1 and 2, we find that 316 terms were identified as essential by nine or more of the educators (299 + 17). Column 4 gives that result as a cumulative number of terms identified as essential by the given number of educators (nine or more educators identified 316 terms as essential).

The survey results are worth considering because they indicate that the number of terms that educators agree are essential is smaller than one might expect. Of

FIGURE 7.2 Mathematics Terms Deemed Essential for All High School Graduates			
Number of Educators Who Agreed That a Given Term Is Essential	Number of Terms on Which They Agreed	Percentage	Cumulative Agreement
10	299	40.4	
9	17	2.3	9 or more 316
8	39	5.3	8 or more 355
7	26	3.5	7 or more 381
6	23	3.1	6 or more 404
5	69	9.3	5 or more 473
4	53	7.2	4 or more 526
3	8	1.4	3 or more 534
2	23	3.1	2 or more 598
1	41	5.5	
0	143	19.3	

Note: For a discussion of how the 741 mathematics terms were identified, see Marzano, 2002. Percentages do not add up to 100 because numbers have been rounded.

course, the criterion as to the percentage of mathematics educators who must identify a term as essential is arbitrary. However, using the intuitively appealing criterion of "a majority of mathematics educators" (i.e., six or more in the context of my study), then 404 of the 741 terms, or 54.5 percent, were identified as necessary for all students to know before high school graduation (see Figure 7.2, column 4).

Whatever the appropriate criterion might be, these findings suggest that not all of the terms taught in mathematics are considered essential. Indeed, 19.3 percent of the terms in my study were not identified by any of the mathematics educators as essential (see the last row in Figure 7.2), and only 40.4 percent were identified by all 10 educators as essential. If the other subject areas followed the same patterns, then we would estimate that only about 55 percent, or 4,358 of the 7,923 terms in the Appendix, would be identified by a majority of subject matter specialists as essential. Looking again at Figure 7.1, which suggests that 4,096 terms can be addressed in a K–10 direct instruction program, we may conclude that almost all of the essential terms for all 11 subject areas could be addressed using the approach described in this book. Although at first blush a national or state-level effort to identify the essential versus supplementary terms might seem advisable, I believe that such an effort is the right and responsibility of local education agencies. This is not to say that national or state efforts would not be useful or welcome, but it is ultimately the responsibility of educators within individual schools and districts to make the final determination of what is or is not essential because they know best the needs and wants of their students and community.

One District's Efforts

Some schools and districts in the United States have made efforts to identify essential terminology. One notable example is Community Consolidated School District 15 in Palatine, Illinois. To identify what they refer to as "core vocabulary terms" in grades 2 through 6 and to ensure that these terms are taught in every school in the district, they developed a program referred to as Vocabulary for Increased Achievement, or VIA (Community Consolidated School District 15, 2003). The district brought together subject matter specialists and generalists to select terms from the Illinois state standards documents and their district curriculum guides. They targeted four subject areas—language arts, mathematics, science, and social studies. After identifying key vocabulary terms for grades 2 through 6, they organized the words into categories important to each subject area. To illustrate, here are a few of the terms in each of the categories identified for grade 6:

Language Arts
  Genres: *myths*
  Text elements: *tone*
  Word study: *etymology*
  Writing: *figurative language*

Grammar: *prepositional phrase*
Research: *primary source*
Speaking/listening: *debate*

Science
Earth science: *plates*
Physical science: *energy source*
Space science: *solstice*

Social Studies
Culture: *social pyramid*
Economics: *surplus*
Geography: *migration*
Government: *tyranny*
History: *civilization*

Mathematics
Computation and concept of numbers: *exponent*
Functions and algebra: *linear equation*
Geometry and measurement: *congruence*
Statistics and data analysis: *frequency*

In addition to identifying core terms, the VIA project articulated a robust philosophy of vocabulary development and a well-designed pedagogy. Its stated philosophy includes many of the principles and characteristics highlighted in this book. For example, the VIA philosophy includes these beliefs:

- Words form the basis of background knowledge critical to learning.
- Words are learned gradually over time.
- Schools should ensure that background knowledge is adequately developed in all students.

Similarly, the articulated pedagogy contains many of the techniques described in this book, including these:

- A focus on descriptions as opposed to definitions
- Use of linguistic and nonlinguistic representations
- An emphasis on multiple exposures
- Integration of wide reading and direct instruction
- An emphasis on student interaction regarding key terms

Finally, the VIA program uses systematic assessment of knowledge of the key terms to identify the progress of their students in grades 2 through 6.

The VIA program as constructed by Community Consolidated School District 15 is only one way that a district might go about crafting a systematic program of direct vocabulary instruction. An important aspect of their effort is that they did, in fact, develop a districtwide program so that they can ensure that all students will receive adequate exposure to key subject area terms. In other words, they have not left the important issue of academic vocabulary up to the idiosyncratic decision of individual teachers.

Epilogue

This book has described a system of education that would consciously and explicitly address a critical problem facing U.S. schools: the fact that students come to school with widely varying levels of academic background knowledge because of differences in their access to academically oriented experiences outside of school. I believe that such differences in access constitute the greatest alterable inequality separating students who live in or near poverty from those who do not. Stated more directly, I believe that if schools systematically address academic background knowledge using the approach I have described, they can make major strides in closing the achievement gap between educationally advantaged and disadvantaged students. Given that my recommendations would require instructional approaches that are well within our current means and structure, a case might be made that schools that do not address this issue are remiss in their duties if they truly ascribe to the principle that all students have the right to the best education possible. It is my hope that this book will both inspire and guide schools and districts that have not as yet addressed this critical issue to design programs to enhance academic background knowledge.

Technical Notes

This section contains technical notes referred to in the text.

Technical Note 1

To compute the average correlation between background knowledge and academic achievement, I first analyzed the correlations from the studies reported in Chapter 1 to determine *outliers,* using techniques reported by Tukey (1977). An outlier is a correlation that does not "fit" within a given set. It is either much larger or much smaller than the other correlations. I then transformed the remaining correlations using the Fisher Z transformation and computed the average of these transformed correlations. This step is necessary because differences between correlations do not constitute an equal interval scale. That is, differences between large correlations are not mathematically equal to differences between small correlations. The average Z transformed correlation was then transformed back to the original metric.

Technical Note 2

Throughout the book, I report a number of correlations between sets of variables. Most often one of these variables is academic achievement. The first example in Chapter 1 uses academic background knowledge as the other variable and reports a correlation of .66 between the two. One way to interpret a correlation is in a "predictive sense"—the extent to which performance on one variable predicts performance on the other variable. In the examples in this book, academic achievement is typically the variable that is being predicted. The correlation between the "predicted" variable (e.g., academic achievement) and the "predictor" variable can be used to establish an equation representing the relationship between the two. The general form of that equation (frequently referred to as a regression equation) is as follows:

(Predicted Z score) = (Predictor Z score) x (correlation)

To understand this equation, it is necessary to understand what a Z score is. A Z score is a transformation of a raw score to standard deviation units. A Z score of 1.00 means that a given raw score is one standard deviation above the mean of the distribution; a Z score of 2.00 means that a given raw score is two standard deviations above the mean; and so on. A useful aspect of Z scores is that they can be easily translated into percentile points on the unit normal distribution. A Z score of .00 means that an individual is at the 50th percentile; a Z score of 1.00 means that a person is at the 84th percentile; a score of –1.00 means that a person is at the 16th percentile. These conversions are accomplished by consulting a table depicting the unit normal distribution.

From the equation, we see that the Z score of the predicted variable can be computed by multiplying the Z score on the predictor variable by the correlation. For example, assume that a certain student has a Z score of 1.00 on the predictor variable. (In the first example in Chapter 1, that variable is academic background knowledge.) Because the correlation between academic background knowledge and academic achievement is .66, we multiply the Z score of 1.00 times .66. Thus, the formula predicts that someone with a Z score of 1.00 on academic background knowledge will have a predicted Z score on academic achievement of .66.

The prediction equation also demonstrates that a Z score of .00 on the predictor variable translates into a Z score of .00 on the predicted variable. In other words, a person with the mean score on the predictor variable will have the mean score on the predicted variable. This allows us to make inferences about changes in the predicted variable associated with changes in the predictor variable. It is easiest to do this if we begin with the assumption that a person starts at the mean on the predictor variable and the predicted variable—that is, the person is at the 50th percentile on both variables. In the case of the first example in Chapter 1, we assumed that the student starts at the 50th percentile both in terms of academic background knowledge and academic achievement. Because the regression equation predicts that a Z score of 1.00 in academic background knowledge translates into a Z score of .66 on academic achievement, we can infer the following: an increase in academic background knowledge from a Z score of .00 to 1.00 is associated with an increase in academic achievement of a Z score from .00 to .66. Translating this into percentile form, we can say that an increase in the predictor variable of one standard deviation is associated with an increase in the predicted variable from the 50th percentile to the 75th percentile because a Z score of .66 represents the 75th percentile on the unit normal distribution.

In the text I have stated that an "increase" of one standard deviation in the predictor variable is associated with an "increase" in the predicted variable. This terminology is based on theoretical as opposed to statistical criteria because a prediction equation like the one above tells us nothing about causality. In the examples used in the book, I have inferred causality from the research and theoretical literature.

Technical Note 3

Figure 1.4 (p. 8) and others in this book were constructed from a correlation coefficient. A correlation coefficient can be interpreted in terms of the binomial effect size display (BESD). To employ the BESD, the predictor variable is thought of as being dichotomized into two distinct groups. In the BESD illustration used in Figure 1.4, the dichotomized independent variable is being born in or near poverty versus not being born in or near poverty. Similarly, the predicted variable is dichotomized into success or failure on some criterion measure. In this book, the predicted variable is generally conceptualized as success or failure on some form of achievement test.

A common convention when using the BESD is to assume that the expectation for the predicted variable is a success rate of 0.50. To compute the BESD, the correlation coefficient is divided by 2 and then added to and subtracted from 0.50. For example, if the correlation between predictor and predicted is 0.50, then 0.50 ÷ 2 = 0.25. The proportion of subjects in the experimental group that would be expected to "succeed" on the predicted variable is computed as 0.50 + 0.25 = 0.75. The proportion of subjects in the experimental group that would be expected to "fail" on the criterion measure is 0.50 − 0.25 = 0.25. The converse of these computations is used for the control group. Rosenthal and Rubin (1982) make the case for the use of BESD as a realistic representation of the size of the treatment effect when the outcome variable is continuous, provided that the groups are of equal size and variance.

The correlation used to compute the BESD in Figure 1.4 was derived from Smith, Brooks-Gunn, and Klebanov (1997). They report standardized beta weights for the relationship between family income and success on a number of academic measures controlled for ethnicity, parent education, and family structure (e.g., single-parent home versus two-parent home, intact home versus divorced-parent home). Given that these beta weights control for the same factors and address students of the same age range as represented in the equations from Smith and colleagues, they can be legitimately aggregated using a weighted average after transforming them via the Fisher Z algorithm. That weighted average was .26.

Technical Note 4

A vote-counting procedure based on the assumption of equal sample sizes (Bushman, 1994) was used to estimate the effect size for the SSR studies as reported by Pilgreen (2000, pp. 106–108). This procedure can be used when one does not know the actual effect size in a set of studies but does have information regarding the number of studies in a set for which the experimental group significantly (i.e., probability less than or equal to .05) outperformed the control group. This was provided in the Pilgreen data. It was necessary, however, to estimate the sample sizes of the groups and assume that those sample sizes were approximately equal. Bushman (1994) advises that when sample sizes do not differ greatly, one can use a representative average value. In this case, I computed effect sizes using two assumed sample sizes—one fairly liberal, the other fairly conservative. One value was 25 students in each of the experimental and control groups; the other value was 50 students in each of the experimental and control groups. The estimated effect size under the assumption of a sample size of 25 was .40 with a 95 percent confidence interval of .29 to .54. The estimated effect size under the assumption of a sample size of 50 was .28 with a 95 percent confidence interval of .18 to .37. Both of these intervals result in a rejection of the null hypothesis. I selected the larger effect size for reporting in the text because it seemed more representative of the sample size of studies that are typical in education. Also, given Pilgreen's report that in pre/post case studies of SSR, students gained 10 months in reading comprehension in a 4-month period, the larger estimated effect size seemed more representative of the true effect size than the smaller.

I used the same basic process for the Krashen (2000) data. The estimated effect size under the assumption of a sample size of 25 was .87 with a 95 percent confidence interval of .59 to 1.30. The estimated effect size under the assumption of a sample size of 50 was .59 with a 95 percent confidence interval of .42 to .95. Both of these intervals result in a rejection of the null hypothesis. For the reasons cited above, I selected the larger effect size for reporting in the text.

In addition to estimating effect sizes using vote-counting procedures, I used Stouffer's method of combining Z scores (see Rosenthal, 1991) to estimate the combined significance level of the SSR studies. Although a combined significance level of .05 was already established from the confidence intervals reported above, the Stouffer method was considered less restrictive and, therefore, less conservative. It was assumed that studies showing a significant difference in favor of the experimental group had a Z score of +1.96, and that studies showing a significant difference in favor of the control group had a Z score of −1.96. Studies that showed no significant difference between experimental and control groups were assumed to have a Z score of .00.

The combined Z score for the Pilgreen data was 3.14, indicating a one-tailed significance level of .001. The combined Z score for the Krashen data for SSR studies more than one year in length was 5.25, indicating a one-tailed significance level of .00001.

Technical Note 5

The term *effect size* as used in this book refers to the *standardized mean difference* (d), which is defined as the difference between experimental and control means divided by an estimate of the population standard deviation—hence, the name, *standardized mean difference.*

$$\text{standardized mean difference effect size} = \frac{\text{mean of experimental group} - \text{mean of control group}}{\text{estimate of population standard deviation}}$$

To illustrate the use of an effect size, assume that the achievement mean score of an experimental group is 90 on a standardized test and that the mean of a control group is 80. Also assume that the estimate of the population standard deviation is 10. The effect size would be

$$\frac{90 - 80}{10} = 1.0$$

This effect size can be interpreted in the following way: the mean of the experimental group is 1.0 standard deviations larger than the mean of the control group. Given that adequate control procedures were employed in the study, we might infer, then, that the intervention experienced by the experimental group raises achievement test scores by one standard deviation. Thus, the effect size expresses the differences between means in standardized or Z score form. For a thorough discussion of effect sizes, see Hedges and Olkin (1985).

Appendix

In this section, 7,923 vocabulary terms are listed for 11 subject areas:

1. Mathematics	5. Geography	9. Physical education
2. Science	6. Civics	10. The arts
3. English language arts	7. Economics	11. Technology
4. History	8. Health	

The terms for all subject areas are reported at four levels:

Level 1: grades K–2	Level 3: grades 6–8
Level 2: grades 3–5	Level 4: grades 9–12

Twenty-eight standards documents served as the source for the 7,923 terms. I identified these terms using a linguistic analysis process as described in Marzano (2002). I do not offer them as a definitive listing. Rather, I encourage districts and schools to adapt and supplement the lists in any way they see fit, depending on how a given subject area is taught. The following sections describe the sources used to construct the list in each subject area, along with unique characteristics of the various subject area lists.

Mathematics

The following documents were used as the source for the mathematics terms:

National Council of Teachers of Mathematics (NCTM). (1989). *Curriculum and evaluation standards for school mathematics.* Reston, VA: Author.
National Council of Teachers of Mathematics (NCTM). (2000). *Principles and standards for school mathematics.* Reston, VA: Author.

Kendall, J. S., & Marzano, R. J. (McREL). (2000). *Content knowledge: A compendium of standards and benchmarks for K–12 education* (3rd ed.). Alexandria, VA: Association for Supervision and Curriculum Development.

Council for Basic Education (CBE). (1998). *Standards for excellence in education.* Washington, DC: Author.

The 1989 NCTM document was the initial standards document for mathematics. It was updated and replaced by the NCTM 2000 publication. The McREL document uses the two NCTM documents and a number of other national and state documents. The CBE document uses the 1989 NCTM document and selected state documents.

Science

The following documents were used as the source for the science terms:

National Research Council (NRC). (1996). *National science education standards.* Washington, DC: National Academy Press.

American Association for the Advancement of Science (Project 2061). (1993). *Benchmarks for science literacy.* New York: Oxford University Press.

National Science Teachers Association (NSTA). (1993). *Scope, sequence, and coordination of secondary school science. Vol. 1. The content core.* Washington, DC: Author.

Kendall, J. S., & Marzano, R. J. (McREL). (2000). *Content knowledge: A compendium of standards and benchmarks for K–12 education* (3rd ed.). Alexandria, VA: Association for Supervision and Curriculum Development.

Council for Basic Education (CBE). (1998). *Standards for excellence in education.* Washington, DC: Author.

The NRC document is commonly considered the official standards document for science. However, the Project 2061 document is widely used and provides guidance in terms of expectations for different grade levels, as does the NSTA document. The McREL document includes these and other national and state documents. The CBE document uses the Project 2061 document only.

English Language Arts

The following documents were used as the source for the English language arts terms:

National Council of Teachers of English (NCTE) and the International Reading Association (IRA). (1996). *Standards for the English language arts.* Urbana, IL, and Newark, DE: Authors.

Crafton, L. K. (1996). *Standards in practice: Grades K–2.* Urbana, IL: National Council of Teachers of English.

Sierra-Perry, M. (1996). *Standards in practice: Grades 3–5.* Urbana, IL: National Council of Teachers of English.

Wilhelm, J. D. (1996). *Standards in practice: Grades 6–8.* Urbana, IL: National Council of Teachers of English.

Smagorinsky, P. (1996). *Standards in practice: Grades 9–12.* Urbana, IL: National Council of Teachers of English.

Kendall, J. S., & Marzano, R. J. (McREL). (2000). *Content knowledge: A compendium of standards and benchmarks for K–12 education* (3rd ed.). Alexandria, VA: Association for Supervision and Curriculum Development.
Council for Basic Education (CBE). (1998). *Standards for excellence in education.* Washington, DC: Author.
Teachers of English to Speakers of Other Languages, Inc. (TESOL). (1997). *ESL standards for pre-K–12 students.* Alexandria, VA: Author.
National Standards in Foreign Language Education Project (NSFLE). (1996). *Standards for foreign language learning: Preparing for the 21st century.* Lawrence, KS: Author.

The document jointly published by NCTE and IRA is considered the informal national standards document for the English language arts. (For a discussion as to why the document is referred to as the "informal" standards document, see Kendall & Marzano, 2000.) The document describes standards in very general terms. However, the "standards in practice" documents (Crafton, 1996; Sierra-Perry, 1996; Wilhelm, 1996; Smagorinsky, 1996) provide descriptions of the standards applied to K–12 education. The McREL document uses these resources and other state and national documents. The CBE document uses two state documents. The TESOL and NSFLE documents were included as sources for the English language arts terms because they both describe knowledge and skills important to an understanding and use of the English language.

The English language arts terms in this Appendix do not include specific literary works or authors. Readers seeking such a list should consult the McREL and CBE documents.

History

The following documents were used as the source for the history terms:

National Center for History in the Schools (NCHS). (1994). *National standards for history for grades K–4: Expanding children's world in time and space.* Los Angeles: Author.
National Center for History in the Schools (NCHS). (1994). *National standards for United States history: Exploring the American experience.* Los Angeles: Author.
National Center for History in the Schools (NCHS). (1994). *National standards for world history: Exploring paths to the present.* Los Angeles: Author.
National Center for History in the Schools (NCHS). (1996). *National standards for history: Basic edition.* Los Angeles: Author.
National Council for the Social Studies (NCSS). (1994). *Expectations of excellence: Curriculum standards for social studies.* Washington, DC: Author.
Kendall, J. S., & Marzano, R. J. (McREL). (2000). *Content knowledge: A compendium of standards and benchmarks for K–12 education* (3rd ed.). Alexandria, VA: Association for Supervision and Curriculum Development.
Council for Basic Education (CBE). (1998). *Standards for excellence in education.* Washington, DC: Author.

The history terms in the Appendix are organized in a manner that is somewhat different from that used in the documents listed. The NCHS documents organize the history standards into four basic categories: historical thinking, K–4 standards,

U.S. history, and world history. The historical thinking standards address general skills like chronological thinking and historical analysis and interpretation. These skills are intended to be applied across all grade levels and all topics. The K–4 standards address general topics such as families and communities in the past and the present, general concepts from U.S. history, and the history of specific states. The U.S. history standards are designed for grades 5 through 12, as are the world history standards. The McREL document (which draws on the NCHS documents and a variety of other state and national sources) follows the same basic model, although it is more specific regarding grade-level intervals. The CBE document uses the NCHS documents and includes historical thinking standards, U.S. history standards, and world history standards. Finally, the NCSS document identifies general knowledge and skills, many of which overlap with the K–4 standards and the historical thinking standards from the NCHS documents. For the purposes of this book, I decided to collapse the common terms from the following sources into a single list entitled General History: the K–4 history standards from the NCHS documents, the historical thinking standards from the NCHS documents, the NCSS standards, and the information mentioned in both the U.S. and the world history standards. Thus, the terms in the General History list in the Appendix include general terms important to social studies, historical thinking, K–4 history (as defined by the NCHS documents), and the overlap in the U.S. history standards and the world history standards. Like the terms for the other subject areas, the General History terms are organized into four levels spanning the K–12 sequence of grades: Level 1: K–2; Level 2: 3–5; Level 3: 6–8; and Level 4: 9–12. The other two lists of history terms in this Appendix are entitled U.S. History and World History. These lists are organized into three grade-level intervals: Level 2: 3–5; Level 3: 6–8; and Level 4: 9–12. Levels 2 and 3 include slightly different grade levels than the corresponding levels in the NCHS documents. However, the use of documents from different organizations (i.e., NCHS, NCSS, McREL, and CBE) allowed for viable inferences as to the classification of terms into the four levels used in this Appendix.

Geography

The following documents were used as the source for the geography terms:

Geography Education Standards Project (GESP). (1994). *Geography for life: National geography standards.* Washington, DC: National Geographic Research and Exploration.

Kendall, J. S., & Marzano, R. J. (McREL). (2000). *Content knowledge: A compendium of standards and benchmarks for K–12 education* (3rd ed.). Alexandria, VA: Association for Supervision and Curriculum Development.

Council for Basic Education (CBE). (1998). *Standards for excellence in education.* Washington, DC: Author.

The GESP document is considered the official standards document for geography. The McREL document uses the GESP document and a number of other national and state documents. The CBE document uses the GESP document only. The geography list includes relatively few names of specific locations. Obviously, this is not an exhaustive list of all the names and places a district or school might want to teach in the context of a geography course. For example, states and capitals are not listed, nor are important cities and countries around the world. The specific locations that appear on the list are there because they exemplify some important concept in geography, not because they represent important locations in and of themselves.

Civics

The following documents were used as the source for the civics terms:

Center for Civic Education (CCE). (1994). *National standards for civics and government.* Calabasas, CA: Author.
Kendall, J. S., & Marzano, R. J. (McREL). (2000). *Content knowledge: A compendium of standards and benchmarks for K–12 education* (3rd ed.). Alexandria, VA: Association for Supervision and Curriculum Development.
Council for Basic Education (CBE). (1998). *Standards for excellence in education.* Washington, DC: Author.

The CCE document is considered the official standards document for civics. The McREL document uses it and a number of other state and national documents. The CBE document uses the CCE document only.

Economics

The following documents were used as the source for the economics terms:

National Council on Economic Education (NCEE). (1997). *Voluntary national content standards in economics.* New York: Author.
Kendall, J. S., & Marzano, R. J. (McREL). (2000). *Content knowledge: A compendium of standards and benchmarks for K–12 education* (3rd ed.). Alexandria, VA: Association for Supervision and Curriculum Development.

The NCEE document is considered the official standards document for economics. The McREL document uses it and a number of other state and national documents. The CBE does not address economics.

Health

The following documents were used as the source for the health terms:

Joint Committee on National Health Education Standards (JCNHES). (1995). *National health education standards: Achieving health literacy.* Reston, VA: Association for the Advancement of Health Education.

Kendall, J. S., & Marzano, R. J. (McREL). (2000). *Content knowledge: A compendium of standards and benchmarks for K–12 education* (3rd ed.). Alexandria, VA: Association for Supervision and Curriculum Development.

The JCNHES document is considered the official standards document for health. The McREL document uses it and a number of other state and national documents. The CBE document does not address health.

Physical Education

The following documents were used as the source for the physical education terms:

National Association for Sport and Physical Education [NASPE]. (1995). *Moving into the future: National standards for physical education: A guide to content assessment.* St. Louis: Mosby.
Kendall, J. S., & Marzano, R. J. (McREL). (2000). *Content knowledge: A compendium of standards and benchmarks for K–12 education* (3rd ed.). Alexandria, VA: Association for Supervision and Curriculum Development.

The NASPE document is considered the official standards document for physical education. The McREL document uses it and a number of other state and national documents. The CBE does not address physical education.

The Arts

The following documents were used as the source for the arts terms:

Consortium of National Arts Education Associations (CNAEA). (1994). *National standards for arts education: What every young American should know and be able to do in the arts.* Reston, VA: Music Educators National Conference.
Kendall, J. S., & Marzano, R. J. (McREL). (2000). *Content knowledge: A compendium of standards and benchmarks for K–12 education* (3rd ed.). Alexandria, VA: Association for Supervision and Curriculum Development.
Council for Basic Education (CBE). (1998). *Standards for excellence in education.* Washington, DC: Author.

The CNAEA document is considered the official standards document for the arts. The McREL document uses the CNAEA document and a number of other national and state documents. The CBE document uses the CNAEA document only. The terms in this Appendix are organized in a slightly different manner from the standards in the source documents listed above. The CNAEA and CBE documents organize the standards into four categories: dance, music, theater, and the visual arts. The McREL document uses these four categories and a fifth entitled "art connections." The Appendix includes terms in the four basic categories: dance, music, theater, and the visual arts. It also includes a fifth category entitled Arts General. This category includes terms that are commonly found in all or a majority of the four other categories.

Technology

The following documents were used as the source for the technology terms:

International Technology Education Association (ITEA). (2000). *Standards for technology literacy: Content for the study of technology.* Reston, VA: Author.

International Society for Technology in Education (ISTE). (2000). *National educational technology standards for students: Connecting curriculum and technology.* Eugene, OR: Author.

Project 2061, American Association for the Advancement of Science. (1993). *Benchmarks for science literacy.* New York: Oxford University Press.

National Business Education Association (NBEA). (1995). *National standards for business education: What America's students should know and be able to do in business.* Reston, VA: Author.

Kendall, J. S., & Marzano, R. J. (McREL). (2000). *Content knowledge: A compendium of standards and benchmarks for K–12 education* (3rd ed.). Alexandria, VA: Association for Supervision and Curriculum Development.

The ITEA document is commonly considered the official standards document for technology. The ISTE document is also widely used. The Project 2061 document and the NBEA document contain sections specific to the use of technology. The McREL document uses these and other state and national documents. The CBE document does not address technology.

VOCABULARY TERMS

Readers should note that proper names are listed alphabetically by first name as opposed to last name. Also, some entries are alphabetized on the basis of the article *the*.

Mathematics, Level 1

above
addition
area
behind
below
between
calendar
cardinal number
chance
circle
clock
coin
corner
day
decreasing pattern
difference
direction
distance
estimate answer
foot (measurement)

graph
greater than
grouping
guess and check
height
hour
in front
inch
increasing pattern
inside
left
length
less than
lists
location
measuring cup
minute
model
money
near
number

number line
numeral
numeric pattern
ordinal number
orientation
outcome
outside
pattern
pattern extension
pound
prediction
rectangle
right
second (time)
set
shape combination
shape division
shape pattern
similarity
size
sound pattern

Mathematics, Level 1 (*cont'd*)
square
standard measures of time
standard measures of weight
subtraction
sum
table
temperature
temperature estimation
temperature measurement
time interval
triangle
under
volume
week
whole number
width
year
zero

Mathematics, Level 2
2-dimensional shape
2-dimensional shape
    combination
2-dimensional shape
    decomposition
2-dimensional shape slide
2-dimensional shape turn
2-dimensional space
3-dimensional shape
3-dimensional shape
    combination
acute angle
addend
addition algorithm
angle
angle measurement tool
angle unit
area
associative property
bar graph
basic number combinations
capacity
centimeter
certainty (probability)
circumference

classes of triangles
cluster
common denominator
common fractions
commutative property
conservation of area
constant
corresponding angles
corresponding sides
cube
cylinder
data
data cluster
data collection method
decimal
decimal addition
decimal division
decimal estimation
decimal multiplication
decimal subtraction
diagram
different size units
distributive property
dividend
divisibility
division
elapsed time
English system of
    measurement
equation
equilateral triangle
equivalent forms
equivalent fractions
equivalent representation
estimation
estimation of fractions
estimation of height
estimation of length
estimation of width
even numbers
event likelihood
expanded notation
extreme value
faces of a shape
factors
flip transformation

fraction
fraction addition
fraction division
fraction multiplication
fraction subtraction
fractions of different size
front-end digits
front-end estimation
function
geometric pattern
geometric patterns extension
gram
greatest common factor
growing pattern
histogram
horizontal axis
identity property
improbability
improper fraction
inequality
inequality solutions
intersection of shapes
invalid argument
investigation
irrelevant information in a
    problem
isosceles triangle
least common multiple
line graph
linear pattern
mass
mean
measurement
measures of central tendency
measures of height
measures of length
measures of width
median
meter
metric system
midpoint
mixed numbers
mode
multiple
multiplication
negative number

number of faces
number pairs
number sentence
number triplet
obtuse angle
odd numbers
open sentence
order of operations
parallel lines
parallelogram
parallelogram formula
part to whole
path
pattern addition
pattern subtraction
percent
perimeter
perpendicular lines
pie chart
positive number
prime factorization
prime number
prism
probability
process of elimination
product
proof
pyramid
quotient
rectangle formula
rectangular prism
reduced form
relative distance
relative magnitude
relative magnitude of fractions
relative size
relevant information in a
    problem
remainder
repeating pattern
restate a problem
reversing order of operations
rhombus
right angle
rotation
rounding

ruler
same size units
sample
scale
shape similarity
shape symmetry
shape transformation
shrinking pattern
sphere
standard vs. nonstandard units
studies
subset
subtraction algorithm
surface area
survey
symbolic representation
tallies
time zone
trial & error
triangle formula
truncation
unit conversion
unit differences
unlike denominators
valid argument
variability
Venn diagram
verbal representation of a
    problem
verification
vertical axis
volume measurement
volume of irregular shapes
volume of rectangular solids

Mathematics, Level 3
3-dimensional shape cross
    section
3-dimensional space
addition of fractions
algebraic expression
algebraic expression expansion
algebraic representation
algebraic step function
alternate interior angle
angle bisector

approximate lines
area model
area of irregular shapes
array
axis of symmetry
base 10
base 60
benchmarking
biased sample
blueprint
box & whisker plot
certainty of conclusions
circle formula
circumference formula
combining like terms
complementary angle
complementary event
complex problem
composite number
congruence
conjecture
constant difference
constant rate of change
constant ratio
convert large number to small
    number
convert small number to large
    number
coordinate geometry
coordinate plane
coordinate system
counter example
counting procedure
cube number
cube root
cubic unit
data display error
data extreme
data gap
data set
deductive argument
deductive prediction
defining properties of
    shapes/figures
dilation
dispersion

Mathematics, Level 3 (*cont'd*)

distance formula
enlarging transformation
equal ratios
equation systems
experiment
exponent
exponential notation
fair chance
formula for missing values
frequency
frequency distribution
graphic representation of
   function
graphic solution
grid
growth rate
inductive reasoning
input/output table
integer
intercept
intersecting lines
irregular polygon
iterative sequence
large sample
limited sample
line symmetry
linear arithmetic sequence
linear equation
linear geometric sequence
linear units
logic ALL
logic AND
logic IF/THEN
logic NONE
logic NOT
logic OR
logic SOME
mathematical expression
maximum
method selection
minimum
multiple problem-solving
   strategies
multiple strategies for proofs
multiplication algorithm

mutually exclusive events
networks
nominal data
nondecimal numeration
   system
nonlinear equation
nonlinear function
nonroutine vs. routine
   problems
number property
number systems
number theory
odds
ordered pairs
outliers
overestimation
parallel figures
pattern division
pattern multiplication
pattern recognition
percents above 100
percents below 1
perimeter formula
perpendicular bisector
perspective
pictorial representation
place holder
planar cross section
plane
plane figure
polygon
precision of measurement
prime factor
problem formulation
problem space
problem types
projection
proportion
proportional gain
quadratic equation
quadrilateral
random number
random sample
random variable
range
range of estimations

rate
rate of change
rational number
rectangular coordinates
recursive sequence
reference set
reflection transformation
relative frequency
relatively prime
reliability
Roman numeral
root
rotation symmetry
sample selection techniques
sample space
sampling error
scale drawing
scale map
scale transformation
scatter plot
scientific notation
sequence
shrinking transformation
significant digits
similar proportions
similarity vs. congruence
simplification
slide transformation
slope
slope intercept formula
solid figure
solution algorithm
solution probabilities
spreadsheet
square number
square root
square units
stem & leaf plot
straight edge & compass
substitution for unknowns
supplementary angle
table representation of
   functions
table representation of
   probability
tessellation

tetrahedron
theoretical probability
thermometer
trapezoid formula
tree diagram model
triangle sides
underestimation
unit size
unknown
variable
variable change
vertex
volume formula
volume of cylinder
volume of prism
volume of pyramid
work backward
written representation

Mathematics, Level 4
absolute error
absolute function
absolute value
acceleration
add radical expressions
addition counting procedure
algebraic function
angle of depression
arc
area under curve
asymptote of function
base e
binary system
bivariate data
bivariate data transformation
bivariate distribution
Cartesian coordinates
categorical data
central angle
central limit theorem
chord
circle without center
circular function
classes of functions
combination
complex number

compound event
compound interest
conditional probability
confidence interval
conjugate complex number
continuity
continuous probability
    distribution
control group
correlation
cosine
critical paths method
curve fitting
curve fitting median method
decibel
density
dependent events
derivation
dilation of object in a plane
direct function
direct measure
discrete probability
discrete probability
    distribution
divide radical expressions
domain of function
empirical verification
equivalent forms of equations
equivalent forms of
    inequalities
expected value
experimental design
experimental probability
exponent
exponential function
factorial
factorial notation
Fibonacci sequence
finite graph
force
formal mathematical induction
fraction inversion
function composition
function notation
geometric function
global/local behavior

imaginary number
independent events
independent trials
indirect measure
inflection
interest
inverse function
irrational number
isometry
law of large numbers
law of probability
limit
line equation
line segment
line segment congruence
line segment similarity
line through point not on a
    line
linear
log function
logarithm
logarithmic function
mathematical theories
matrix
matrix addition
matrix division
matrix equation
matrix inversion
matrix multiplication
matrix subtraction
minimum/maximum of
    function
monitor progress of a problem
monomial
Monte Carlo simulation
multiply radical expressions
natural log
natural number
nature of deduction
negative exponent
normal curve
number subsystems
parallel box plot
parameter
parameter estimate
parametric equation

Mathematics, Level 4 (*cont'd*)

periodic function
permutation
phase shift
pi
point of tangency
polar coordinates
polynomial
polynomial addition
polynomial division
polynomial function
polynomial multiplication
polynomial solution by
   bisection
polynomial solution by sign
   change
polynomial solution successive
   approximation
polynomial subtraction
population
postulate
powers
precision of estimation
probability distribution
proof paragraph
protractor
Pythagorean theorem
quartile deviation
radical expression
radical function
radius
random sampling technique
range of function
rational function
real numbers
real-world function
reciprocal
recurrence equation
recurrence relationship
recursive equation
reflection in plane
reflection in space
regression coefficient
regression line
relative error
representativeness of sample

Richter scale
right triangle geometry
roots & real numbers
roots to determine cost
roots to determine profit
roots to determine revenue
rotation in plane
sample statistic
sampling distribution
scalar
series
series circuit
sigma notation
similar figures
sine
sinusoidal function
smallest set of rules
speed
spurious correlation
standard deviation
statistical experiment
statistical regression
statistic
step function
strategy efficiency
strategy generation technique
subtract radical expressions
successive approximations
summary statistic
surface area cone
surface area cylinder
surface area sphere
synthetic geometry
systems of inequalities
tangent
term
theorem
theorem direct proof
theorem indirect proof
transversal
treatment group
trigonometric ratio
trigonometric relation
truth table proof
two-way tables
U.S. customary system

unit analysis
univariate data
univariate distribution
upper/lower bounds
validity
variance
vector
vector addition
vector division
vector multiplication
vector subtraction
velocity
vertex edge graph

Science, Level 1
air
animal features
balance
behavior pattern
boulder
burning
chart
circular motion
cloud
color
computer
daily weather pattern
day
death
dinosaur
dissolving
distance
diversity of life
Earth materials
Earth's gravity
Earth's rotation
egg
energy
food
freezing
gas
growth
habitat
heat
horsetail tree
individual differences

insect
light
liquid
liquid water
location
machine
magnet
magnification
magnifier
mammoth
mixture
month
Moon
motion
night
observation
ocean
parent
parent/offspring similarity
pebble
plant
plant growth
position
precipitation
prediction
prehistoric animals
properties of light
pulling
pushing
reasoning
requirements for life
rock characteristics
ruler
salt water
sand
science
scientist
seasonal change
seasonal weather pattern
shape
shelter
similarities & differences
    among organisms
size
sky
soil

solid rock
sound
star
star age
star brightness
states of matter
straight-line motion
Sun's position
Sun's size
teamwork
temperature
the senses
thermometer
universe
vibration
water
weather
weather conditions
weather patterns
week
weight
wind
year
zigzag motion

Science, Level 2
ability to support life
acceleration
air movement
animal product
apparent movement of the
    planets
apparent movement of the
    stars
apparent movement of the
    Sun
applied force
astronomical distance
astronomical object
astronomical size
astronomy
battery
bedrock
beneficial change
birth
body of water

boiling point
bones/no bones
calculator
cause & effect
change of direction
change of motion
change of speed
changes in the Earth's surface
characteristics of air
charge attraction
charge repulsion
classification of substances
competition
composition of matter
condensation
conduction
conductivity
conductor
conservation of mass
conservation of matter
constellation
control of variables
controlled experiment
cooling
core
data analysis
data interpretation
data presentation
density
detrimental change
disease
drought
Earth's axis
Earth's orbit
Earth's surface
Earth's temperature
earthquake
electrical charge
electrical circuit
electrical current
electricity
energy transfer
engineering
environment
environmental changes
environmental conditions

Science, Level 2 *(cont'd)*
erosion
evaporation
external cue
extinction
food chain
food web
force strength
forms of energy
forms of water
formula
fossil
fossil evidence
fresh water
friction
gases of the atmosphere
generator
glacial movement
glacier
graduated cylinder
graph
ground water
heat conduction
heat transfer
herbivore
history of science
inherited characteristic
land form
landslide
life cycle
light absorption
light emission
light reflection
light refraction
living organism
logical argument
magnetic attraction
magnetic repulsion
mass
measurement of motion
melting point
metal
microscope
migration
mineral
Moon's orbit

Moon's phases
naturalistic observation
nutrients
ocean currents
offspring
oil
omnivore
ongoing process of science
organism
outer space
phase change
photosynthetic plants
physical properties
physical setting
pitch
planet
plant organ
plant product
plant root
plant/animal
pollution
population
population density
position over time
predator
prehistoric environment
prehistoric organisms
properties of soil
properties of sound
properties of water
question formulation
recycle
relative position
replicable experiment
reproducible result
reproduction
resource availability
rock breakage
rock composition
rock cycle
scientific equipment
scientific evidence
scientific experiment
soil color
soil composition
soil texture

Solar System
solubility
stored energy
survival of organisms
technology
telescope
tide
volcanic eruption
water capacity
weathered rock
weathering
wind patterns

Science, Level 3
acquired trait
adaptive characteristics
air mass circulation
alternative explanation of
    data
animal nervous systems
asexual reproduction
asteroid
asteroid impact
asteroid movement patterns
atmosphere
atmospheric composition
atmospheric layers
atmospheric pressure
atom
atomic arrangement
balanced force
behavioral change in
    organisms
behavioral response to stimuli
bias
body plan
carrying capacity
celestial body
cell
cell division
cell growth
characteristics of life
chemical change
chemical compound
chemical element
chemical energy

chemical properties of
    substances
chemical reaction
circulatory system
classification of organisms
climate
climate change
climatic pattern
closed system
color of light
comet
comet impact
comet movement patterns
common ancestry
concentration of reactants
confirmation by observation
conflicting interpretations
conservation of energy
constant speed
continuation of species
crustal deformation
crustal plate movement
crystal
debris
deceleration
decomposer
digestive system
direction of a force
direction of motion
displacement of results
Earth system
Earth's age
Earth's atmosphere
Earth's climate
Earth's crust
Earth's layers
eclipse
ecological role
ecosystem
egg cell
electric current
electrical energy
element stability
emergence of life forms
energy source
erosion resistance

ethics in science
evaluation of science process
evidence from sedimentary
    rock
excretory system
experimental confirmation
experimental control
external feature
faulty reasoning
filtering
food oxidization
forms of matter
fossil record
fundamental unit of life
fungus
galaxy
Galileo
gene
geologic evidence
geologic force
geological shift
gravitational force
Greek basic four elements
habits of mind
heat convection
heat emission
heat energy
heat radiation
heat retention
hereditary information
homeostasis
host
hydrosphere
hypothesis
hypothesis testing
igneous rock
immune system
inertia
infection
informed subject
infrared radiation
insulator
intellectual honesty
interdependence of organisms
internal cue
internal structure

invertebrate
kinetic energy
lever arm
life form change
life-sustaining functions
light scattering
light transmission
light wavelength
light year
lithosphere
logic
Louis Pasteur
mantle
Marie Curie
mathematical model
mechanical energy
mechanical motion
metal reactivity
metamorphic rock
meteor
meteor impact
meteor movement patterns
Milky Way galaxy
molecular arrangement
molecular motion
molecule
multicellular organism
muscular system
mutualism
nervous system
Newton's Laws of Motion
nonmetal reactivity
nonreactive gas
nuclear reaction
organ
organ system
organism system failure
oxidation
oxygen
parasite
particle ring
peer review
percolation
photosynthesis
physiological change
Pierre Curie

Science, Level 3 *(cont'd)*

planet composition
planet orbits
planet size
planet surface features
plant tissue
polygenic trait
predation
prey
properties of elements
pulley
radiation
reaction rate
recrystallization
recycling of matter
reproductive system
research question
respiration
respiratory system
right of refusal
risk & benefit
rock layer movement
rusting
satellite
scientific interpretation
scientific method
scientific skepticism
screening
sediment deposition
sedimentary rock
sedimentation
separation method
sexual reproduction
skeletal system
soil erosion
soil fertility
Solar System formation
specialized cell
specialized organ
specialized tissue
species
species diversity
speed
sperm
sperm cell
sunlight reflection

surface area of reactants
surface run-off
taxonomy
theoretical model
tissue
tolerance of ambiguity
unbalanced force
unicellular organism
unity of life
universal solvent
vertebrate
visible light
water cycle
wavelength

Science, Level 4

abiotic components of
    ecosystems
accelerator
acid/base reactions
actual mass
advection
age of the universe
Albert Einstein
Alfred Wegener
amino acid sequence
anatomical characteristic
Antoine Lavoisier
atmospheric change
atomic bomb
atomic bonding principles
atomic configuration
atomic energy
atomic mass
atomic motion
atomic nucleus
atomic number
atomic reaction
atomic theory
atomic weight
Avogadro's hypothesis
Bernoulli's principle
Big Bang theory
biochemical characteristic
biological adaptation
biological evolution

biological molecule
breakdown of food
    molecules
buoyancy
carbon
carbon atom
carbon cycle
carbon dioxide
catalyst
cell function
cell membrane
cell nucleus
cell organelle
cell wall
cellular communication
cellular differentiation
cellular energy conversion
cellular regulation
cellular response
cellular waste disposal
charged object
Charles Darwin
Charles Lyell
chemical bond
chemical organization of
    organisms
chemical properties of
    elements
chemical reaction rate
chloroplast
chromatography
chromosome
chromosome pair
composition of the universe
convection
convection current
Copernican revolution
Copernicus
Coulomb's law
criteria for acceptance
crystalline solid
cytoplasm
data reduction
decay rate
degree of kinship
derived characteristic

Science, Level 4 (cont'd)
periodic table of the elements
photosynthesizing organism
phylogenetics
plate boundary
plate collision
plate tectonics
potential energy
pressure
properties of reactants
properties of waves
protein
protein structure
protein synthesis
proton
Ptolemy
quantum of energy
radical reaction
radio wave
radioactive dating
radioactive decay
radioactive isotope
rate of nuclear decay
recessive trait
recombination of chemical
    elements
recombination of genetic
    material
relative mass
relative motion
release of energy
reproductive capacity
reproductive value of traits
revision of scientific theories
rock sequence
rules of evidence
sea floor spreading
segregation
seismic wave
selective gene expression
semiconductor
sex cell
sex chromosomes
sex-linked trait
shared characteristic
sound wave

space probe
special theory of relativity
speciation
speed of light
spontaneous nuclear reaction
star composition
star destruction
star formation
star size
star system
star temperature
star types
stellar energy
storage of genetic information
Sun's radiation
superconductor
survival value of traits
synthetic polymer
thermal equilibrium
torque
transforming matter and/or
    energy
transport of cell materials
transporting matter and/or
    energy
ultraviolet radiation
unequal heating of air
unequal heating of land
    masses
unequal heating of oceans
vacuole
viscosity
water wave
wave amplitude
wave packet
wave source
weight of subatomic particles
x-ray

**English Language Arts,
Level 1**
alphabet
author
back cover
beginning consonant
blend

book
cartoon
chapter
character
composition
comprehension
consonant blend
conversation
cover
date
dictionary
discussion
drawing
ending consonant
everyday language
fairy tale
first name
folktale
follow/give directions
front cover
group discussion
guest speaker
keyboarding
language
last name
letter
letter–sound relationship
listening skill
long vowel
lowercase
magazine
main character
main idea
map
margin
mental image
message
movie
newspaper
number word
order of events
parts of a book
photographer
picture book
picture dictionary
poem

predictable book
prewriting
print
publish
purpose
question
reread
respond to literature
retell
rhyme
sentence
short vowel
sight word
sign
speech
spelling
spelling pattern
symbol
table of contents
take turns
television program
textbook
theater
title
title page
typing
uppercase
videotape
villain
vocabulary
vowel combination
vowel sound

English Language Arts, Level 2

abbreviation
action verb
action word
actor
adjective
adverb
advertisement
affix
animation
antonym
apology

apostrophe
appendix
asking permission
audience
audiotape
auxiliary verb
brainstorm
capitalization
card catalog
cause and effect
central idea
chapter title
character development
chart
checklist
children's literature
chronological order
citation
closing sentence
colon
comma
command
commercial
common noun
compare & contrast
complete sentence
complex sentence
compound word
concluding statement
conclusion
consonant substitution
construct meaning
content-area vocabulary
context clue
contraction
contrast
cue
cursive
custom
declarative sentence
decode
definition
detail
diary
direct quote
directions

director
discussion leader
double negative
draft
drama
e-mail
edit
encyclopedia
ending
essay
example
explanation
expression
fable
facial expression
fantasy
fiction
first person
form
friendly letter
genre
gesture
glossary
grammar
graphic artist
graphic organizer
graphics
greeting
guide words
heading
headline
host
hostess
how question
humor
illustration
imagery
indentation
index
inference
Internet
interrogative sentence
introduction
investigate
invitation
irregular plural noun

English Language Arts, Level 2 (cont'd)
journal
key word
learning log
legend
letter of request
linking verb
list
listening comprehension
literature
meaning clue
memory aid
minor character
miscue
mood
motive
multimeaning word
multiple drafts
multiple sources
mystery
myth
negative
news
newspaper section
nonfiction
notes
noun
novel
numerical adjective
object
opinion
oral presentation
oral report
organization
outline
pamphlet
paragraph
passage
past tense
peer review
pen pal
period
personal letter
personal pronoun
phone directory

phonetic analysis
phrase
pitch
plot
plot development
point of view
posing a question
possessive noun
possessive pronoun
posture
preface
prefix
preposition
prepositional phrase
presentation
preview
prior knowledge
pronoun
pronunciation
proofread
prop
proper noun
punctuation
question mark
quotation
quotation marks
r-controlled
radio program
rating
reading strategy
reading vocabulary
regular plural noun
regular verb
request
revise
rhyming dictionary
role playing
root word
rules of conversation
scan
science fiction
second person
sensory image
sentence structure
sequential order
setting

short story
signature
singular noun
skim
sound effect
source
special effect
spoken text
stay on topic
story element
story map
story structure
subject
subject-verb agreement
suffix
summarize
summary
summary sentence
supporting detail
suspense
syllabication
syllable
symbolism
synonym
table
tall tale
target language
tense
text
thank you letter
theme
theme music
thesaurus
third person
time line
tone
topic sentence
typeface
usage
verb
voice
voice level
volume
Web site
when question
where question

why question
word choice
word family
word search
written directions
written exchange

English Language Arts, Level 3

action segment
active listener
adjective clause
adjective phrase
adverb clause
adverb phrase
almanac
Anglo-Saxon affix
Anglo-Saxon root
argumentation
atlas
author's purpose
autobiography
background knowledge
bibliography
biographical sketch
biography
body language
body of the text
broadcast
broadcast advertising
business letter
camera angle
camera shot
caption
catalog
CD-ROM
character trait
children's program
chronology
clarification
climax
close-up
closing
clue
common feature
comparative adjective

compile
composition structure
compound sentence
compound verb
conjunction
contract
convention
coordinating conjunction
criticism
cross-reference
current affairs
demonstrative pronoun
derivation
description
descriptive language
diagram
dialect
dialogue
document
documentary
editorial
elaboration
electronic media
enunciation
episode
etiquette
etymology
exclamation mark
exclamatory sentence
explicit/implicit
exposition
extend invitation
extraneous information
eye contact
facilitator
fact vs. opinion
familiar idiom
familiar interaction
feature story
feedback
figurative language
figure of speech
film director
flashback
follow-up sentence
footnote

foreign word
foreshadowing
formal language
formal speech
format
fully developed character
gender
generalization
glittering generality
grammatical form
Greek affix
Greek root
high-frequency word
historical fiction
historical theme
homonym
homophone
hyphen
imperative sentence
inconsistency
independent clause
informal language
information source
interjection
interpretation
interview
intonation
irregular verb
italics
jargon
juxtaposition
knowledge base
language convention
layout
lecture
line (in a play)
literal phrase
log
logic
logical argument
logo
manner of speech
mass media
mechanics (language)
media type
metaphor

**English Language Arts,
Level 3** (cont'd)
meter
modifier
multimedia presentation
musical
narration
native culture
native speaker
news broadcast
news bulletin
nonverbal cue
object pronoun
objective view
oral tradition
pacing
page format
parallel episodes
parallel structure
paraphrase
peer-response group
periodical
personal narrative
personification
perspective
persuasion
phrase grouping
physical description
physical gesture
plagiarism
poetic element
polite form
political cartoonist
political speech
positive adjective
predicate adjective
present tense
private audience
problem-solution
producer
programming
projection
pronominal adjective
proper adjective
proverb
public audience

public opinion trend
publication date
pull-down menu
quiz show
*Reader's Guide to Periodical
    Literature*
recitation
recurring theme
reference source
relative pronoun
relevant detail
rephrasing
report
representation
research paper
resolution
resource material
restatement
rhythm
sales technique
salutation
saying
scriptwriter
self-correction
sentence combining
shades of meaning
simile
simple sentence
sitcom
skit
slang
slanted material
small talk
software
sound system
special interests
specialized language
speech pattern
speed reading
stereotype
stress
stylistic feature
subject pronoun
subjective view
subliminal message
subordinate character

subordinating conjunction
subplot
superlative adjective
supernatural tale
syllabic system
syntax
synthesize
tabloid newspaper
talk show
target audience
technical directions
technical language
tempo
tension (in a story)
textual clue
time lapse
transition
translate
trickster tale
verb phrase
verbal cue
vernacular dialect
viewer perception
viewpoint
visual aid
voice inflection
word borrowing
word origin
word play

**English Language Arts,
Level 4**
acronym
advertising code
advertising copy
aesthetic purpose
aesthetic quality
allegory
alliteration
allusion
ambience
ambiguity
American literature
American Psychological
    Association
analogy

ancient literature
anecdotal scripting
anecdote
annotated bibliography
appeal to authority
appeal to emotion
appeal to logic
archetype
articulation
artifact
assonance
attack ad hominem
author's bias
autobiographical narrative
ballad
bandwagon
belief system
bias
Bible
biographical narrative
blurring of genres
bolding
British literature
bylaw
celebrity endorsement
censorship
characterization
cinematographer
circumlocution
clarity of purpose
clincher sentence
cognate
coherence
cohesion
collective noun
commercialization
compound adjective
compound noun
compound personal pronoun
compound-complex sentence
computer-generated image
concept
conceptual map
conjunctive adverb
connotative meaning
consonance

consumer document
context
contrasting expressions
controlling idea
copyright law
correlative conjunction
counter argument
couplet
credibility
credit
criteria
critical standard
cultural agency
cultural expression
cultural influence
cultural nuance
cultural theme
cutline
dash
debate
deconstruct
delivery
denotative meaning
dictation
diction
digressive time
direct address
directionality
divided quotation
drama-documentary
dramatic dialogue
dramatic mood change
emotional appeal
emphasis
epic
ethics
exaggerated claim
excerpt
expressive writing
extended quotation
external/internal conflict
false causality
faulty mode of persuasion
FCC regulation
feature article
fictional narrative

field study
film review
filter (in photography)
friendly audience
future perfect verb tense
hierarchic structure
Homeric Greek literature
hostile audience
hyperbole
idiom
incongruity
indefinite adjective
indefinite pronoun
inflection
interior monologue
internal conflict
interrogative pronoun
irony
job application
job interview
Latin affix
Latin root
leave-taking
limited point of view
literary criticism
literary device
literature review
logical fallacy
logographic system
lyric poem
marketing
media-generated image
medieval literature
medium
memorandum
methodology
microfiche
Modern Language Association
modern literature
modulation
mythology
narrator
negotiate
neoclassic literature
norm
noun clause

English Language Arts, Level 4 (*cont'd*)

noun phrase
nuance
ode
omniscient point of view
onomatopoeia
opening monologue
overgeneralization
overstatement
overview
packaging
parable
parody
past perfect verb tense
pastoral
performance review
persona
personal space
philosophical assumption
poise
policy statement
present perfect verb tense
primary source
production cost
progressive verb form
propaganda
proposition of fact speech
proposition of policy speech
proposition of problem speech
proposition of value speech
questionnaire
reaction shot
readability
red herring
redraft
reflexive pronoun
repeats
resume
rhetorical device
rhetorical question
romantic period literature
sarcasm
satire
secondary source
semicolon

set design
soap opera
sociocultural context
soliloquy
somber lighting
speech action
speed writing
standard English
status indicator
stream of consciousness
structural analysis
style sheet format
subvocalize
telephone information service
temporal change
text boundary
text feature
text structure
thesis
thesis statement
transparency
truth in advertising
understatement
universal theme
visual text
warranty
word processing
word reference

General History, Level 1

Abraham Lincoln
America
American Revolution, 1776
ancient time
archeological evidence
argument
automobile
beginning
behavior
belief
Benjamin Franklin
bow and arrow
bridge
building
calendar time
camel caravan

cause
celebration
ceremony
chariot
Christmas
Christopher Columbus
city
colonial community
common good
community
country
cowboy
crop
cultural tradition
daily life
dance
day
decade
democracy
disagreement
domesticated animal
education
ending date
England
English colony
environment
equality
event
expansion
explorer
fable
family history
family life
farm
father of our country
folktale
Fourth of July
freedom
future
generation
geography
George Washington
goods
government
group membership
harvest festival

heroism
history
holiday
houses of worship
housing
human rights
hunger
hunter/gatherer
idea
independence
individual rights
invention
job
journey
law
leader
legend
liberty
Liberty Bell
lifestyle
local history
Martin Luther King Jr.
Martin Luther King Jr. Day
Memorial Day
middle
money
month
monument
myth
nation
national flag
national holiday
Native American
newcomer
nonmotorized vehicle
oral tradition
origin
past
photograph
picture time line
pioneer
place-name
plant cultivation
Pledge of Allegiance
Plymouth
pony express

prairie
present
printing press
radio
recent past
recreation
region
regional folk hero
regional song
religion
resistance
respect for others
responsibility
revolution
role
rules
satellite system
sculpture
senior citizen home
services
society
soup kitchen
state
steam engine
steamship
surplus food
symbol
tall tale
team member
technology
telegraph
temple
territory
Thanksgiving
Thomas Jefferson
time line
today
tomorrow
tool
town
trade
trail
transportation
travel
United States
vote

war
week
wheel
White House
worker
world
year
yesterday

General History, Level 2
A.D.
abolition movement
abolitionist
acceptable behavior
Adolf Hitler
Africa
African American
African slave trade
agriculture
aircraft carrier
Alaska
Alexander Graham Bell
alliance
Allied Powers
Amelia Earhart
American Indian chief
American society
American symbol
Americas, the
ancestor worship
ancient Greece
ancient Rome
Angel Island
annexation
Anno Domini
anti-Chinese movement
aqueduct
archeologist
archeology
architect
architecture
armed forces
artifact
artistic expression
Asia
Asian American

General History, Level 2

(cont'd)

Asian Pacific settler
assembly line
Astoria
astrolabe
attitudes
author's interpretation
autobiography
aviation
Aztec
ballad
Bantu migrations in Africa
B.C., Before Christ
B.C.E., Before the Common Era
behavior consequence
behavior pattern
Bering land bridge
Betty Zane
big business
Bill of Rights
Billy the Kid
biography
Black Hawk War
blue-collar worker
Booker T. Washington
Boston Tea Party
Braille alphabet
Brer Rabbit
Britain
British Isle
bronze tool-making technology
California
camel
campaign
Canada
canal system
Caribbean
caste system
castle
cattle herders
C.E.
Central Africa
Central America
century
Cesar Chavez

character trait
Cherokee
Cherokee Trail of Tears
China
Chinese community
Chinese New Year
Christian
Christianity
chronology
Cinco de Mayo
citizenship
civil liberties
civil rights
civil rights movement
civil war
Civil War (U.S.)
Clara Barton
class
climate changes
coal mining
coffee trade
Cold War
colonial government
colonial period
colonist
colony
Columbian Exchange
Columbus
commercial advertising
commercial center
Common Era
common man
communication technology
communism
compass
computer technology
conquest
constitution
convent
corruption
country of origin
court
craft
credibility
Cuba
Cuban Missile Crisis

cultural contact
cuneiform
custom
Daniel Boone
Davey Crockett
debt
Declaration of Independence
delegated power
democratic values
developing country
development
diplomacy
direct experience
discovery
disease
document
dugout Phoenician ship
Dust Bowl
Dutch
early Middle Ages
earnings
earthquake
East Asia
Eastern Europe
Eastern Hemisphere
economic interdependence
economic system
Egypt
Egyptian time
Eleanor Roosevelt
elected representative
electricity
Elizabeth Blackwell
Ellis Island
emancipation
Emancipation Proclamation
emperor
empire
employment
Enlightenment
entertainment industry
equal rights
era
Eric the Red
Erie Canal
ethnic diversity

ethnic tradition
Europe
European colonization
European Crusades
European explorer
European settler
expedition
extended family
eyewitness account
factory
family alliance
family farm
family role
famine
Far West
farming methods
Ferdinand Magellan
fertilizer
first inhabitant
fishing community
flooding pattern
food production
food storage
forced relocation
foreign policy
foreign trade
former master
former slave
France
Francisco Franco
Franklin D. Roosevelt
Frederick Douglass
freedom of expression
freedom of religion
freedom of speech
French colony
French Revolution
frontier
frontiersman
Galileo
geographic border
geology
George Bush
George W. Bush
George Washington Carver
Gerald Ford

Germany
Geronimo
gold production
Great Depression
group behavior
group expectations
gunpowder
Hanging Gardens of Babylon
Harriet Tubman
Hawaii
Hawaiian culture
hemisphere
Henry Ford
hieroglyphic
historian
historic figure
historical document
historical map
home country
home front
homeless
Hopi
household appliance
human cost
hymn
immigrant
immigration
Incan Empire
Incan highway
independence movement
Indian time
indigenous people
industrial development
Industrial Revolution
industrial society
infectious disease
institution
interest group
international conflict
Internet, the
interpretation
interstate highway system
Inuit
iron
iron tools and weapons
Iroquois

Islam
Islamic law
Israel
Italy
Jackie Robinson
Jacques Cartier
James Armistead
Japan
Jedediah Smith
Jesus of Nazareth
Jew
Jewish time
Joe Magarac
John Glenn
John Henry
Jonas Salk
Judaism
justice
kingdom
labor
Labor Day
labor movement
land use
landowner
landscape
Latin America
law and order
League of Nations
Lee Iaccoca
leisure activity
lesson of history
life experience
Lincoln Memorial
literacy
literacy rate
local resource
London
long-distance trade
Louis Pasteur
low-income area
lunar year
luxury goods
Lydia Darragh
majority rule
Mali
manor

General History, Level 2
(cont'd)
manufacturing
Marco Polo
Marie Curie
mass advertising
mass media
mass production
Mayan calendar
Mayflower Compact
media
medical advance
Medieval Europe
merchant
Mexican-American war
Mexican migrant worker
Mexico
middle class
Middle East
middle passage
migrant
migration
military power
mill
mining town
minority rights
missionary
mode of communication
modern democratic
    thought
modernization
monk
Monroe Doctrine
Moslem
mother country
motive
motorized vehicle
motto
mountain man
mummification
Muslim
Muslim time
Nathan Beman
national park
national symbol
Native American ancestors

Native American land
    holdings
Native American tribe
natural environment
natural resource
naval warfare
navigation
New England
New England colonies
New England mill town
New Orleans
New York
newspaper account
Nez Perce
nonviolent resistance
norm
Norse long ship
North America
nuclear technology
occupation
ocean currents
official
Old Northwest
outlaw
overland trade route
overseas trade
Pacific, the
Pacific Rim economy
Pacific Theater
Palestine
parables
Paris
patriot
pattern of change
Paul Bunyan
peacekeeper
peasant
Pecos Bill
period of history
personal values
Philadelphia
physical geography
pictograph
pilgrim
plague
planned city

plantation
plantation colony
point of view
policy issue
political cartoon
political geography
pollution
popular culture
popular figure
popular uprising
population
population growth
postwar period
pottery
poverty
power by the people
Presidents Day
principles
primary source
private life
production
professional sport
property ownership
protest
proverb
Pueblo
Puerto Rico
Puritan values
pyramids
race relations
racial group
rail transportation
railroad construction
ranching
rapid transit
reconstruction
reform
reformer
religious freedom
religious revival
reservation
revolutionary government
right to hold office
right to life, liberty, and the
    pursuit of happiness
right to vote

right to work
ritual
road system
rocketry
Roman Empire
Roman Republic
Roman system of roads
Rome
Rosa Parks
ruling class
rural area
Russia
Russian peasantry
Sacramento
Sally Ride
San Antonio
San Francisco
Scandinavia
school attendance
scientific breakthrough
secondary source
separation of church and state
separation of powers
settlement
settler
Seven Years' War
ship design
silver production
Sioux
Sitka
slave
slave holder
slave rebellion
slave trade
slogan
smuggling
social class
social reform
solar system
solar year
Sojourner Truth
Southeast Asia
Southwest
Southwest Asia
Soviet Union
space exploration

Spain
Spanish-American War
Spanish colony
spectator sport
square rigger
St. Augustine
statehood
Statue of Liberty
steam locomotive
steel construction
street gang
submarine
suburb
sugar cane
superstition
Susan B. Anthony
systems of roads
tactic
tax
Tecumseh
Ten Commandments
tenant
Tenochtitlán
textile industry
Timbuktu
tobacco
tolerance
trade route
tradition
transport system
transportation hub
tribute
turning point in human
   history
twentieth century
unification
United Nations
United States Constitution
university
urban center
urban community
vaccine
Vasco da Gama
Versailles
Versailles Treaty
Veterans Day

veterans' memorial
Vietnam
Vietnam War
Vietnamese boat people
Vincennes
volunteer
voting rights
W. E. B. DuBois
weaving
Western Europe
Western Hemisphere
white-collar worker
Williamsburg
women's movement
Woodrow Wilson
working conditions
workplace
world economy
world population growth
World War I
World War II
written code
written language
written record
Zheng He

General History, Level 3
adaptation
agrarian society
agribusiness
agricultural economy
agricultural lifestyle
agricultural technology
anthropologist
antibiotics
armed revolution
astronomical discovery
astronomy
atomic bomb
authoritarian rule
Batu
Benin
Bill Clinton
birth rate
black majority
blind respect

General History, Level 3

(cont'd)

boundary dispute
bourgeoisie
British rule
bronze casting
brush painting
business practice
capitalism
capitalist economy
Catholic Christianity
Catholic Church
chance event
charter document
chattel slavery
checks and balances
child labor
Chinese Revolution
Christian beliefs
civil disobedience
civil service examination
civil service reform
civilian
civilian population
civilization
clergy
coerced labor
cohesion
collectivization
colonization
colony in Massachusetts
commercialization
communal life
communist country
Communist Party
conflict resolution
conservation movement
conservatism
contemporary democracy
convert
cosmos
court packing
crop rotation
cross-cultural contact
cultural exchange
cultural heritage

cultural integration
daily survival skill
dating methods
death rate
debtor class
demographic shift
depression
desegregation
discrimination
disease microorganism
disenfranchisement
dissent
divided loyalties
domestic crop
dowry
Dutch colonization
economic power
economy
Egyptian civilization
emigration
employment opportunity
English Common Law
environmental change
epic
epidemic disease
equal opportunity
equal protection of the laws
ethical belief
ethical systems
ethnic art
ethnic conflict
ethnic group
ethnic identity
ethnic minority
ethnic origin
evolution
exodus
extractive mining
fair employment practice
fascism
Federalist Party
feminism
feminist movement
final solution
financing
flora

foreign capital investment
foreign market
fortification
founders
framers
fraternal organization
French colonization
fundamental value
gender role
global communication
global market
gridiron pattern
group overlap
Haitian Revolution
hierarchy
historical account
historical fiction
historical narrative
hoarding
Holocaust
hostility
human intention
human nature
Iberia
immigration screening
imperial policy
imperialism
import
individual status
industrialization
infant mortality rate
inheritance law
innate ability
international market
international relations
interpretation
intervention
Iraq
Islamic beliefs
isolationism
jazz
Jesus Christ
Jewish monotheism
Jewish refugee
Jewish resistance movement
Korean War

labor force
labor union
learned behavior pattern
liberal democracy
limitations on government
linguistic diversity
literary narrative
long-distance migration
Lost Generation
lynching
Magna Carta (1215)
mandate
marine transportation
marital status
maritime rights
maritime technology
maritime trade route
Marshall Plan
mass consumer economy
matrilineal family
memento
middle-class culture
migrant worker
militant religious movement
military mobilization
military tactic
military unit
modern art
monarchy
monastery
monasticism
monsoon wind
moral reform
moral responsibility
moral values
mortality rate
mosque
mound builder
multiple-tier time line
mural
Muslim Empire
nation-state
national bank
national self-rule
nativism
Nazi

Nazi-Soviet Non-Aggression
    pact of 1939
neutrality
nobility
nomadic people
North American mound-
    building people
North American plains society
nuclear politics
obsidian
occupational specialization
open range
open shop
organized labor
Paris Peace Accord of 1973
participatory government
pathogen
patriarchal society
peasantry
People's Republic of China
Persian Gulf
perspective
philanthropist
Philippine annexation
philosophical movement
philosophy
political alliance
political border
polygamous marriage
pooled resources
port city
port of entry
Portugal
Portuguese caravel
post–World War I
post–World War II
Post Vincennes
price war
private property
private white academy
professional sector
protective tariff
Protestant Christianity
Protestant Reformation
public education
public opinion

Puritanism
racial minority
rapid industrialization
rationing
reform government
reform legislation
religious dissenter
removal policy
ritual sacrifice
Roman occupation of Britain
Russian absolutism
Russian Revolution of 1917
saint
scientific method
secession
secular ruler
secular state
seed drill
segregation
semilunar calendar
separatist movement
service industry
Sicily
significant event
social agency
social attitudes
Social Darwinism
social factor
social issue
social status
Socialist Party
sovereign state
spoils system
standard of behavior
standard of living
state bureaucracy
states' rights
status
steppe lands
stereotype
stimuli
stock breeding
stratification
strike
strip mining
subculture

General History, Level 3
(cont'd)
superpower rivalry
tariffs
telecommunication
temperance
territorial expansion
terrorism
theater of conflict
third party
totalitarian regime
trade balance
trade union
trading triangle
transformation
transmission of beliefs
transmission of culture
tribal identity
urbanization
war crime
water rights
weaponry
welfare
white-collar sector
woman suffrage
Woodrow Wilson's Fourteen
    Points
working-class culture
world history
world power
world war

General History, Level 4
abortion
absolutism
adaptation
affluence
African American community
amnesty
animal domestication
anticommunist movement
anti-Semitism
aristocratic power
arms embargo
arms limitations
artisan

assimilation
atomic diplomacy
autonomous power
bank recharter
barbarian
bilingual education
biological evidence
bipolar centers of power
black market
border conflict
breakup of Soviet Union
British colony
British imperialism
British monarch
capitalist country
cartography
casualty rate
Catholic clergy
centralized monarchy
chemical warfare
Chinese Communist Party
Christian denomination
church-state relations
city planning
civic center
class conflict
class relations
colonial rule
commodity price
common refuse
compulsory education
conscription
constitutional ideal
constitutionalism
consumer's rights
consumer culture
containment policy
contemporary life
continuity
conventional warfare
corporation
Covenant of the League
    of Nations
creditor
critical text analysis
cultural continuity

cultural identity
cultural preservation
defense policy
defense spending
demobilization
democratization
demographics
depression of 1873–1879
depression of 1893–1897
détente
diffusion
disease pandemic
distribution of powers
due process
duke
Dutch merchant class
Dutch West Indies
economy
economic dependency
economic disparity
economic reforms
educational reform
enemies of the state
energy crisis
English Parliament
entrepreneur
entrepreneurial spirit
environmental degradation
environmentalism
ethical dilemma
ethnicity
evangelical argument
evangelical movement
exchange of fauna
exchange of flora
expansionism
expansionist foreign policy
Federalist
food plant domestication
fraud
free enterprise
free labor system
free trade
freedom of the press
fundamentalism
generational conflict

genetically determined
    behavior
genocide
geopolitics
global economy
global trade
globalizing trend
government subsidy
gradation
group identity
guerilla warfare
hearsay
hereditary social system
heredity
historical context
historical continuity
humanism
ideological conflict
ideology
imperial presidency
inalienable right to freedom
income gap
individualism
industrial parity
inflammatory
inflation
instinctive behavior
integration
intellectual life
internal trade
international economy
investigative technique
investment
iron metallurgy
Islamic state
Islamization
Jewish scapegoating
jihad
labor relations
legal code
liberalism
liberation theology
male-dominated job
market revolution
martyr
materialism

mercantilism
mercenary
Mexican Revolution
militarism
military-industrial complex
military preparedness
millennialism
mining economy
mobilization
moderate thinking
monetary policy
monotheism
mulatto
multiculturalism
multilateral aid organization
multinational corporation
Muslim country
nation building
national autonomy
national debt
national identity
national market
national security
national socialism
nationalism
Native American origin story
native population
natural history
neocolonialism
new scientific rationalism
noble savage
nonunion worker
nullification
oil crisis of 1970s
one man one vote
opposition group
oppression
outward migration
Parliament
parliamentary government
periodize
Philippines
Pop Art
postindustrial society
primate
prior experience

privatization
profit motive
profiteering
propaganda
propaganda campaign
property rights
Protestant clergy
province
psyche
public policy
quadrant
racial role
radicalism
rationalism
reactionary thinking
Realism
realpolitik
recession
recurrent pandemic
Red Russian
Red Scare
redistribution of wealth
refugee population
religious evangelism
reparation payment
repertoire
representative government
republicanism
resettlement
retaliation
reunification
rights of the disabled
rigid class
Russian Chronicle
Russian Revolution of 1905
sanctioned country
scientific racism
second front
sectionalism
secular ideology
sedentary agriculture
self-determination
social democratization
socialism
socioeconomic group
South Africa

General History, Level 4

(cont'd)

sovereignty
sphere of influence
stagnation of wages
staple crop production
state constitution
status quo
subsistence method
suburbanization
supply-side economics
system of alliances
traditional cultural identity
UN resolution
United States intervention
universal language
urban bourgeoisie
U.S. domestic energy policy
U.S. foreign policy
U.S. Smoot-Hawley Tariff
U.S.S.R.
Utopian community
volunteerism
wartime diplomacy
wartime inflation
welfare state
Western values
women in the clergy
workforce
world geopolitics
writ of habeas corpus

U.S. History, Level 2

1492
1896 election
1920s
13th Amendment
14th Amendment
15th Amendment
16th Amendment
17th Amendment
18th Amendment
19th Amendment
Age of Exploration
Alamo
Alexander Hamilton

American Expeditionary Force
Andrew Jackson
Antietam
Arab-Israeli crisis
Articles of Confederation
Axis Powers
Battle of Bull Run
Black Reconstruction
Boston
Brown v. Board of Education (1954)
Cabeza de Vaca
Camelot image
Cayuga
Charles Finney
Chickasaw removal
Chickasaw
Choctaw removal
coal mine strike
Confederacy
Confederate Army
Connecticut Compromise
Constitutional Convention
cotton gin
Cree removal
December 7, 1941
Democratic Party
escaped slave
European Theater
Fort Sumter
Fourteen Points
Francisco Vasquez de Coronado
Fredericksburg
Freedmen's Bureau
freedom ride
French Quebec
French settlement
fur trade
General Robert E. Lee
GI Bill
Golden Door
Great Awakening
Great Plains
Harlem Renaissance
Harry S. Truman

Herbert Hoover
Hispanic American
"I Have a Dream" speech
indentured servant
industrial North
internment of Japanese Americans
Jacqueline Kennedy
James Monroe
Jenne
Jim Bowie
Jim Crow
Jimmy Carter
John Adams
John F. Kennedy
John Hancock
King James I
Know-Nothing Party
Latino
Lexington and Concord
Louisiana
Louisiana Purchase
lower South colony
Lyndon B. Johnson administration
Manassas
manifest destiny
Mary McLeod Bethune
Mid-Atlantic colony
minstrel show
Missouri Compromise
Mohawk
Mormon
Mother Mary Jones
Mt. Rushmore
National Organization for Women
New Deal
New Federalism
New Frontier
New Jersey Plan
New Mexico
Northeast
Oneida
Onondaga
Open Door policy

Oregon
P. T. Barnum
Panama Canal
Pearl Harbor
Pennsylvania
Peter Cartwright
post–Civil War period
pre-Columbus
Prohibition
Reagan revolution
Revolutionary War
Richard Henry Lee
Richard Nixon
Ronald Reagan
Sam Houston
Samuel Adams
Santa Fe
Second Great Awakening
Seminole removal
Seneca
sharecropper
Shays Rebellion
Shiloh
Silent Majority
Songhai
spinning jenny
stock market crash of 1929
suffrage movement
Supreme Court
taxation without
    representation
Texas
Texas War for Independence
    (1836)
the East
the North
the South
the West
Theodore Roosevelt
thirteen colonies
Thomas Nast
Trail of Tears
Treaty of Guadalupe Hidalgo
Treaty of Paris
Underground Railroad
Union Army

U.S. territory
Vicksburg
Virginia Plan
War of 1812
Warren Court
Watergate
westward expansion
Whiskey Rebellion
William H. Taft
yeoman farmer

U.S. History, Level 3

1960 presidential campaign
African-American Union
    soldier
American dream
American foreign policy
American identity
American West
Anne Hutchinson
antebellum period
Anti-Federalist
anti-immigrant attitude
antislavery ideology
Article III of the Constitution
Atlantic slave trade
Bacon's rebellion
Battle for Britain
Benjamin Franklin's
    autobiography
big stick diplomacy
Calvin Coolidge
Camp David Accords
Charles Evans Hughes
Christian evangelical
    movement
Church of Jesus Christ of
    Latter-day Saints
closed shop
Compromise of 1850
Compromise of 1877
Congress
Congressional authority
Continental Congress
Dawes Severalty Act of 1887
Declaration of Sentiments

Democrat
Democratic-Republican Party
dollar diplomacy
domestic policy
domestic program
Dr. Francis Townsend
Dred Scott decision
Dwight D. Eisenhower
Eisenhower Doctrine
election of 1800
election of 1912
Engel v. Vitale
English Bill of Rights (1689)
Equal Rights Amendment
Fair Deal
family assistance program
farm labor
featherbedding
federal Indian policy
federalism
Filipino insurrection
First Amendment
First Congress
First Lady
flawed peace
free exercise clause
French and Indian War
Garvey movement
gentleman's agreement
Glorious Revolution
Great Society
Hiram Johnson
Huey Long
impeachment
Industrial Workers of the
    World
Iranian hostage crisis
James Buchanan
James Madison
Jay's Treaty
John Marshall
Joseph McCarthy
Judiciary Act of 1789
Kennedy assassination
Ku Klux Klan
Lewis and Clark expedition

U.S. History, Level 3 (cont'd)
Little Rock 1957
Loyalist
Malcolm X
Marbury v. Madison (1803)
Massachusetts
McCarthyism
midnight judge
modern republicanism
NAACP
Navigation Acts
new freedom
new nationalism
Normandy Invasion
Northwest Ordinance of 1787
Oregon territory
pardon of Richard Nixon
party system
Paxton Boys Massacre
Populism
Populist Party
Progressive era
Progressive movement
Reconstruction amendments
Republican
Republican Party
return to domesticity
Robert La Follette
Roosevelt coalition
Rust Belt
Scopes trial
Seneca Falls Convention
share the wealth
shot heard round the world
Soviet espionage
Sun Belt
Tenure of Office Act
thirteen virtues
Townsend Plan
Transcendentalism
trans-Mississippi region
Truman Doctrine
U.S. Supreme Court
universal white male suffrage
Virginia
Warren G. Harding

Whig Party
Works Progress Administration
WPA project

U.S. History, Level 4
18th century republicanism
accession of Elizabeth I
affirmative action
Agricultural Adjustment Act
Algonkian
Alien and Sedition Acts
American Communist Party
American Federation of Labor
Americanization
Arizona
Asian Civil Rights Movement
baby boom generation
Bank Recharter Bill of 1832
Battle of Saratoga
Bay of Pigs
black legend
Carolina regulators
Carrie Chapman Catt
Chesapeake
CIO
"City Upon a Hill" speech
Civil Rights Act of 1964
Civil Works Administration
Civilian Conservation Corps
Committee for Industrial
   Organizations
Constitution of 1787
covenant community
crabgrass frontier
crop lien system
Cross of Gold speech
Dartmouth College v. Woodward
   (1819)
D-Day
de facto segregation
de jure segregation
Democratic nominee
Desert Storm
downtown business area
East Asian Co-Prosperity
   Sphere

economic depression of 1819
economic depression of 1837
economic depression of 1857
election of 1960
emerging capitalist economy
Emilio Aguinaldo
European land hunger
evil empire
executive branch
farm labor movement
federal judiciary
fireside chats
First New Deal
Five Civilized Tribes
Four Freedoms speech
French Declaration of the
   Rights of Man
full dinner pail
Gay Liberation Movement
gay rights
General Ulysses S. Grant
General William T. Sherman
Gettysburg Address
GI Bill on higher education
Gibbons v. Ogden (1824)
Good Neighbor Policy
Grand Alliance
Great Migration
Greenback Labor Party
hammering campaign
Hernando Cortes
Hetch Hetchy controversy
Indian laborer
Indian Reorganization Act of
   1934
International Ladies Garment
   Workers Union
Iran-Contra affair
James K. Polk
Japanese American
Jay Gardoqui Treaty of 1786
Jefferson Davis
John Collier
John F. Kennedy presidency
John Locke
John White

Kansas-Nebraska Act
King's Mountain
Kuwait
La Raza Unida
labor conflicts of 1894
legislative branch
Leisler's Rebellion
Lone Star Republic
mainstream America
Mark Hanna
Maryland
McCulloch v. Maryland
Midwest
Mississippian culture
Mormon migration to the
    West
mound center in Cahokia,
    Illinois
mound center in the
    Mississippi valley
National Democratic Party
National Industrial Recovery
    Act
National Recovery
    Administration
National Republican Party
National Woman Suffrage
    Association
New Klan
New Woman
New York City draft riots of
    July 1863
Northwest Territory
November 10 proposal
Old Hickory
Omaha Platform of 1892
Panama Revolution of 1903
parochial school
Peace of Paris
Plessy v. Ferguson (1896)
post–Cold War era
Public Works Administration
Quaker
Radical Republicans
relocation center
Roe v. Wade

Roger Williams
Roosevelt Corollary
Rural Electrification
    Administration
Sacco and Vanzetti trial
Scots-Irish
Second New Deal
secondary education
Shaysites
South Carolina
spirit of individualism
Tennessee Valley Authority
    Act
Texas Revolution (1836–1845)
Theodore deBry
Title VII
traditional American family
two-party system
Two Treatises on Government
Upton Sinclair
U.S. Communist Party
Victorian value
war bond
War on Poverty
War Powers Act of March
    1942
West Indian colony
William Jennings Bryan
William McKinley
Wilmot Proviso
Zuni

World History, Level 2
1948 UN Declaration of
    Human Rights
African heritage
Afro-Eurasia
Age of Enlightenment
Alfred the Great
Americas
Andes
Arab Palestinian
Ashikaga period
Ashoka
Athenian democracy
Atlantic basin

Augustus
Australia
Aztec Empire
Aztec "Foundation of Heaven"
Baghdad
Balkans
Bartholomew de las Casas
Battle of Hastings
Benito Mussolini
Berlin blockade
Black Sea
Bombay
Boxer Rebellion
Brahmanism
Brazil
British East India Company
Buddha
Buddhism
Buenos Aires
Byzantine Empire
Byzantium
Cairo
Canton
capture of Constantinople
Carthage
cavalry warfare
celestial empire
Central Asia
Central Asian steppes
Central Iberia
Central Powers
Charlemagne
chivalry
Christian community
Christopher Columbus
Cicero
Cincinnatus
class system
Classical Greek art and
    architecture
clay pottery
Commodore Matthew Perry
Confucianism
Confucius
Constantine
Copernicus

World History, Level 2 *(cont'd)*

Cortes journey into Mexico
court of Heian
cowboy culture
Cro-Magnon
czar
Czar Nicholas II
daily prayer (Salat)
dharma
Diderot
discovery of diamonds
discovery of gold
Dr. Sun Yatsen
Duchy of Moscow
East Africa
Eastern Roman Empire
Edmund Cartwright
elite status
English civil war
English Revolution of 1688
Eurasia
Eurasian society
European colonial rule
European conquest
European Economic
    Community
European opium trade
father of modern Egypt
feudal society
founding of Rome
French East India company
French invasion of Egypt in
    1798
Garibaldi
Garibaldi's nationalist redshirts
Genghis Khan
goddesses
gods
Great Canal of China
Greek city-state
Greek gods and goddesses
Guangzhou
Gupta Empire
Haitian Revolution
Hajj
Han Empire

Hebrew Torah
Hegira (Hirjah)
Hellenist culture
Hellenistic art
Henri Matisse
Hinduism
hominid
Huang He (Yellow River)
    civilization
human community
Hundred Years' War
Hungarian revolt
imperial conquest
independent lord
India
Indian Ocean
Indian spice
Indonesia
Indus Valley
industrial age
international trade routes
invention of paper
Ireland
Jakarta tales
James Hargreaves
James Watt
Japanese feudal society
Japanese tea ceremony
Jewish civilization
John Kay
Joseph Stalin
Julius Caesar
Justinian
Kaaba
Kilwa
King Affonso II of the Kongo
    and Po
King Alfred of England
knight
knightly class
Korea
Kush culture
Lenin
Liberty, Equality, Fraternity
maize cultivation
Malaysia

Mali Empire
Marcus Aurelius
Maurya empire
Mayan city-state
Mayan pyramids
Mayan religion
Mediterranean region
Meiji Japan
Mesoamerica
Mesopotamia
middle passage
Ming Dynasty
Moche civilization
modern China
Mohenjo-Daro
Mughal Empire
Muhammad
Muhammad Ali of Egypt
Mycenaean Greek culture
Napoleon Bonaparte
Napoleonic period
Nazi holocaust
Nazi war against the Jews
Neanderthal
Nero
Netherlands
New Kingdom
New Testament
New Zealand
Newton
Nile Delta
Nile Valley
Norse invasion
North Africa
Nubia
Oceania
Olmec civilization
Ottoman Empire
Pablo Picasso
Pacific Islands
Pan-Arabism
Paul the Apostle
Peru
Pharaoh
Phoenicia
Pompeii

pre-European life in the
   Americas
Qur'an/Koran
Ramadan
Rasputin
Reformation
Renaissance
Richard Arkwright
Safavid Empire
Samurai class
scientific revolution
Scipio Africanus
serf
Shah Abbas I
Shang Dynasty
Sheba
Siberia
siege of Troy
silk roads
Singapore
Socrates
Solomon
Song Dynasty
Songhai Empire
South America
South Korea
South Pacific
Southern Iberia
Soviet invasion of
   Czechoslovakia
Spanish Civil War
spice trade
Stonehenge
Sub-Saharan Africa
Suez Canal
Suleiman the Magnificent
Sunna
Swahili
Syria
Taj Mahal, India
Tang China
Tang Empire
Teotihuacan civilization
Tiberius Gracchus
Tigris-Euphrates Valley
Tokugawa shogunate

Tokyo
trans-Atlantic slave trade
Turkey
Turkic Empire
West Africa
Western Roman Empire
William the Conqueror
Winston Churchill
Zapotec civilization
Zheng He maritime
   expeditions
Zulu empire

World History, Level 3
Abbasid Empire
Abd al Quadir
African resistance movement
Agustin de Iturbide
Akbar
Albert Einstein
alchemy
Alfred Krupp
Algeria
Alps
American Indian nation
Ammianus Marcellinus
Anasazi
Anatolia
Andean region
apartheid
Arab Muslim
arranged marriage
Aryan culture
Ashanti
Asian art form
Assyria
Assyrian Empire
Axis country
Babylonian Empire
Baltic region
Bantu
Barbados
Berlin
Bismarck's "Blood and Iron"
   speech
Buddhist beliefs

Cape Region
Carolingian Empire
Catherine the Great
Catholic Reformation
Cecil Rhodes
Central Europe
Ceylon
Champa
Chandogya
Chandragupta
Charles Darwin
China's 1911 Republican
   Revolution
Chinese Revolution of 1911
Christian Europe
Christian religious art
Christian soldier
classical civilization
Cleisthenes
Clothilde
Clovis
colonial Africa
commercial agriculture
Communist party in China
Conference of Versailles
Congress of Vienna
constitutional monarchy
Coptic Christians
courtly ideals
courtly love
creation myths of Babylon
creation myths of China
creation myths of Egypt
creation myths of Greece
creation myths of Sumer
Creole
Creole-dominated revolt of
   1821
Crete
Crimean War
Crusades
Cultural Revolution
Dahomey
Dai Vet
Daoism/Taoism
Darius I

World History, Level 3 (*cont'd*)

Darius the Great
democratic despotism
division of Germany and
   Berlin
division of the subcontinent
Dorothea Lange
Dutch Republic
dynastic politics
Early Middle Ages
East India Company
East Indies
Eastern Mediterranean
Elizabeth I
Ellora
Emmeline Pankhurst
empire-builder
Epic of Gilgamesh
Estates-General
Ethiopia
European imperialism
European monarchy
European resistance
   movement
fascist aggression
fascist regime
Father Miguel Hidalgo
feudal lord
feudalism
Francis Bacon
Frankish Empire
Gangetic states
Gangzhou (Canton)
Ghana
Glorious Revolution of 1688
Gothic cathedral
Great Leap Forward
Great Plague
Great Powers in Europe
Great Reform Bill 1832
Greco-Roman antiquity
Greece
Greek art
Greek Christian civilization
Greek drama
Greek rationalism

Greenland
Grimke sisters
griot "keeper of tales"
Haiti
Heian
Hellenistic period
Helsinki Accords
herding societies
Hermit Kingdom
high culture entertainment
High Middle Ages
High Renaissance
Hittite people
Holland
Homo erectus
Homo sapiens
Ibn Battuta
Ice Age
imperial absolutism
Indian culture
Indo-Aryan people
Indo-European language
Indo-Gangetic plain
Indonesian archipelago
Inner Asia
Isfahan
Italian Renaissance
James Maxwell
Janissary Corps
Japanese modernization
Jean Jaures
Jose Clemente Orozco
Kalash church
Kamakura period
Karl Marx
karma
Kathe Kollwitz
khans
Khoisan group
kingdom of Aksum
kinship group
Kongo
Korean culture
kulak
Kuomintang
Lalibela church

lateen sails
Lenin's New Economic Policy
Leo Africanus
Lucretia Mott
Lunda
Macedonia
Machu Picchu
Mahdist state
Mahmud II
Malayo-Polynesia
Manchu Empire
Manchu
Mandate of Heaven
manorialism
Mao Zedong
Mao's program
Maroon society
Mauryan-Buddhist power
medieval Christian society
medieval theology
megalithic stone building
megalopolis
Menelik II
Meroitic period
Middle Ages
Middle Kingdom
Minoan Crete
Mohandas Gandhi
Mohandas Gandhi's call for
   nonviolent dissent
Monarch Mansa Musa
Mongol conquest of 1206
Moroccan resistance
   movement
Napoleon's invasions
Neolithic agricultural society
neutral nation
Newfoundland
Niger River
nirvana
North Atlantic Treaty
   Organization
Oaxaca
Old Kingdom
Old Regime France
Opium War

oracle bone inscription
Orosius
paleolithic cave painting
Panchatantra
papacy
pastoral nomadic people
Persia
Persian Empire
Peter Stolypin
Peter the Great
Pizarro
Poland
polis
Polynesia
post-Mao China
Priscus
Punic Wars
Queen Hatshepsut
Quin Empire
Ramsay MacDonald
Ramses II
Raymond Poincaré
Reagan-Gorbachev summit
    diplomacy
reconquest of Spain
reincarnation
Renaissance humanism
René Descartes
Robert Owen's New Lanark
    System
Roman Catholic Church
Romanticism
Rosa Luxemburg
royal court
Rule of St. Benedict
Samarkand
Samori Ture
Sassanid Empire
Saudi Arabia
Saxon peoples
Scythian society
second industrial revolution
seizure of Constantinople
Selim III
Shiba Kokan
Shinto

Svetaketu
Siam
Sigmund Freud
Solon
Sotabu screen
South Asia
Soviet bloc
Soviet domination
Soviet invasion of Afghanistan
Spanish Muslim society
squire
St. Petersburg, "window on
    the west"
Stalin's purge
Stanley Baldwin
story of Olaudah Equiano
    (Gustavus Vassa)
Sudan
the Gracchi
three piece iron
Thutmose III
Tiananmen Square protest
Timur the Lame (Tamerlane)
Tippu Tip
Toltecs
Torah
Toussaint L'Ouverture
trench warfare
trial of Galileo
Trojan war
Turkic migration
Turkestan
unification of Germany
unification of Italy
United States foreign policy
Upanishad
U.S. isolationist policy
Vedas
Vedis gods
warrior culture
Warsaw Pact
West Asia
Western and Eastern
    European societies
Western art and literature
Western culture

White Sea
Xiongnu society
Zagwé Dynasty
Zanzibar
Zhou Dynasty
Zhu Xi

World History, Level 4
1994 Cairo Conference on
    World Population
Abdul-Mejid
aboriginal population
absolutist state
Abstract Expressionism
Adam Smith
Aegean region
African nationalist movement
African village life
Akbar Islam
Akhenaton (Amenhotep IV)
al-Afghani
Alexander
Alexander of Macedon
alphabetic writing
Amsterdam
Angkor Wat
Anglo-Saxon Boniface
Arab Caliphate
Arab League
Arabia
Arabic
Argentina
Aristotle
art of courtly love
Ataturk
Athens
atonism
Austria
Austro-Hungarian Empire
Babylon
Balfour Declaration
Battle of Tours of 733
Bavaria
Bhati movement
biblical account of Genesis
Bismarck

World History, Level 4 (*cont'd*)
Black Death
Black Legend
Bloody Sunday
Boccaccio
Boer
Boer War
Bolshevik
Brazilian independence
    movement
Britain's modernizing policy
    in India
British West Indies
Brooke
Bruges
Buddhist-Hindu culture
Buddhist monk
Buganda
Byzantine church
Cambodia
Caspian Sea
cassava
Caucasus
caudillo
Cavalier
Cavour
Charter Oath of 1868
Chartist movement
Chile
Chimu society
China's population growth
China's revolutionary
    movement
Chinese workers
Chinese writing system
Christian missionary
Christian monotheism
city-state
Code Napoléon
code of Hammurabi
Conference at San Remo
Constantinople
cremation of Strasbourg Jews
Cubism
Cuzco
Cyrus I

Czar Nicholas I
Dadaism
Damascus
David Siqueiros
Decembrist uprising
Declaration of the Rights of
    Man
Declaration of the Rights of
    Women
Descartes' Discourse on
    Method
Diary of Murasaki Shikibu
Diego Rivera
Diem regime
Dreyfus affair
early modern society
Emperor Aurangzeb
Ems telegram
enclosure movement
encomienda system
Enlightened Despot
Enuma Elish
Erich Remarque
Ernest Hemingway
Ethiopian art
Ethiopian rock churches
Eurasian empire
European country
European Jew
European manorial system
Existentialism
Expressionism
expulsion of Jews and
    Muslims from Spain
foot binding
forced collectivization
Franco-Prussian War
French Estates-General
French salon
French West Indies
Freud's psychoanalytic
    method
Geneva Accords
Genoa
gentry elite
George Orwell

German concept of Kultur
German Empire
German Federal Republic
Germanic peoples
Ghaznavid Empire
Golden Horde
Great Khan Mongke
Great Khan Ogodei
Great War
Great Western Schism
Greek comedy
Greek Orthodox Christianity
Greek philosopher
Greek tragedy
Guatemala
guild
hacienda
Hadith
Hapsburg Empire
Hatt-I-Humayun
Heian period
Herodotus
hominid community
Hun invasions
Hung-wu emperor
Iberian Empire
Iliad
imperial Mughal
Impressionism
Indian concept of ideal
    kingship
Indian uprising of 1857
Iran
Ismail
Italian humanism
Jamal al-Din
Japanese invasion of China
Jenn-jeno
Jewish and Arab inhabitants
    of Palestine
Jewish diaspora
Jewish flight to Poland and
    Russia
Jiang Jieshi
Joan of Arc
John of Plano Carpini

World History, Level 4 *(cont'd)*
White Paper Reports on
    Palestine
White Russian
world influenza pandemic
    1918–1919
Young Turk movement
Yuan Dynasty
Zionist Movement
Zoroastrianism

Geography, Level 1
airport
America
area
barrier
body of water
California
city
city park
climate
climate change
coast
cold climate
community
community project
competition
construction
country
creek
crop
custom
dam
desert
direction
distance
downtown
elevation
exploration
factory
family
farming
fishing
flood
forest
fuel

globe
government
graph
highway
hill
home
hospital
hotel
housing
lake
land
local community
location
map
measurement
mile
mountain
museum
nation
neighborhood
ocean
park
pattern
pipeline
place
plant population
population
position
railroad
rainfall
region
river
road
rural region
seasons
settlement
shelter
ship
shopping center
soil
sports stadium
state
stream
temperature
timber
town

transportation
United States
urban area
vegetation
village
weather
wildlife
world
yard size

Geography, Level 2
accessibility
aerial photograph
Africa
agricultural practice
agriculture
air conditioning
air pollution
Alaska
Antarctic Circle
Appalachian Mountains
Arizona
artifacts
Asia
atmosphere
billboards
boomtown
boundary
Canada
capacity
capital
cardinal direction
central business district
chart
city center
civil war
coal mining
coastal area
colonization
Colorado mining town
    (19th century)
communication route
conservation issue
contagious disease
continent
county

Geography, Level 2 *(cont'd)*
situation
smog
social class
society
soil conservation
soil region
solar energy
South
South America
South Pole
Spain
storage
style of homes
suburban area
technology
territory
Texas
timber cutting
time zone
topographic map
tornado
tourist center
township
trade pact
trade route
trade wind
transportation route
transportation system
vegetation region
volcano
volume
water availability
water basin
water crossing
water pollution
waterway
West Coast
wetland
wind storm
windward

Geography, Level 3
acid rain
adaptation
Algeria

alphanumeric system
alternative energy source
Amsterdam
architectural style of buildings
arid climate
assimilation
Australia
average family size
axis
barrier island
Belgium
bicycle lane
biome
biosphere
Boston
boundary dispute
Brenner Pass
building style
Burma Pass
Canberra
Capitol Hill
central place
cheap labor
Chile
China
Chinatown
Chinese textile
clearing of forest
climate region
Congo
conservationist
contemporary system of
    communication
Cumberland Gap
data set
database
decentralization
Delaware River
demographic change
demographic information
density
density of population
developed country
developing country
diamond trade
diesel machinery

dispersion
division (of Earth's surface)
downstream
drainage basin
dry-land farming technique
earth-moving machinery
earthquake-resistant
    construction
earthquake zone
economic alliance
ecosystem
electric car
energy-poor region
energy industry
energy source
equilibrium
Ethiopia
ethnic composition
evacuation route
Everglades
export
fall line of the Appalachians
fauna
feeding level
flat-map projection
flood-control project
floodplain
flora
fungi
Gateway Arch—St. Louis
geographic factor
global impact
global warming
Golden Gate Bridge—San
    Francisco
Great American Desert
grid
hemisphere
historic preservation
Hong Kong
housing development
Huang Ho
human process
hurricane
hurricane shelter
hurricane tracks

hydroelectric power
imported resource
Indians
Indonesia
industrial center
industrial district
infant mortality rate
infrastructure
interdependence
internal structure
Inuit
involuntary migration
Iraq invasion of Kuwait (1991)
Irish immigrant
isthmus
Italy
Jamaican sugar
Japanese occupation of
    Manchuria (1930s)
Khyber Pass
land-locked
land-use data
land-use pattern
language region
leeward
levee
life form
linkage
literacy rate
lithosphere
Little Italy
local scale
major parallel
marine climate
marine vegetation
meridian
Mesopotamia
midaltitude
migrant population
military campaign
military installation
mobility
Moslems
multiculturalism
nationalism
natural resource

natural vegetation
natural wetlands
Netherlands
New Delhi
Nile Valley
nitrogen cycle
nonrenewable resource
nuclear-waste storage
ocean circulation
ocean pollution
Ogallala Aquifer
old-growth forest
Opera House—Sydney,
    Australia
origin
overfishing
overpopulation
Pakistan
paper factory
pedestrian walkway
pesticide
petroleum
Philippine archipelago
Philippines
physical environment
physical geography
physical variation
plant species
political region
political unit
population concentration
population density
population distribution
population growth rate
population region
population structure
postal zone
prevailing wind
prime meridian (Greenwich
    meridian)
principal line
principal meridians
production site
public housing
public transit
raw material

recession
reforestation
region of contact
regional boundary
regrowth
religious facility
renewable resource
residential pattern
resource management
ridge-and-valley pattern
Riviera
runoff
rust belt
satellite-based communi-
    cations system
Saudi Arabia
savanna
school district
sea wall
seasonal pattern of life
semiarid area
settlement pattern
shifting civilization
Siberia
Sikhs
Singapore
single-industry city
soil erosion
soil fertility
solar power
South Africa
Soviet Union
spatial
spatial arrangement
spatial perception
spatial scale
spread of bubonic plague
spread of disease
standard of living
steel-tipped plow
strait
strip mining
suburbanization
Sunbelt
system
Tacoma Strait

Geography, Level 3 *(cont'd)*
tariff
technological hazard
telephone area code
temperature fluctuation
terrace
terraced rice fields
The Hague
thematic map
topography
Tower Bridge—London
trade advantage
transportation hub
Trenton
triangular trade route
Tropic of Cancer
Tropic of Capricorn
tropical rain forest
truck-farming community
tsunami
tundra
Twin Peaks
urban commuting
use of explosives
Vietnamese
voluntary migration
Washington
water spring
water supply
watershed
work animal
World Court
Yucatan Peninsula

Geography, Level 4
absolute location
acculturation
agribusiness
agricultural soil
AIDS
airborne emission
air-mass circulation
alluvial fan
Americentric
aquifer
artesian wells

atmospheric pressure cells
atmospheric warming
Basque minority
Bible Belt
biodiversity
biological magnification
British Empire
bubonic plague
Buddhism
Burkina Faso
carbon cycle
Caribbean Basin
Carolingian Empire
carrying capacity
cartogram
cartographer
census data
census district
center-pivot irrigation
Central Europe
central place theory
chemical cycle
chemical fertilizer
Chernobyl nuclear accident
choropleth map
circuit-court district
climate graph (climagraph)
coastal ecosystem
coastal flood zone
command economy
commodity flow
Common Market
comparative advantage
complementarity
concentrated settlement form
concentration of services
concentric zone model
congressional district
container company
contaminant
contemporary economic trade
   network
continental climate
continental drift
cost-distance
crude birth rate

crude death rate
cultural diffusion
cultural landscape
culture hearth
culture region
cycling of energy
decolonization
deforestation
demographic transition
demography
depleted rain forests of central
   Africa
deposition
desertification
diffusion
diffusion of tobacco smoking
distance decay
distribution of ecosystems
doubling time
drought-plagued Sahel
dust storm
dynamic system
eastern Australia
eastern United States
ecology
economic dominance
economic incentive
economically developing
   nation
edge city
environmental degradation
environmental determinism
equinox
erosional agent
ethnic elitism
ethnic enclave
ethnic minority
ethnicity
ethnocentrism
Eurocentric
European Union
eutrophication
exurban area
facsimile transmission service
fanshed
feedback loop

fertility rate
flow map
flow of energy
flow pattern
flow resource
flowchart
foreign capital
foreign market
formal region
free-trade zone
French colonization of
　Indochina
friction
friction of distance
functional region
gentrification
Geographic Information
　Systems
geographic technology
geomorphology
GIS
global market
global migration pattern
Great Barrier Reef
Great Plains Dust Bowl
greenhouse effect
greenway
Gross Domestic Product
Gross National Product
groundwater quality
groundwater reduction
habitat destruction
Han dynasty
hazardous waste handling
health care facility
High Plains
high-latitude place
hinterland
hub-and-spoke
human adaptation
human control over nature
human-induced change
Hutus
hybridization of crops
hydrilla
hydrologic cycle

hydrosphere
indigenous people
Industrial Revolution
industrialization
intermediate directions
international debt crisis
interstate highway system
intervening opportunity
introduction of species
Iran
Iraq
Jerusalem
Kurds
lake desiccation
lake ecosystem
land degradation
landform relief
land value
landmass
land-survey system
Latin America
law of retail gravitation
life experience
light-rail system
location principle
Malaysian rain forest
market economy
megalopolis
mental map
mercantilism
metropolitan corridor
microclimate
midlatitude forest
migration counterstream
migration stream
molybdenum
monoculture
moraine
multinational organization
municipality
NAFTA
nation-state
natural population increase
network
Nicaragua
North Korea

Nova Scotia
oblate spheroid
ocean ecosystem
Ontario
OPEC
overcutting of pine forest
oxygen cycle
ozone depletion
ozone layer
perceptual region
peripheral area
petroleum consumption
phosphate reserves
physical process
physiography
physiological population
　density
planned city
plant community
plate tectonics
population pyramid
Portuguese
post-reunification Germany
power bloc
primary data
primary economic activity
primate city
principal parallels
profitability
pull factors
push factors
racial minority
rain shadow
rate of natural increase
rate of resource consumption
reduction of species diversity
regional planning district
regionalization
relative humidity
relative location
religious ties
relocation strategy
remote sensing
resource base
Ring of Fire
Roman Empire

Geography, Level 4 (cont'd)
rural-to-urban migration
rutile sand
Rwanda
salinization
salt accumulation
sand movement
secondary economic activity
sector model
sediment
seismic activity
sequence occupance
silting
Sinocentric
Social Security number
social welfare of workers
socioeconomic status
soil acidification
soil creep
soil salinization
solar radiation
South Korea
Southeast Asia
Spanish settlement
stage of life
statutory requirement
sub-Arctic environment
sub-Saharan Africa
subsistence agriculture
subsistence farming
sustainable development
sustainable environment
synergy
systemic
tectonic plate
tectonic process
tertiary economic activity
the Pampas in Argentina
theory of comparative
    advantage
thermal
threshold
threshold population
tidal process
toxic dumping
toxic waste handling

transnational corporation
transportation corridor
transregional alliance
travel effort
tropical soil degradation
tungsten
Turkey
Tutsis
Ukraine
urban heat island
urban morphology
urbanization
volcanism
voting ward
ward
weathering
wilderness area
world atmospheric circulation
world temperature increase
zoned use of land
zoning regulation

Civics, Level 1
accept responsibility for one's
    actions
agreement
authority
citizen
control
duty
education
election
flag
good law
good rule
government
honesty
individual
justice
law
leader
nation
national anthem
official
open-mindedness
order

Pledge of Allegiance
police authority
power
privacy
qualifications
race
religion
respect for law
respect for the rights of others
responsibility
rights
rule
school
symbol
take turns
territory
trade
transportation
truth
United States
volunteer
vote
war

Civics, Level 2
absence of rules and laws
abuse of power
alien
American holiday
American society
benefits
Bill of Rights
campaign
candidate
Chamber of Commerce
citizenship
city council
civic responsibility
civic-mindedness
clean air laws
Columbus Day
common good
community
compromise
Congress
consent of the governed

consider the rights and
   interests of others
courts
Declaration of Independence
democracy
diplomacy
discrimination
discrimination based on age
discrimination based on
   disability
discrimination based on
   ethnicity
discrimination based on
   gender
discrimination based on
   language
discrimination based on
   religious belief
diversity
elected representative
equal opportunity
equal pay for equal work
evidence
executive branch
Fourth of July
freedom of religion
freedom of speech
geographical representation
governor
great seal
Greek democracy
health services
highest law of the land
human rights
individual liberty
individual responsibility
individual rights
invasion of privacy
jury duty
Labor Day
labor union
law enforcement
lawmaker
leadership
legislator
liberty and justice for all

life, liberty, and the pursuit of
   happiness
local government
Martin Luther King Jr.
mayor
Memorial Day
military force
military intervention
national origin
national park
national security
negotiation
nobility
oath of office
patriotism
peaceful demonstration
personal responsibility
petition
political candidate
political office
political party
politics
pollution
population growth
poverty
prejudice
president
presidential election
Presidents Day
privilege
P.T.A.
public good
public office
public policy
public servant
public utilities
pure food and drug laws
quality of life
racial discrimination
racial diversity
reform
refugee
religious belief
religious discrimination
representation
representative

revolution
right to a fair trial
right to choose one's work
right to criticize the
   government
right to join a political party
right to public education
right to vote
royalty
rule by the people
rule of law
school board
school prayer
self-discipline
self-governance
senator
slavery
special interest group
state government
state legislature
state senator
Statue of Justice
Statue of Liberty
Supreme Court
taxes
Thanksgiving
trade agreement
treaty
tribal council
tribal government
Uncle Sam
unemployment
United States citizenship
United States Constitution
unlimited government
value
Veterans Day
volunteerism
welfare
world leader

Civics, Level 3
AFL-CIO
Aid to Families with
   Dependent Children
allegiance

Civics, Level 3 (cont'd)

ambassador
American citizenship
American Revolution
American tribal government
armed forces service
arms control
bias
binding agreement
cabinet
capital punishment
central government
charitable group
citizenship by birth
civil rights
civil rights movement
civilian control of the military
coining money
colonial charters
commander in chief
Common Cause
Confederate States of America
conflict management
constitutional law
corrective justice
covert action
criminal law
curfew
customs search
death penalty
debate
delegated powers
demographics
demonstration
domestic policy
dress code
due process
economic aid
economic incentive
economic sanctions
economic security
English Parliament
enumerated powers
Environmental Protection Act
environmental protection
    movement

equal justice for all
equal protection of the law
equal rights under the law
equity
ethical dilemma
ethnic diversity
ex post facto
executive power
fair notice of a hearing
fair trial
federal court
federal income tax
First Amendment
foreign aid
foreign policy
foreign relations
form a more perfect union
Founders
Framers
freedom of assembly
freedom of association
freedom of conscience
freedom of petition
freedom of press
freedom of residence
freedom to emigrate
freedom to marry whom one
    chooses
freedom to travel freely
French Revolution
fundamental principles of
    American democracy
gender diversity
general election
Gettysburg Address
Greenpeace
gun control
habeas corpus
hate speech
immigration
impeachment
income tax
indentured servitude
informed citizenry
institution (political)
interest group

international law
International Red Cross
interstate commerce
interstate highways
judicial branch
judicial power
just compensation
juvenile
labor movement
landmark decision
Latin America
League of Women Voters
legal recourse
legislative branch
legislative power
legislature
letter to the editor
licensing
limited government
local election
lower court
loyal opposition
majority rule
Marbury v. Madison
Martin Luther King Jr.'s
    "I Have a Dream"
Mayflower Compact
Medicaid
Medicare
minimum wage
minority rights
NAACP
national defense
nation-state
NATO
naturalization
Nineteenth Amendment
nomination
OAS
Parliament
parliamentary system
People's Republic of China
picket
political life
political appointment
popular sovereignty

prayer in public school
preamble
Preamble to the Constitution
president's cabinet
presumption of innocence
prime minister
principle
private life
private property
property tax
protest
public agenda
public life
public opinion poll
public trial
Pure Food and Drug Act
recall election
representative democracy
representative government
revenue
right of appeal
right to acquire/dispose of
    property
right to copyright
right to counsel
right to enter into a lawful
    contract
right to equal protection of the
    law
right to establish a business
right to hold public office
right to join a labor union
right to join a professional
    association
right to know
right to patent
right to privacy
right to property
Roman Republic
rule of men
Senate
separation of church and state
separation of powers
shared power
Sixteenth Amendment
slander

Social Security
sovereign state
sovereignty
speedy trial
state constitution
state court
state election
state sales tax
state sovereignty
states' rights
suffrage
suffrage movement
Supreme Being
tariff
tax revenue
terrorism
The Federalist Papers
the press
totalitarian system
treason
trial by jury
union
United Nations
United Nations Charter
Universal Declaration of
    Human Rights
U.S. v. Nixon
veto power
Virgin Islands
vote of no confidence
voter registration
World Council of Churches
World Court

Civics, Level 4
abortion
adversary system
advice and consent
affirmative action
"all men are created equal"
allocation of power
American constitutional
    democracy
Americans with Disabilities
    Act
Amnesty International

anarchy
Antarctic Treaty
Anti-Federalist
arbitrary rule
arbitration
Article I of the Constitution
Article I Section 7
Article I Section 8
Article II of the Constitution
Article III of the Constitution
Articles of Confederation
authoritarian system
bilateral agreement
body politic
boycott
bribery
British constitution
Brown v. Board of Education
bureaucracy
capricious rule
caste system
charter local government
chauvinism
checks and balances
Chief Joseph's "I Shall Fight
    No More Forever"
Chinese Revolution
citizenry
citizens and subjects
civil disobedience
civil law
civil liberties
civil rights legislation
Civil War amendments
civilian review board
civility
class boundaries
class system
"clear and present danger"
    rule
Cold War
collective decision
common law
communism
Communist International
concurrent power

Civics, Level 4 (*cont'd*)

congressional district
congressional election
conservative
constituency
Constitutional amendment
constitutional democracy
constitutionalism
constitutionality of laws
consumer product safety
copyright
cruel and unusual punishment
democratic legislature
Democratic Party
direct democracy
direct popular rule
distribution of power
divine law
divine right
domestic tranquility
double jeopardy
E Pluribus Unum
electoral system
eminent domain
English Bill of Rights
Enlightenment
equal protection clause
Equal Rights Amendment
established religion
establishment clause
estate tax
ethnicity
European Union
excise tax
exclusionary rule
Federal Communications
    Commission
Federal Reserve
federal supremacy clause
federalism
Federalist
Food and Drug
    Administration
Fourteenth Amendment
franchise
free enterprise

free exercise clause
freedom to choose
    employment
freedom to enter into
    contracts
fundamental rights
GATT
general welfare
general welfare clause
Head Start
Helsinki Accord
higher court review
House of Commons
House of Lords
humanitarian aid
ideology
illegal search and seizure
immigration policy
impartial tribunal
imperial power
inalienable rights
incorporation
independent judiciary
independent regulatory agency
International Monetary Fund
jingoism
judicial review
junta
jurisdiction
legislation
legislative districting
legitimacy
libel
liberal
liberalism
Lincoln's "House Divided"
litigation
lobbying
Magna Carta
market economy
Marshall Plan
monarchy
Monroe Doctrine
moral obligation
Most Favored Nation
    Agreements

multilateral agreement
multinational corporation
NAFTA
National Education
    Association
national interest
nationalism
natural law
natural rights
Ninth Amendment
Northwest Ordinance
op-ed page
Organization of American
    States
organized crime
organized labor
patent
perjury
personal autonomy
political cartoon
political culture
political efficacy
political ideology
political philosophy
political rights
popular will
power of the purse
power to declare war
primary election
private domain
private sector
proportional system
Protestant Reformation
Puritan ethic
referendum
republic
Republican Party
reserved power
right to due process of law
right to life
school voucher
scope and limit
search and seizure
self-determination
self-evident truths
service group

sexual harassment
social contract
social equity
social issue
social welfare
Sojourner Truth's "Ain't I a
    Woman?"
state bill of rights
statute law
supremacy clause
system of checks and balances
Tenth Amendment
term limitation
third party
time, place, manner
    restrictions
two-party system
unenumerated rights
UNICEF
union movement
unitary government
urban decay
urban riot
vigilantism
warrant
"We the People . . ."
winner-take-all system
Woodrow Wilson's "Fourteen
    Points"
World Bank
World War I
World War II
zoning

Economics, Level 1
advertising
bank
business
buyer
coin
cost
debt
dime
dollar
earn
goods

job
labor
loss
money
needs
penny
poverty
price
quarter
sale
save
sell
seller
services
skills
spending
wants
worker

Economics, Level 2
advantage
barter
benefit
borrow
business firm
capital
capital goods
capital resource
competition
competitive market
consumer
consumption
contract
contract negotiation
credit
currency
customer service
division of labor
earnings
economy
employer
employment
entrepreneur
firm
funds
goods/services exchange

household
incentive
income
income tax
innovation
invention
investment
investor
limited budget
limited resources
loan
market
natural resource
partnership
payment
penalty
price decrease
price increase
producer
product
profit
profit opportunity
purchasing power
rent
resource
resource scarcity
revenue
reward
risk
salary
savings
scarcity
shortage
specialization
surplus
tax
trade
trade barrier
trade-off
training
value
wage

Economics, Level 3
average price level
carrying money

Economics, Level 3 (*cont'd*)
central authority
checking account
command economic system
commercial bank
contract labor
cost of production
credit policy
decentralization
disincentive
earned income
economic incentive
economic indicator
economic specialization
equilibrium
exchange rate
export
exporting firm
finance
foreign exchange market
foreign trade
free trade
fringe benefit
full-time employment
funding
Gross Domestic Product
human capital
human resource
import
inflation
inflation rate
interest
intermediary
labor force
labor market
labor union
large firm
law of supply and demand
market clearing price
market economy
market exchange
national defense spending
national economy
negative incentive
nonprofit organization

nonrival product
opportunity benefit
opportunity cost
output per hour
output per machine
output per unit of land
output per worker
part-time employment
positive incentive
private market
production
productivity
property rights
public project
quota
relative price
rent control
risk reduction
sales tax
savings account
self-employment
self-sufficiency
shared consumption
side effect
special interest group
specialized economic
    institution
standard currency
standard of living
storing money
substitute product
supplier
surcharge
system of weights and
    measures
tax deduction
tax exemption
tax reduction
total benefit
total cost
total market value
unemployment
unemployment rate
wage rate
work rule

Economics, Level 4
absolute advantage
aggregate demand
aggregate supply
allocation method
bait and switch
balanced budget
budget constraint
budget deficit
budget surplus
business deduction
capital stock
capitalism
circulation of money
collective bargaining
collusion
communism
comparative advantage
complementary product
consumer fraud
Consumer Price Index
consumer spending
consumer tastes
cooperative
corporate spending
cost-benefit ratio
cost-push inflation
current interest rate
cyclical unemployment
default on a loan
deferment of loan
deficit
deflation
demand-pull inflation
demand curve
depression
deregulation
discount rate
disposable income
Dow Jones
durable goods
economic risk
economic theory
economics
elasticity

expected rate of inflation
expenditure
externalities
Federal Reserve System
federal spending
federal tax revenue
financial institution
fiscal policy
fixed income
fixed rate of interest
free enterprise
frictional employment
frictional unemployment
functional distribution of
    income
government directive
government employee
government security
government spending
grant
home office
income distribution
incorporation
interest payment
interest rate
labor force immobility
large-scale investment
liability rules
macroeconomics
marginal benefit
marginal cost
marketplace
maximum employment
medical coverage
medical expenditure
microeconomics
monetary policy
money supply
monopoly
national debt
national government
    spending
natural monopoly
negative externality
net export

nominal Gross Domestic
    Product
nominal interest rate
nondurable goods
nonexclusion
nonprice competition
oligopoly
open market purchase
payroll tax
per capita GDP
personal distribution of
    income
personal income
physical capital
positive externality
prevailing price
price ceiling
price control
price floor
price stability
private investment
    spending
production cost
production method
production output
property tax
proprietor's income
public service commission
public welfare
public works
real cost
real GDP
real interest rate
recession
redistribution of income
regulation
rental income
research and development
reserve requirement
return on investment
seasonal unemployment
service charge
shareholder
shift in demand curve
shift in supply curve

social security
social security withholding
socialism
speculation
standard measure (of
    unemployment rate)
standard measures
standard weights
state revenue
stock
stock market
stockholder
structural unemployment
subsidy
supply curve
tariffs
tax revenue
telecommuting
transaction cost
transfer payment
transportation cost
underground economy
virtual company
Wall Street
warranty
work experience
workers' compensation

Health, Level 1
911
abuse
argument
birth
bleeding
blood
bruise
conflict
congestion
cough
cut
death
dentist
diet
disease
divorce

Health, Level 1 *(cont'd)*

doctor
drug
emergency
exercise
extended family
family member
fat
feelings
feelings of others
fever
fire safety
food group
food handling
gums
hand washing
harmful substance
health
helmet
hospital
human body
illness
injury
listening skill
marriage
medicine
nails
name calling
nurse
paramedic
police officer
pollution
precaution
rash
rest
risk
safety rule
scratch
simple injury
skin
stranger
symptom
tooth decay
traffic safety
water safety
wheezing

Health, Level 2

acne
activity level
alcohol
calorie
cooking temperature
dental floss
dietitian
disability
drug abuse
early detection and treatment
environment
exercise program
fiber
first- (second-, third-) degree
    burn
first aid
food label
growth cycle
health goal
health screening
healthy relationship
HMO
infant
infectious disease
lifestyle
medical personnel
medication
minor burn
mood swing
mouth guard
neighborhood safety
nonprescription drug
nonviolent conflict
    resolution
nutritional value
obesity
old age
over-the-counter medicine
overeating
parenthood
peer pressure
personal health goal
physical fitness
physician
poison

pregnancy
prescription medicine
protective equipment
psychological health
puberty
public health clinic
recreation safety
refusal skill
responsibility
self-control
sexual abuse
sexual maturation
smoking
social pressure
spoiled food
stress
stress management
sunscreen
tobacco abuse
treatment
voice change
warning label
weight gain
weight loss
well-being

Health, Level 3

abdominal thrust maneuver
adolescence
adolescent independence
alcohol abuse
American Heart Association
American Lung Association
anemia
anorexia
asthma
bacteria
body system
bulimia
cancer
cardiopulmonary
    resuscitation
chronic disease
community agency
community health
conception

conflict resolution
counseling
CPR
cultural belief
denial
dental health
depression
diabetes
Diabetes Association
discrimination
domestic violence
drug-seeking behavior
drug dependency
drunk and drugged driving
eating disorder
emergency plan
emotional abuse
emphysema
family history
food additive
food refrigeration
food storage
handicapping condition
health-care provider
health fad
health risk
heart disease
Heimlich maneuver
hygiene
immunization
injury-prevention strategy
long-term consequence
lung cancer
malnutrition
maturation
mental health clinic
mental health
neglect
negotiation skill
other-directed violence
personal health assessment
personal hygiene
plaque
pollutant
prejudice
prevention

risk factor
safe driving
safety hazard
self-directed violence
self-esteem
self-examination
short-term consequence
solid-waste contamination
storage temperature
tolerance for frustration
tolerance level
weight maintenance

Health, Level 4
abstinence
advocacy service
alcohol dependency
antioxidant
assertive consumerism
benign
biopsy
breast examination
caffeine dependency
carcinogenic
child-care center
child abuse
cirrhosis
clinical depression
cocaine
communicable disease
conflict prevention strategy
consumer health service
coping strategy
date rape
dating relationship
degenerative disease
diet aid
dietary supplement
drug-related problem
drug of choice
DSS regulation
emotional health
environmental health
environmental tobacco
    smoke
EPA

fad diet
family intervention
FDA
federal agency
female sexuality
fetus
food-production control
gender differences
genetic inheritability
health-care product
health insurance
household-waste disposal
immune system
inhalants
interpersonal conflict
life cycle
male sexuality
malignant
marijuana
medical history
melanoma
middle age
needle sharing
nicotine
nutrition plan
OSHA
osteoporosis
paranoia
pathogen
penis
perinatal care
prenatal care
psychotherapy
refuse
regular examination
rehabilitation
reproduction
Right to Know law
sexual activity
social isolation
state agency
substance abuse
teenage pregnancy
testicle
tobacco dependency
vagina

Physical Education, Level 1
ability
activity
arm preparation
balance
body shape
breathing rate
catch
circling
climbing
coach
exercise
flexibility
galloping
game
game rule
glove
goal
gymnasium
headstand
heart rate
hopping
jogging
joint
jump rope
jumping
kick & strike
landing
lifting
losing
lunging
outdoor activity
overhand throw
pass a ball
perspiration
player
practice
race
ready position
riding
running
score
sit-&-reach position
skill
skipping
sliding

speed
sport
stretching
take-off
team sport
throwing
throwing arm
turn taking
turning
twisting
underhand throw
winning

Physical Education, Level 2
arm & shoulder stretch
athlete
athletic equipment
balance board
baseball
basketball
basketball chest pass
bat
batting
body control
boxer
championship
competitive sport
conditioning
cool-down
course
court
curl-up
cyclist
defensive strategy
distance walk/run
diver
endurance
endurance activity
fielding
fitness level
fitness standard
follow-through
foot dribble
football
gymnastics
hand dribble

hockey
ice skates
increased heart rate
individual sport
lifestyle
lifetime sport
locomotor skill
motor skill
movement control
movement pattern
muscle soreness
muscular endurance
muscular strength
net & invasion game
nonlocomotor skill
object-control skill
offensive strategy
opponent
personal challenge
personal space
physical fitness level
physical fitness test
physical injury
power
procedure
professional sport
proper nutrition
pull-up
pulse rate
punt
push-up
racing start
racket
racket sport
recovery rate
recreational league
rhythmical skill
rink
risk taking
self-assessment
self-expression through
     physical activity
serve the ball
shoot the ball
sideline
skate

skis
soccer dribble
softball
sport etiquette
sport-specific skill
sports apparatus
sports club
sportsmanship
stealing the ball
striking pattern
swimming
temporary tiredness
tennis
timed walk/run
to make a play
track
training
transition movement
traveling pattern
trunk twist
warm-up
weight-bearing activity
wheelchair sports

Physical Education, Level 3
advanced movement skill
aerobic
aerobic capacity
anaerobic
calisthenics
cardiorespiratory endurance
cardiorespiratory exertion
dual sport
emotional health
exclusionary behavior
eye-hand coordination
fat body mass
feedback
fitness goal
freestyle swimming
frequency of training
game plan
handicapped athlete
health benefit
heart-rate recovery
heart-rate reserve

inclusive behavior
intramural sport
irregular heart rate
isometric exercise
lean body mass
leisure activity
manual dexterity
mental health
movement concept
muscle cramp
overtraining
overuse injury
psychological benefit
physiological benefit
range of motion
relaxation techniques
resistance training
resting heart rate
self-image
self-talk
spatial awareness
spike the ball
stress reduction
target heart rate
threshold
visualization
volleyball
weight control
weight training

Physical Education, Level 4
abdomen
aquatics
autonomous phase of learning
ballistic stretching
biomechanics of movement
body composition
cardiovascular efficiency
center of gravity
circuit training
equilibrium
extracurricular sport
fast-twitch muscle
health-enhancing level of
    fitness
international competition

interval training
law of specificity
leadership role
mental imagery
overload principle
personal fitness program
physiological factor
progression principle
progressive overload
rate of perceived exertion
respiratory efficiency
reversibility
sedentary lifestyle
situational awareness
slow-twitch muscle
specificity principle
sport facility
sport psychology
static balance
static stretch

Arts General, Level 1
applause
art
artist
audience
clapping
costume
dance
entertainer
film
music
pattern
sequence
stage
theater

Arts General, Level 2
accompaniment
art form
artistic purpose
balance
beat
diction
emphasis
form

Arts General, Level 2 (*cont'd*)
genre
improvisation
interpretation
lighting
mood
movement
originality
performance
performer
personal preference
professional
repetition
rhythm
scenery
set
setting
structure
style
subject matter
symbol
technical component
tempo
theme
timing
tone
visual artist
visual arts
work of art

Arts General, Level 3
AB form
ABA form
aesthetic criteria
aesthetics
art medium
artistic choice
audience response
aural element
body alignment
breath control
costuming
cultural context
emotional response
ensemble
expression

function of art
historical context
historical influence
historical period
kinetic element
performing arts
presentation
rehearsal
repertoire
scene
tension
texture
traditional art forms
transition
variation

Arts General, Level 4
artistic process
contemporary music
craftsmanship
emotional dimension
integration of art forms
media
technique
unity of the arts
universal concept

Dance, Level 1
bend
dancer
distance
ending
fall
forward
height
hop
landing
leap
middle
sideward
skip
straight
strength
stretch
turn
twist

Dance, Level 2
balance
body position
body shape
dance phrase
dance step
energy
flexibility
focus
folk dance
following
in step
leading
line
mirroring
movement element
partner skill
personal space
rhythmic completion
shape
slide
supporting weight
taking weight
traditional dance
weight shift

Dance, Level 3
abstracted gesture
agility
angle
articulation of movement
ballet
call and response
canon
chance reordering
classical dance
collapse
combination of movements
complementary shapes
contrasting shapes
coordination
dab
diagonal
directionality
elevation
float

glide
initiation of movement
injury-prevention strategy
jazz dance
level in relation to floor
movement quality
movement sequence
narrative
pantomime
punch
recovery
reordering
restructure
round
social dance
spatial pattern
square dance
sustain
swing
tap dance
theatrical dance
vibratory
warm-up technique

Dance, Level 4
abstract dance
alignment
axial movement
Balinese dance
base of support
bharata natyam dance
body-part articulation
body image
central initiation
choreographic
choreographic process
choreographic structure
distal initiation
dynamic qualities or efforts
Ghanaian dance
noh dance
kinesphere
kinesthetic awareness
line of gravity
locomotor movement
Middle Eastern dance

modern dance
movement elevation
movement phrase
movement theme
musicality
nonlocomotor movement
palindrome
penultimate movement
percussive
projection
rhythmic acuity
rondo
skeletal alignment
tempi
theme and variation
time element

Music, Level 1
body sound
instrument
loudness
lullaby
melody
musician
partner song
piano
sing
song
strum
swaying
symbol for note
voice

Music, Level 2
accent
alto
arrangement
art song
band instrument
bass
chord
classroom instruments
compose
composer
conductor
cue

diminuendo
Dixieland music
dotted note
drum machine
duet
echo
eighth note
electronic instrument
electronic sound
elements of music
embellishment
flat
folk
forte
fretted instrument
gospel music
guitar
half note
harmony
key signature
keyboard
keyboard instruments
legato
levels of difficulty
major key
march
measure
MIDI
minor key
Musical Instrument Digital
    Interface
musical phrase
musical piece
musical staff
nontraditional sound
notation
orchestra conductor
orchestral instrument
patriotic song
percussion instrument
pitch
posture
progression
quarter note
recorder
repeat

Music, Level 2 (*cont'd*)

rest

rhythmic variation

ritard

rock music

round

scale

sequencer

sharp

sixteenth note

skipping

snapping

soprano

staccato

staff

standard notation

string instrument

symbol for articulation

synthesizer

tenor

tie

time signature

traditional sound

treble clef

ukulele

whole note

work song

Music, Level 3

a capella

articulation

barbershop quartet

bass clef

blues

bow control

chorded zithers

chorus

classical

coda

composition

crescendo

dynamic change

dynamic level

harmonic accompaniment

harmonic instrument

hymn

instrumental literature

interval

intonation

jazz

jingle

level-1 difficulty

level-2 difficulty

level-3 difficulty

level-4 difficulty

level-5 difficulty

madrigal

mallet instruments

marcato

melodic embellishment

melodic instrument

melodic line

melodic ostinato

melodic phrase

meter

meter change

meter signature

music in four parts

music in two and three

    parts

oboe

opera

phrasing

pitch notation

playing by ear

playing position

pop

presto

quartet

range

recorder-type instruments

refrain

release

rhythmic ostinato

sight read

sonata

stick control

suite

sympathy

symphonic

syncopation

timbre

tonality

traditional sound source

trio

triple meter

wind instrument

Music, Level 4

accelerando

acoustic instrument

alla breve

allegro

andante

Broadway musical

chord progression

compositional device

compositional technique

consonance

contour

decrescendo

dissonance

duple meter

expressive device

instrumental score

instrumentation

inversion

oratorio

ostinato

pentatonic melody

pentatonic tonality

point of climax

register

retrograde

rhythmic phrase

rubato

staves

swing

tempo marking

vocal literature

vocal score

Theater, Level 1

act

actor

dramatic play

story

writer

Theater, Level 2
acting skill
action
cast
character
classroom dramatization
dialogue
drama
line
makeup
production
prop
role
social pretend play
villain

Theater, Level 3
archetype
atmosphere
avocation
character motivation
characterization
classical
constructed meaning
direction
director
dramatic media
dramatization
electronic media
empathy
formal production
informal production
locale
new art forms
nonlocomotor movement
oral element
physical environment
pitch
playwright
production value
publicity
script
sensory recall
set design
staging
study guide

superhero
suspense
theater literacy
trickster
visual element
vocal pitch

Theater, Level 4
acting method
aesthetic achievement
American theater
dramatic text
heritage
musical theater
oral symbol
physical & chemical
    properties of lighting,
    color, electricity
production requirement
promotional plan
stage management
unified production concept
visual symbol

Visual Arts, Level 1
brush
camera
paint

Visual Arts, Level 2
art material
art process
art technique
art tools
artwork
balance
canvas
cardboard
casting
clay
color
color variation
complementary color
composition
construction
contrast

cool color
depth
elicited response
knife
medium
metal
models
oil paint
overlapping
perspective
plastic
scissors
sculpture
shading
shape
size variation
stone
varying color
varying size
videotape
viewer
visual structure
warm color
watercolor
wood

Visual Arts, Level 3
art elements
art history
brayers
contemporary meaning
definition
design element
easel
expressive features
form
hue
intensity
kiln
laser
lathe
line
motion
placement
press
space

Visual Arts, Level 3 (*cont'd*)
spatial characteristic
temporal structure
texture
value
visual concept

Visual Arts, Level 4
art criticism
art object
halftone
highlight
negative space
organizational principle
positive space
shadow edge

Technology, Level 1
backspace key
computer
computer program
diskette
enter key
escape key
floppy disk
hand position
home row
Internet
keyboard
login
menu
monitor
mouse
power-up
power supply
printer
reboot
return key
space bar
special keys
World Wide Web

Technology, Level 2
alphanumeric keys
back-up

connecting cable
copy
copyright law
cursor
data
data deletion
data records
data retrieval
data storage
database
delete key
desktop
disk drive
download
e-mail
edit
electronic form
file folder
function keys
graphics
hard disk
hard drive
hardware
help system
home page
information exchange
information retrieval
Internet browser
load a program
memory
modem
multiple solutions
online
print form
software
software piracy
speed of communication
storage
storage device
stored data
technical difficulty
troubleshooting
upload
virus
word processor

Technology, Level 3
automated machine
bulletin board system
capacity
CD-ROM
central processing unit
computer fraud
computer hacking
copyright violation
data access
data display
data processing
data update
decoder
designed object
desktop publishing software
digitized
disassembly
document formatting
e-learning
feedback
file management
format
formatting
function
human-operated machine
icon
input device
Internet Service Provider
Intranet
invasion of privacy
local network system
malfunction
man-made object
misconnected
mismatched
navigation (Internet)
network
nonphysical object
output
output device
programming command
programming language
record management
search techniques

sort techniques
special purpose program
specialized machine
spreadsheet
steps in the design process
system failure
tape drive
text format
touch screen
URL
virus setting
voice recorder

Technology, Level 4
artifact
batch production
binary
biotechnology
bit
Boolean search
byte
chat room
chip
closed-loop system
coordinated subsystems
CPU
debug
dedicated line
design principle
dual effect
e-paper

encoder
export a file
external storage
feedback system
field
frame
gigabyte
hardware limitations
hardware platform
hardware trade-off
HTML
import a file
information transfer
initialize
intelligent system
iterative process
kilobyte
linear system
listserv
machine-to-machine
macro
magnetic field
mail merge
mathematical modeling
megabyte
merge files
microprocessor
modified design
natural object
open-loop system
operating system

optimized solution
overdesign
patent
performance testing
peripheral device
person-to-machine
person-to-person
pixel
RAM
rate of diffusion
recursive process
redundancy
repetitive process
scanner
service provider
simple system
simulation
software application
sound recorder
spam
story board
streaming
subsystem
system design
systems thinking
telecommunications
telecomputing
template
transmitter
usenet newsreader
Web ring

References

Adams, M. J. (1990). *Beginning to read: Thinking and learning about print.* Cambridge, MA: MIT Press.

Alexander, P. A. (1984). Training analogical reasoning skills in the gifted. *Roeper Review, 6*(4), 191–193.

Alexander, P. A., Kulikowich, J. M., & Schulze, S. K. (1994). How subject-matter knowledge affects recall and interest. *Review of Educational Research, 31*(2), 313–337.

Allington, R. L. (1984). Content coverage and contextual reading in reading groups. *Journal of Reading Behavior, 16,* 85–96.

Ames, W. S. (1964). The understanding vocabulary of first grade pupils. *Elementary English, 41,* 64–68.

Anders, P. L., Bos, C. S., & Filip, D. (1984). The effect of semantic feature analysis on the reading comprehension of learning disabled students. In J. Niles & L. A. Harris (Eds.), *Changing perspectives in research in reading/language processing and instruction* (Vol. 33). Rochester, NY: National Reading Conference.

Anderson, J. R. (1983). *The architecture of cognition.* Cambridge, MA: Harvard University Press.

Anderson, J. R. (1990). *Cognitive psychology and its implications.* New York: W. H. Freeman.

Anderson, J. R. (1995). *Learning and memory: An integrated approach.* New York: John Wiley & Sons.

Anderson, R. C., & Freebody, P. (1981). Vocabulary knowledge. In J. T. Guthrie (Ed.), *Comprehension and teaching: Research reviews* (pp. 77–117). Newark, DE: International Reading Association.

Anderson, R. C., & McGaw, B. (1973). On the representation of the meanings of general terms. *Journal of Experimental Psychology, 101,* 301–306.

Anderson, R. C., Wilson, P. T., & Fielding, L. G. (1986). Growth in reading and how children spend their time outside of school. *Reading Research Quarterly, 23,* 285–303.

Atwell, N. C. (1987). *In the middle.* Portsmouth, NH: Heinemann.

Axinn, W., Duncan, G. J., & Thornton, A. (1997). The effects of parents' income, wealth and attitudes on children's completed schooling and self-esteem. In G. J. Duncan & J. Brooks-Gunn (Eds.), *Consequences of growing up poor.* New York: Russell Sage Foundation.

Bakhtin, M. M. (1986). *Speech genres and other late essays.* Austin: University of Texas Press.

Beck, I. L., & McKeown, M. G. (1985). Teaching vocabulary: Making the instruction fit the goal. *Educational Perspectives, 23*(1), 11–15.

Beck, I. L. & McKeown, M. G. (1991). Conditions to vocabulary acquisition. In R. Barr, M. Kamil, P. Mosenthal, & P. D. Pearson (Eds.). *Handbook of reading research* (Vol. II, pp. 789–814). New York: Longman.

Beck, I. L., McKeown, M. G., & Kucan, L. (2002). *Bringing words to life: Robust vocabulary instruction.* New York: Guilford Press.

Becker, W. C. (1977). Teaching reading and language to the disadvantaged: What we have learned from field research. *Harvard Educational Review, 47*(4), 518–543.

Becker, W. C., Dixon, R., & Anderson-Inman, L. (1980). *Morphographic and root word analysis of 26,000 high frequency words.* Eugene, OR: University of Oregon, College of Education.

Beckwith, R., Miller, G. A., & Tengi, R. (1993). *Design and implementation of the WordNet lexical database and searching software* [Online]. Available: http://engr.smu.edu/~rada/wnb/#8

Berliner, D. C. (1992, February). *Educational reform in an era of disinformation.* Paper presented at the American Association for Teacher Education, San Antonio, TX.

Bloom, B. S. (1976). *Human characteristics and school learning.* New York: McGraw-Hill.

Bodrova, E., & Leong, D. J. (1996). *Tools of the mind: Vygotskian approach to early childhood education.* Columbus, OH: Merrill.

Bonser, F. G., Burch, L. H., & Turner, M. R. (1915). Vocabulary tests as measures of school efficiency. *School and Society, 2,* 714–718.

Boulanger, D. F. (1981). Ability and science learning. *Journal of Research in Science Teaching, 18*(2), 113–121.

Bradshaw, G. L., & Anderson, J. R. (1982). Elaborative encoding as an explanation of levels of processing. *Journal of Verbal Learning and Verbal Behavior, 21,* 165–174.

Brandenburg, G. C. (1918). Psychological aspects of language. *Journal of Educational Psychology, 9,* 313–332.

Breland, H. M., Jones, R. J., & Jenkins, I. (1994) *The College Board vocabulary study.* New York: College Board Publications.

Brewster, C., & Fager, J. (1998). *Student mentoring.* Portland, OR: Northwest Regional Educational Laboratory.

Britton, J., Burgess, T., Martin, N., McLeod, A., & Rosen, H. (1975). *The development of writing abilities* (pp. 11–18). London: MacMillan.

Brooks-Gunn, J., Duncan, G. J., & Maritato, N. (1997). Poor families poor outcomes: The well-being of children and youth. In G. J. Duncan & J. Brooks-Gunn (Eds.), *Consequences of growing up poor* (pp. 1–17). New York: Russell Sage Foundation.

Burger, H. C. (1984). *The wordtree.* Merriam, KS: The Wordtree.

Bushman, B. J. (1994). Vote-counting procedures in meta-analysis. In H. Cooper & L. V. Hedges (Eds.), *The handbook of research synthesis* (pp. 193–213). New York: Russell Sage Foundation.

Calkins, L. M. (1986). *The art of teaching writing.* Portsmouth, NH: Heinemann.

Carey, S. (1978). Child as word learner. In M. Halle, J. Bresnan, & G. Miller (Eds.), *Linguistic theory and psychological reality* (pp. 264–293). Cambridge, MA: MIT Press.

Carroll, J. B. (1971). *Learning from verbal discourse in educational media: A review of the literature.* Princeton, NJ: Educational Testing Service. (ETS RM 71-61)

Carroll, J. B., Davies, P., & Richman, B. (1971). *The American Heritage word frequency book.* New York: American Heritage Publishing.

Cattell, R. B. (1987). *Intelligence: Its structure, growth and action* (Rev. ed.). Amsterdam: North Holland Press. (Original work published 1971)

Center for Civic Education. (1994). *National standards for civics and government.* Calabasas, CA: Author.

Chen, Z. (1996). Children's analogical problem solving: The effects of superficial, structural, and procedural similarities. *Journal of Experimental Child Psychology, 62*(3), 410–431.

Chen, Z. (1999). Schema induction in children's analogical problem solving. *Journal of Educational Psychology, 91*(4), 703–715.

Chen, Z., Yanowitz, K. L., & Daehler, M. W. (1996). Constraints on accessing abstract source information: Instantiation of principles facilitates children's analogical transfer. *Journal of Educational Psychology, 87*(3), 445–454.

Chi, M. T. H., Feltovich, P. J., & Glaser, R. (1981). Categorization and representation of physics problems by experts and novices. *Cognitive Science, 5,* 121–152.

Chomsky, N. (1957). *Syntactic structures.* The Hague: Moutan.

Chomsky, N. (1965). *Aspects of a theory of syntax.* Cambridge, MA: MIT Press.

Clark, H. H., & Clark, E. V. (1977). *Psychology and language.* San Diego, CA: Harcourt Brace Jovanovich.

Cole, J. C., & McLeod, J. S. (1999). Children's writing ability. The impact of the pictorial stimulus. *Psychology in the Schools, 36*(4), 359–370.

Collins. (1987). *Collins COBUILD English language dictionary.* London: Author.

Collins, A. M., & Quillian, M. R. (1969). Retrieval time for semantic memory. *Journal of Verbal Learning and Verbal Behavior, 8,* 240–247.

Community Consolidated School District 15. (2003). VIA: Vocabulary for Increased Achievement. Palatine, IL: Author.

Conger, R. D., Conger, K. J., & Elder, G. H., Jr. (1997). Family economic hardship and adolescent adjustment: Mediating and moderating processes. In G. J. Duncan & J. Brooks-Gunn (Eds.), *Consequences of growing up poor* (pp. 288–310). New York: Russell Sage Foundation.

Consortium of National Arts Education Associations. (1994). *National standards for arts education: What every young American should know and be able to do in the arts.* Reston, VA: Music Educators National Conference.

Corcoran, M., & Adams, T. (1997). Race, sex, and the intergenerational transmission of poverty. In G. J. Duncan & J. Brooks-Gunn (Eds.), *Consequences of growing up poor* (pp. 461–517). New York: Russell Sage Foundation.

Core Knowledge Foundation. (1999). *Core knowledge sequence: Content guidelines for grades K–8.* Charlottesville, VA: Author.

Core Knowledge Foundation. (1999). *About core knowledge* [Online]. Available: http://www.coreknowledge.org/CKproto2/about/index.htm

Council for Basic Education. (1998). *Standards for excellence in education.* Washington, DC: Author.

Covington, M. V. (1992). *Making the grade: A self-worth perspective on motivation and school reform.* New York: Cambridge University Press.

Crafton, L. K. (1996). *Standards in practice: Grades K–2.* Urbana, IL: National Council of Teachers of English.

Craik, F. I. M., & Lockhart, R. S. (1972). Levels of processing: A framework for memory research. *Journal of Verbal Learning and Verbal Behavior, 11,* 671–684.

Csikszentmihalyi, M. (1990). *Flow: The psychology of optimal experience.* New York: Harper & Row.

Cuff, N. B. (1930). Vocabulary tests. *Journal of Educational Psychology, 21,* 212–220.

Dagher, Z. R. (1995). Does the use of analogies contribute to conceptual change? *Science and Education, 78*(6), 601–614.

Dale, E. (1965). Vocabulary measurement: Techniques and major findings. *Elementary English, 42,* 82–88.

Dale, E., & O'Rourke, J. (1986). *Vocabulary building.* Columbus, OH: Zaner Bloser.

D'Anna, C. A., Zechmeister, E. B., & Hall, J. W. (1991). Toward a meaningful definition of vocabulary size. *Journal of Reading Behavior, 23,* 109–122.

Dennett, D. C. (1969). *Content and consciousness.* London: Routledge & Kegan Paul.

Dennett, D. C. (1991). *Consciousness explained.* Boston: Little, Brown & Co.

Dochy, F., Segers, M., & Buehl, M. M. (1999). The relationship between assessment practices and outcomes of studies: The case of research on prior knowledge. *Review of Educational Research, 69*(2), 145–186.

Dolch, E. (1936). How much word knowledge do children bring to grade 1? *Elementary English Review, 13,* 177–183.

Dolch, E. W., & Leads, D. (1953). Vocabulary tests and depth of meaning. *Journal of Educational Research. 47,* 181–189.

Dorso, F. T., & Shore, W. J. (1991). Partial knowledge of word meanings. *Journal of Experimental Psychology: General, 120,* 190–202.

Drum, P. A., & Konopak, B. C. (1987). Learning word meanings from written context. In M. G. McKeown & M. E. Curtis (Eds.), *The nature of vocabulary acquisition* (pp. 73–87). Hillsdale, NJ: Erlbaum.

Dupuy, H. P. (1974). *The rationale, development and standardization of a basic word vocabulary test* (DHEW Publication No. HRA 74-1334). Washington, DC: U.S. Government Printing Office.

Durkin, D. (1979). What classroom observations reveal about reading comprehension instruction. *Reading Research Quarterly, 14,* 481–533.

Elwood, M. I. (1939). A preliminary note on the vocabulary test in the revised Stanford-Binet scale. *Journal of Educational Psychology, 30,* 632–634.

English, F. W. (2000). *Deciding what to teach and test: Developing, aligning, and auditing the curriculum.* Thousand Oaks, CA: Corwin Press.

English, L. D. (1997). Children's reasoning in classifying and solving computational word problems. In L. D. English (Ed.), *Mathematical reasoning: Analogies, metaphors and images* (pp. 191–220). Mahwah, NJ: Lawrence Erlbaum.

Evans, K. S. (1996). Creating spaces for equity? The role of positioning in peer-led literature discussions. *Language Arts, 73,* 194–202.

Fellbaum, C. (1993). *English verbs as a semantic net* [On-line]. Available: http://engr.smu.edu/~rada/wnb/#8

Fellbaum, C., Gross, D., & Miller, K. (1993). *Adjectives in WordNet* [On-line]. Available: http://engr.smu.edu/~rada/wnb/#8

Fish, S. (1980). *Is there a text in this class? The authority of interpretive communities.* Cambridge, MA: Harvard University Press.

Fisher, P. J. L., Blachowicz, C. L. Z, Costa, M., & Pozzi, L. (1992, December). *Vocabulary teaching and learning in middle school cooperative literature study groups.* Paper presented at the National Reading Conference, San Antonio, TX.

Flick, L. (1992). Where concepts meet percepts. Stimulating analogical thought in children. *Science and Education, 75*(2), 215–230.

Fry, E. B., Fountoukidis, D. L., & Polk, J. K. (1985). *The new reading teacher's book of lists* (2nd ed.). Englewood Cliffs, NJ: Prentice Hall.

Fulwiler, T. (1986). The argument for writing across the curriculum. In A. Young & T. Fulwiler (Eds.), *Writing across the disciplines: Research into practice* (pp. 21–32). Portsmouth, NH: Boynton/Cook.

Galda, L., & Cullihan, B. E. (2003). Literature for literacy: What research says about the benefits of using trade books in the classroom. In J. Flood, D. Lapp, J. R. Squires, & J. M. Jensen (Eds.), *Handbook of research on teaching the English language arts* (2nd ed., pp. 640–648). Mahwah, NJ: Erlbaum.

Gentner, D., & Markman, A. B. (1994). Structural alignment in comparison: No difference without similarity. *Psychological Science, 5*(3), 152–158.

Geography Education Standards Project. (1994). *Geography for life: National geography standards.* Washington, DC: National Geographic Research and Exploration.

Glaser, R., & Linn, R. (1993). Forward. In L. Shepard, *Setting performance standards for student achievement* (pp. xiii–xiv). Stanford, CA: National Academy of Education, Stanford University.

Gottfried, G. M. (1998). Using metaphors as modifiers: Children's production of metaphoric compounds. *Journal of Child Language, 24*(3), 567–601.

Graves, M. F. (1984). Selecting vocabulary to teach in the intermediate and secondary grades. In J. Flood (Ed.), *Promoting reading comprehension* (pp. 245–260). Newark, DE: International Reading Association.

Graves, M. F. (1986). Vocabulary learning and instruction. In E. Z. Rothkopf & L. C. Ehri (Eds.), *Review of research in education* (Vol. 13, pp. 49–89). Washington, DC: American Educational Research Association.

Graves, M. F., & Slater, W. H. (1987, April). *The development of reading vocabularies in rural disadvantaged students, inner-city disadvantaged students, and middle-class suburban students.* Paper presented at the meeting of the American Educational Research Association, Washington, DC.

Greenfield, P. M. (1998). The cultural evolution of IQ. In U. Neisser (Ed.), *The rising curve: Long-term gains in IQ and related measures* (pp. 81–123). Washington DC: American Psychological Association.

Grossman, J. B., & Johnson, A. (2002). Assessing the effectiveness of mentoring programs. *The Prevention Researcher, 9*(1), 8–11.

Haggard, M. R. (1982). The vocabulary self-collection strategy: An active approach to word learning. *Journal of Reading, 27,* 203–207.

Hall, V. C., Chiarello, K. S., & Edmonson, B. (1996). Deciding where knowledge comes from depends on where you look. *Journal of Educational Psychology, 88*(2), 305–313.

Hall, W. E., & Cushing, J. R. (1947). The relative value of three methods of presenting material. *Journal of Psychology, 24,* 57–62.

Hanks, P. (1987). Definitions and explanations. In J. M. Sinclair (Ed.), *Looking up* (pp. 116–136). London: Collins.

Harris, A. J., & Jacobson, M. D. (1972). *Basic elementary reading vocabularies.* London: Collier-Macmillan Limited.

Hart, B. & Risley, T. R. (1995). *Meaningful differences in the everyday experience of young American children.* Baltimore, MD: Paul H. Brookes Publishing Co.

Harter, S. (1980). The perceived competence scale for children. *Child Development, 51,* 218–235.

Harter, S. (1999). *The construction of the self: A developmental perspective.* New York: Guilford Press.

Hedges, L. V., & Olkin, I. (1985). *Statistical methods for meta-analysis.* San Diego, CA: Academic Press.

Hernandez, D. J. (1997). Poverty trends. In G. J. Duncan & J. Brooks-Gunn (Eds.), *Consequences of growing up poor* (pp. 18–34). New York: Russell Sage Foundation.

Heurnstein, R. J., & Murray, C. (1994). *The bell curve: Intelligence and class structure in American life*. New York: Free Press.

Hickman, J. (1981). A new perspective on response to literature: Research in an elementary school setting. *Research in the Teaching of English, 15*, 343–354.

Hirsch, E. D., Jr. (1987). *Cultural literacy: What every American needs to know*. Boston: Houghton Mifflin.

Hirsch, E. D., Jr. (Ed.). (1991a). *What your first grader needs to know: Fundamentals of a good first-grade education*. New York: Delta.

Hirsch, E. D., Jr. (Ed.). (1991b). *What your second grader needs to know: Fundamentals of a good second-grade education*. New York: Delta.

Hirsch, E. D., Jr. (Ed.). (1992a). *What your fourth grader needs to know: Fundamentals of a good fourth-grade education*. New York: Delta.

Hirsch, E. D., Jr. (Ed.). (1992b). *What your third grader needs to know: Fundamentals of a good third-grade education*. New York: Delta.

Hirsch, E. D., Jr. (Ed.). (1993a). *What your fifth grader needs to know: Fundamentals of a good fifth-grade education*. New York: Delta.

Hirsch, E. D., Jr. (Ed.). (1993b). *What your sixth grader needs to know: Fundamentals of a good sixth-grade education*. New York: Delta.

Hirsch, E. D., Jr. (Ed.). (1997). *What your first grader needs to know: Fundamentals of a good first-grade education* (Rev. ed.). New York: Delta.

Hirsch, E. D., Jr. (Ed.). (1998). *What your second grader needs to know: Fundamentals of a good second-grade education* (Rev. ed.). New York: Delta.

Hirsch, E. D., Jr., & Holdren, J. (Eds.). (1996). *What your kindergartner needs to know: Preparing your child for a lifetime of learning*. New York: Delta.

Hirsch, E. D., Jr., Kett, J., & Trefil, J. (1988). *The dictionary of cultural literacy: What every American needs to know*. Boston: Houghton Mifflin.

Hirsch, E. D., Jr., Kett, J., & Trefil, J. (1993). *The dictionary of cultural literacy: What every American needs to know* (2nd ed.). Boston: Houghton Mifflin.

Holt, S. B., & O'Tuel, F. S. (1989). The effect of Sustained Silent Reading and Writing on achievement and attitudes of seventh and eighth grade students reading two years below grade level. *Reading Improvement, 26*(4), 290–297.

House, E. R., Emmer, C., & Lawrence, N. (1988, September). *Cultural literacy and testing*. (CSE Technical Report 291). Los Angeles: UCLA Center for Research on Evaluation, Standards, and Student Testing.

Hyerle, D. (1996). *Visual tools for constructing knowledge*. Alexandria, VA: Association for Supervision and Curriculum Development.

International Society for Technology in Education. (2000). *National educational technology standards for students: Connecting curriculum and technology*. Eugene, OR: Author.

International Technology Education Association. (2000). *Standards for technological literacy: Content for the study of technology*. Reston, VA: Author.

Iser, W. (1978). *The act of reading: A theory of aesthetic response*. Baltimore, MD: Johns Hopkins University Press.

Jenkins, J. R., Stein, M. L., & Wysocki, K. (1984). Learning vocabulary through reading. *American Educational Research Journal, 21*(4), 767–787.

Jensen, A. R. (1980). *Bias in mental testing*. New York: Free Press.

Johnson, D. D., & Pearson, P. D. (1984). *Teaching reading vocabulary*. New York: Holt, Rinehart, & Winston.

Johnson, D. D., Toms-Bronowski, S., & Pittleman, S. D. (1982). *An investigation of the effectiveness of semantic mapping and semantic feature analysis with intermediate grade children*. (Program Report 83-3). Madison, WI: Wisconsin Center for Educational Research, University of Wisconsin.

Johnson, D. D., von Hoff Johnson, B., & Schlicting, K. (2004). Logology: Word and language play. In J. F. Baumann & E. J. Kame'enui (Eds.), *Vocabulary instruction: Research to practice* (pp. 179–200). New York: Guilford.

Johnson, D. W., & Johnson, R. T. (1999). *Learning together and alone: Cooperative, competitive, and individualistic learning*. Boston: Allyn & Bacon.

Johnson, D. W., Maruyama, G., Johnson, R. T., Nelson, D., & Skon, L. (1981). Effects of cooperative, competitive and individualistic goal structures on achievement: A meta-analysis. *Psychological Bulletin, 89*(1), 47–62.

Joint Committee on National Health Education Standards. (1995). *National health education standards: Achieving health literacy.* Reston, VA: Association for the Advancement of Health Education.

Just, M. A., & Carpenter, P. A. (1987). *The psychology of reading and language comprehension.* Boston, MA: Allyn & Bacon.

Kame'enui, E. J., Dixon, R. C., & Carnine, D. W. (1987). Issues in the design of vocabulary instruction. In M. G. McKeown & M. E. Curtis (Eds.), *The nature of vocabulary acquisition* (pp. 129–145). Hillsdale, NJ: Erlbaum.

Katz, J., & Fodor, J. (1963). The structure of semantic theory. *Journal of Verbal Learning and Verbal Behavior, 39,* 170–210.

Kendall, J. S., & Marzano, R. J. (2000). *Content knowledge: A compendium of standards and benchmarks for K–12 education* (3rd ed.). Alexandria, VA: Association for Supervision and Curriculum Development.

Kiefer, B. (1986). The child and the picture book: Creating live circuits. *Children's Literature Association Quarterly, 11,* 63–68.

Kintsch, W. (1974). *The representation of meaning in memory.* Hillsdale, NJ: Lawrence Erlbaum and Associates.

Kintsch, W. (1979). On modeling comprehension. *Educational Psychologist, 1,* 3–14.

Krashen, S. D. (2000). Forward. In J. L. Pilgreen, *The SSR handbook: How to organize and manage a sustained silent reading program* (pp. vii–xi). Portsmouth, NH: Heinemann.

Kucera, H., & Francis, W. N. (1967). *Computational analysis of present-day American English.* Providence, RI: Brown University Press.

Kumar, R. C. (1996). *Research methodology: A step-by-step guide for beginners.* Thousand Oaks, CA: Sage Publications.

Landau, S. I. (1984). *Dictionaries: The art and craft of lexicography.* New York: Scribner.

LeDoux, J. E. (1996). *The emotional brain: The mysterious underpinnings of emotional life.* New York: Simon & Schuster.

Lee, A. Y. (n.d.). *Analogical reasoning: A new look at an old problem.* Boulder: University of Colorado, Institute of Cognitive Science.

Lewinski, R. J. (1948). Vocabulary and mental measurement: A quantitative investigation and review of research. *Journal of Genetic Psychology, 72,* 247–281.

Lindfors, J. (1999). *Children's inquiry: Using language to make sense of the world.* New York: Teachers College Press.

Macrorie, K. (1984). *Writing to be read.* Upper Montclair, NJ: Boynton/Cook.

Macrorie, K. (1988). *The I-search paper: Revised edition of searching writing.* Portsmouth, NH: Heinemann.

Madaus, G. F., Kellaghan, T., Rakow, E. A., & King, D. (1979). The sensitivity of measures of school effectiveness. *Harvard Educational Review, 49*(2), 207–230.

Mahan, H. C., & Witmer, L. A. (1936). A note on the Stanford-Binet vocabulary test. *Journal of Applied Psychology, 20,* 258–263.

Malone, T. W. (1981a). Toward a theory of intrinsically motivating instruction. *Cognitive Science, 4,* 333–367.

Malone, T. W. (1981b). *What makes things fun to learn? A study of intrinsically motivating computer games.* Paper presented at the annual meeting of the American Education Research Association annual meeting, Los Angeles, CA.

Markman, A. B., & Gentner, D. (1993a). Splitting the differences: A structural alignment view of similarity. *Journal of Memory and Learning, 32,* 517–535.

Markman, A. B., & Gentner, D. (1993b). Structural alignment during similarity comparisons. *Cognitive Psychology, 25,* 431–467.

Markus, H., & Ruvulo, A. (1990). Possible selves. Personalized representations of goals. In L. Pervin (Ed.), *Goal concepts in psychology* (pp. 211–241). Hillsdale, NJ: Lawrence Erlbaum.

Martinez, M., & Roser, N. L. (2003). Children's response to literature. In J. Flood, D. Lapp, J. R. Squires, & J. M. Jensen (Eds.), *Handbook of research in teaching the English language arts* (2nd ed., pp. 799–813). Mahwah, NJ: Erlbaum.

Marzano, L., & Christensen, N. (1992). *Literacy plus: Games for vocabulary and spelling.* Columbus, OH: Zaner-Bloser.

Marzano, R. J. (2002). *Identifying the primary instructional concepts in mathematics: A linguistic approach.* Englewood, CO: Marzano & Associates.

Marzano, R. J. (2003). *What works in schools: Translating research into action.* Alexandria, VA: Association for Supervision and Curriculum Development.

Marzano, R. J. (2004). The developing vision of vocabulary instruction. In J. F. Baumann & E. J. Kame'enui (Eds.), *Vocabulary instruction: Research to practice* (pp. 100–117). New York: Guilford Press.

Marzano, R. J., & Marzano, J. S. (1988). *A cluster approach to elementary vocabulary instruction.* Newark, DE: International Reading Association.

Marzano, R. J., Pickering, D. J., & Pollock, J. E. (2001). *Classroom instruction that works: Research-based strategies for increasing student achievement.* Alexandria, VA: Association for Supervision and Curriculum Development.

Maslow, A. (1968). *Toward a psychology of being.* New York: Harper.

Maslow, A. (1971). *The farther reaches of human nature.* New York: Viking.

Mason, L. (1994). Cognitive and metacognitive aspects in conceptual change by analogy. *Instructional Science, 22*(3), 157–187.

Mason, L. (1995). Analogy, meta-conceptual awareness and conceptual change: A classroom study. *Educational Studies, 20*(2), 267–291.

Mason, L., & Sorzio, P. (1996). Analogical reasoning in restructuring scientific knowledge. *European Journal of Psychology of Education, 11*(1), 3–23.

McKeown, M. G., & Beck, I. L. (1988). Learning vocabulary: Different ways for different goals. *Remedial and Special Education, 20,* 482–496.

McKeown, M. G., & Curtis, M. E. (Eds.). (1987). *The nature of vocabulary acquisition.* Hillsdale, NJ: Lawrence Erlbaum.

McLanahan, S. S. (1997). Parent absence or poverty: Which matters more? In G. J. Duncan & J. Brooks-Gunn (Eds.), *Consequences of growing up poor* (pp. 35–48). New York: Russell Sage Foundation.

McNemar, Q. (1942). *The revision of the Stanford-Binet scale.* Boston, MA: Houghton-Mifflin.

Medin, D., Goldstone, R. L., & Markman, A. B. (1995). Comparison and choice: Relations between similarity processes and decision processes. *Psychonomic Bulletin & Review, 2*(1), 1–19.

Miller, G. A. (1993). *Nouns in WordNet: A lexical inheritance system* [On-line]. Available: http://engr.smu.edu/~rada/wnb/#8

Miller, G. A., Beckwith, R., Fellbaum, C., Gross, D., & Miller, K. (1993). *Introduction to WordNet: An on-line lexical database* [On-line]. Available: http://engr.smu.edu/~rada/wnb/#8

Nagy, W. E., & Anderson, R. C. (1984). How many words are there in printed school English? *Reading Research Quarterly, 19*(3), 304–330.

Nagy, W. E., Anderson, R. C., & Herman, P. A. (1987). Learning word meaning from context during normal reading. *American Educational Research Journal, 24*(2), 237–270.

Nagy, W. E., & Herman, P. A. (1984). *Limitations of vocabulary instruction* (Tech. Rep. No. 326). Urbana, IL: University of Illinois, Center for the Study of Reading. (ERIC Document Reproduction Service No. ED248498)

Nagy, W. E., & Herman, P. A. (1987). Breadth and depth of vocabulary knowledge: Implications for acquisition and instruction. In M. G. McKeown & M. E. Curtis (Eds.), *The nature of vocabulary acquisition* (pp. 19–35). Hillsdale, NJ: Erlbaum.

Nagy, W. E., Herman, P. A., & Anderson, R. C. (1985). Learning words from context. *Reading Research Quarterly, 20,* 233–253.

National Association for Sport and Physical Education. (1995). *Moving into the future: National standards for physical education: A guide to content assessment.* St. Louis: Mosby.

National Business Education Association. (1995). *National standards for business education: What America's students should know and be able to do in business.* Reston, VA: Author.

National Center for Education Statistics. (2003). *Table 65. Public and private elementary and secondary teachers, enrollment, and pupil/teacher ratios: Fall 1955 to fall 2001* [Online]. Available: http://www.nces.ed.gov/pubs2003/digest02/tables/d005.asp

National Center for History in the Schools. (1994a). *National standards for history for grades K–4: Expanding children's world in time and space.* Los Angeles: Author.

National Center for History in the Schools. (1994b). *National standards for United States history: Exploring the American experience.* Los Angeles: Author.

National Center for History in the Schools. (1994c). *National standards for world history: Exploring paths to the present.* Los Angeles: Author.

National Center for History in the Schools. (1996). *National standards for history: Basic edition.* Los Angeles: UCLA, Author.

National Commission on Excellence in Education. (1983). *A nation at risk: The imperative for educational reform.* Washington, DC: Government Printing Office.

National Council for the Social Studies. (1994). *Expectations of excellence: Curriculum standards for social studies.* Washington, DC: Author.

National Council of Teachers of English and the International Reading Association. (1996). *Standards for the English language arts.* Urbana, IL: Authors.

National Council of Teachers of Mathematics. (1989). *Curriculum and evaluation standards for school mathematics.* Reston, VA: Author.

National Council of Teachers of Mathematics. (2000). *Principles and standards for school mathematics.* Reston, VA: Author.

National Council on Economic Education. (1997). *Voluntary national content standards in economics.* New York: Author.

National Education Goals Panel. (1991). *The national education goals report: Building a nation of learners.* Washington, DC: Author.

National Institute of Child Health and Human Development. (2000). Report of the National Reading Panel. *Teaching children to read: An evidence-based assessment of the scientific research literature on reading and its implications for reading instruction* [Online]. Available: http://www.nichd.nih.gov/publications/nrp/smallbook.htm

National Institute of Child Health and Human Development. (2000). *Report of the National Reading Panel: Teaching children to read.* NIH Publication No. 00-4754. Washington, DC: U.S. Government Printing Office.

National Research Council. (1996). *National science education standards.* Washington, DC: National Academy Press.

National Science Teachers Association. (1993). *Scope, sequence, and coordination of secondary school science: Vol. 1. The context core.* Washington, DC: Author.

National Standards in Foreign Language Education Project. (1996). *Standards for foreign language learning: Preparing for the 21st century.* Lawrence, KS: Author.

Neisser, U. (1982). *Memory observed.* San Francisco, CA: W. H. Freeman.

Neisser, U. (1998). *The rising curve: Long-term gains in IQ and related measures.* Washington DC: American Psychological Association.

Newby, T. J., Ertmer, P. A., & Stepich, D. A. (1995). Instructional analogies and the learning of concepts. *Educational Technology Research and Development, 43*(1), 5–18.

Nist, S. L., & Olejnik, S. (1995). The role of context and dictionary definitions on varying levels of word knowledge. *Reading Research Quarterly, 30,* 172–193.

Nuthall, G. (1999). The way students learn: Acquiring knowledge from an integrated science and social studies unit. *The Elementary School Journal, 99*(4), 303–341.

Odgen, C. K. (1932). *The basic words: A detailed account of uses.* London: Landor & Kegan Paul.

Paivio, A. (1971). *Imagery and verbal processes.* New York: Holt, Rinehart & Winston.

Paivio, A. (1990). *Mental representation: A dual coding approach.* New York: Oxford University Press.

Paivio, A. (1991). Dual coding theory: Retrospect and current status. *Canadian Journal of Psychology, 45,* 255–287.

Peters, H. E., & Mullis, N. C. (1997). The role of family income and sources of income in adolescent achievement. In G. J. Duncan & J. Brooks-Gunn (Eds.), *Consequences of growing up poor* (pp. 340–381). New York: Russell Sage Foundation.

Pilgreen, J. L. (2000). *The SSR handbook: How to organize and manage a sustained silent reading program.* Portsmouth, NH: Boynton/Cook Publishers.

Pilgreen, J., & Krashen, S. (1993, Fall). Sustained Silent Reading with English as a Second Language high school students: Impact on reading comprehension, reading frequency, and reading enjoyment. *School Library Media Quarterly, 22*(1), 21–23.

Potter, M. C., & Faulconer, B. A. (1979). Understanding noun phrases. *Journal of Verbal Learning and Verbal Behavior, 18,* 509–522.

Powell, G. (1980, December). *A meta-analysis of the effects of "imposed" and "induced" imagery upon word recall.* Paper presented at the annual meeting of the National Reading Conference, San Diego, CA. (ERIC Document Reproduction Service No. ED199644)

Project 2061, American Association for the Advancement of Science. (1993). *Benchmarks for science literacy.* New York: Oxford University Press.

Quillian, M. R. (1967). Word concepts: A theory and simulation of some basic semantic capabilities. *Behavioral Science, 12,* 410–430.

Quillian, M. R. (1968). Semantic memory. In M. Minsky, (Ed.), *Semantic information processing.* Cambridge, MA: MIT Press.

Quirk, R., Greenbaum, S., Leech, G., & Svartvik, J. (1972). *A grammar of contemporary English.* London: Longman.

RAND Reading Study Group (2002). *Reading for understanding: Toward a research and development program in reading comprehension.* Prepared for the Office of Educational Research and Improvement (OERI), U.S. Department of Education. Santa Monica, CA: RAND Education.

Rattermann, M. J., & Gentner, D. (1998). More evidence for a relational shift in the development of analogy: Children's performance on a causal-mapping task. *Cognitive Development, 13*(4), 453–478.

Raven, J. C. (1948). The comparative assessment of intellectual ability. *British Journal of Psychology, 39,* 12–19.

Ravitch, D., & Finn, C. E., Jr. (1987). *What do our 17-year-olds know? A report on the first national assessment of history and literature.* New York: Harper and Row.

Ripoll, T. (1999). Why this made me think of that. *Thinking and Reasoning, 4*(1), 15–43.

Rolfhus, E. L., & Ackerman, P. L. (1999). Assessing individual differences in knowledge: Knowledge, intelligence, and related traits. *Journal of Educational Psychology, 91*(3), 511–526.

Rosch, E. (1975). Cognitive representation of semantic categories. *Journal of Experimental Psychology: General, 104,* 192–233.

Rosenblatt, L. (1978). *The reader, the text, the poem: The transactional theory of the literary work.* Carbondale, IL: Southern Illinois University Press.

Rosenthal, R. (1991). *Meta-analytic procedures for social research.* London: Sage Publications.

Rosenthal, R., & Rubin, D. B. (1982). A simple general purpose display of magnitude of experimental effect. *Journal of Educational Psychology, 74*(2), 166–169.

Roser, N., & Juel, C. (1982). Effects of vocabulary instruction on reading comprehension. In J. Niles & L. Harris (Eds.), *New inquiries in reading research* (pp. 110–118). Rochester, NY: National Reading Conference.

Ross, B. H. (1987). This is like that: The use of earlier problems and the separation of similarity effects. *Journal of Experimental Psychology, 13*(4), 629–639.

Rovee-Collier, C. (1995). Time windows in cognitive development. *Developmental Psychology, 31*(2), 147–169.

Ruddell, M. R. (1993). *Teaching content reading and writing.* Boston, MA: Allyn & Bacon.

Sadoski, M. (1983). An exploratory study of the relationships between reported imagery and the comprehension and recall of a story. *Reading Research Quarterly, 19,* 110–123.

Sadoski, M. (1985). The natural use of imagery in story comprehension and recall: Replication and extension. *Reading Research Quarterly, 20,* 658–667.

Sadoski, M., & Paivio, A. (1994). A dual coding view of imagery and verbal processes in reading comprehension. In R. B. Ruddell, M. R. Ruddell, & H. Singer (Eds.), *Theoretical models and processes of reading* (4th ed., pp. 582–601). Newark, DE: International Reading Association.

Sapir, E. (1921). *Language: An introduction to the study of speech.* New York: Harcourt Brace Jovanovich.

Schiefele, U., & Krapp, A. (1996). Topics of interest and free recall of expository text. *Learning and Individual Differences, 8*(2), 141–160.

Schwanenflugel, P. J., Stahl, S. A., & McFalls, E. L. (1997). *Partial word knowledge and vocabulary growth during reading comprehension.* (Research Report No. 76). University of Georgia, National Reading Research Center.

Shapiro, B. J. (1969). The subjective estimation of relative word frequency. *Journal of Verbal Learning and Verbal Behavior, 8,* 248–251.

Shepard, L. (1993). *Setting performance standards for student achievement: A report of the National Academy of Education Panel on the evaluation of the NAEP trial state assessment: An evaluation of the 1992 achievement levels.* Stanford, CA: National Academy of Education, Stanford University.

Shibles, B. H. (1959). How many words does a first grade child know? *Elementary English, 31,* 42–47.

Sierra-Perry, M. (1996). *Standards in practice: Grades 3–5.* Urbana, IL: National Council of Teachers of English.

Sipe, C. L. (1999). Mentoring adolescents: What we have learned. In J. Baldwin Grossman (Ed.), *Contemporary issues in mentoring*. Philadelphia: Public/Private Ventures.

Smagorinsky, P. (1996). *Standards in practice: Grades 9–12*. Urbana, IL: National Council of Teachers of English.

Smith, E. E., & Medin, D. L. (1981). *Categories and concepts*. Cambridge, MA: Harvard University Press.

Smith, J. R., Brooks-Gunn, J., & Klebanov, P. K. (1997). Consequences of living in poverty for young children's cognitive and verbal ability and early school achievement. In G. J. Duncan & J. Brooks-Gunn (Eds.), *Consequences of growing up poor* (pp. 132–189). New York: Russell Sage Foundation.

Smith, M. K. (1941). Measurement of the size of general English vocabulary through the elementary grades and high school. *General Psychological Monographs, 24*, 311–345.

Snow, C. E. (1990). The development of definitional skill. *Journal of Child Language, 17*, 697–710.

Solomon, I. (1995). Analogical transfer and "functional fixedness" in the science classroom. *Journal of Educational Research, 87*(6), 371–377.

Spache, G. (1943). The vocabulary tests of the revised Stanford-Binet as independent measures of intelligence. *Journal of Educational Research, 36*, 512–516.

Stahl, S. A. (1985). To teach a word well: A framework for vocabulary instruction. *Reading World, 24*(3), 16–27.

Stahl, S. A. (1986). Three principles of effective vocabulary instruction. *Journal of Reading, 29*, 662–668.

Stahl, S. A. (1999). *Vocabulary development*. Cambridge, MA: Brookline Books.

Stahl, S. A., & Clark, C. H. (1987). The effects of participatory expectations in classroom discussion on the learning of science vocabulary. *American Educational Research Journal, 24*, 541–556.

Stahl, S. A., & Fairbanks, M. M. (1986). The effects of vocabulary instruction: A model-based meta-analysis. *Review of Educational Research, 56*(1), 72–110.

Stanovich, K. E. (1986). Matthew effects in reading: Some consequences of individual differences in the acquisition of literacy. *Reading Research Quarterly, 21*(4), 360–406.

Stanovich, K. E., & Cunningham, A. E. (1993). Where does knowledge come from? Specific association between print exposure and information. *Journal of Educational Psychology, 85*(2), 211–229.

Sternberg, R. J. (1977). *Intelligence, information processing and analogical reasoning: The componential analysis of human abilities*. Hillsdale, NJ: Erlbaum.

Sternberg, R. J. (1978). *Toward a unified componential theory of human reasoning* (Tech. Rep. No. 4). New Haven, CT: Yale University, Department of Psychology. (ERIC Document Reproduction Service No. ED 154421)

Sternberg, R. J. (1979). *The development of human intelligence* (Tech. Rep. No. 4, Cognitive Development Series). New Haven, CT: Yale University, Department of Psychology. (ERIC Document Reproduction Service No. ED 174658)

Sternberg, R. J. (1985). *Beyond IQ: A triarchic theory of human intelligence*. Cambridge, England: Cambridge University Press.

Sternberg, R. J., & Wagner, R. K. (Eds.). (1986). *Practical intelligence: Nature and origins of competence in the everyday world*. London: Cambridge University Press.

Sticht, T. G., Hofstetter, R. C., & Hofstetter, C. H. (March, 1997). *Knowledge, literacy and power*. San Diego, CA: Consortium for Workforce Education & Lifelong Learning. Available: http://www.coreknowledge.org/CKproto2/about/eval/KnowldgLit&Power.htm

Swanborn, M. S. L., & de Glopper, K. (1999). Incidental word learning while reading: A meta-analysis. *Review of Educational Research, 69*(3), 261–285.

Taba, H. (1962). *Curriculum development: Theory and practice*. New York: Harcourt, Brace, & World.

Tamir, P. (1996). Science assessment. In M. Birenbaum & F. J. R. C. Dochy (Eds.), *Alternatives in assessment of achievements, learning processes, and prior knowledge* (pp. 93–129). Boston: Kluwer.

Teachers of English to Speakers of Other Languages, Inc. (1997). *ESL standards for Pre K–12 students*. Alexandria, VA: Author.

Terman, L. M. (1916). *The measurement of intelligence*. Boston, MA: Houghton-Mifflin.

Terman, L. M. (1918). Vocabulary tests as a measure of intelligence. *Journal of Educational Psychology, 9*, 452–466.

Thorndike, E. L., & Lorge, I. (1944). *The teacher's word book of 30,000 words*. New York: Bureau of Publications, Teacher's College, Columbia University.

Tobias, S. (1994). Interest, prior knowledge and learning. *Review of Educational Research, 64*(1), 37–54.

Tukey, J. W. (1977). *Exploratory data analysis*. Reading, MA: Addison-Wesley.

Tulving, E. (1972). Episodic and semantic memory. In E. Tulving & W. Donaldson (Eds.), *Organization of memory* (pp. 185–191). New York: Academic Press.

Turner, A., & Greene, E. (1977). *The construction of a propositional text base.* Boulder CO: Institute for the Study of Intellectual Behavior, University of Colorado at Boulder.

U.S. Census Bureau. (2003, March). *Table 8. Income in 1999 by educational attainment for people 18 years old and over, by age, sex, race, and Hispanic origin* [Online]. Available: http://www.census.gov/population/www/socdemo/education/ pp. 20–530.

U.S. Census Bureau. (2003, September 25). *Table 1: Number in poverty and poverty rate by race and Hispanic origin: 2001 and 2002* [Online]. Available: http//www.census.gov/hhes/poverty/poverty02/table1.pdf

U.S. Census Bureau. (2003, September 26). *Poverty thresholds for 2002 by size of family and number of related children under 18 years* [Online]. Available: http://www.census.gov/hhes/poverty/threshld/thresh02.html

van Dijk, T. A. (1977). *Text and context.* London: Longman.

van Dijk, T. A. (1980). *Macrostructures.* Hillsdale, NJ: Lawrence Erlbaum.

van Dijk, T. A., & Kintsch, W. (1983). *Strategies of discourse comprehension.* Hillsdale, NJ: Lawrence Erlbaum.

Vygotsky, L. S. (1962). *Thought and language.* Cambridge, MA: MIT Press.

Wahba, N. A., & Bridwell, L. G. (1976). Maslow reconsidered: A review of research on the need of hierarchy theory. *Organizational Behavior and Human Performance, 15,* 212–240.

Wechsler, D. (1949). *Manual, Wechsler intelligence scale for children.* New York: Psychological Corporation.

White, T. G., Sowell, J., & Yanagihara, A. (1989). Teaching elementary students to use word-part clues. *The Reading Teacher, 42,* 302–308.

Whittington, D. (1991). What have 17-year-olds known in the past? *American Educational Research Journal, 28*(4), 759–780.

Wiggins, G., & McTighe, J. (1998). *Understanding by design.* Alexandria, VA: Association for Supervision and Curriculum Development.

Wilhelm, J. D. (1996). *Standards in practice: Grades 6–8.* Urbana, IL: National Council of Teachers of English.

Wilkins, A. J. (1971). Conjoint frequency, category size, and categorization time. *Journal of Verbal Learning and Verbal Behavior, 10,* 382–385.

Zahler, K. A., & Zahler, D. (1989). *Test your countercultural literacy.* New York: Arco.

Zorfass, J. (1991). *Make it happen!* Newton, MA: Education Development Center, Inc.

Index

Note: Page numbers followed by an *f* indicate reference to a figure.

About the Author

Robert J. Marzano is a Senior Scholar at Mid-Continent Research for Education and Learning in Aurora, Colorado; an Associate Professor at Cardinal Stritch University in Milwaukee, Wisconsin; Vice President of Pathfinder Education, Inc.; and President of Marzano & Associates consulting firm in Centennial, Colorado. He has developed programs and practices used in K–12 classrooms that translate current research and theory in cognition into instructional methods. An internationally known trainer and speaker, Marzano has authored 21 books and more than 150 articles and chapters on topics such as reading and writing instruction, thinking skills, school effectiveness, restructuring, assessment, cognition, and standards implementation. Recent ASCD titles include *Classroom Management That Works: Research Based Strategies for Every Teacher* (Marzano, Marzano, & Pickering, 2003), *What Works in Schools: Translating Research into Action* (2003); *A Handbook for Classroom Instruction That Works* (Marzano, Paynter, Pickering, & Gaddy, 2001); and *Classroom Instruction That Works: Research-Based Strategies for Increasing Student Achievement* (Marzano, Pickering, & Pollack, 2001). Additionally, Marzano headed a team of authors who developed *Dimensions of Learning* (ASCD, 1992). His most recent work is *The Pathfinder Project: Exploring the Power of One* (Pathfinder Education, Inc. 2003). Marzano received his B.A. in English from Iona College in New York, an M.Ed. in Reading/Language Arts from Seattle University, and a Ph.D. in Curriculum and Instruction from the University of Washington. He can be contacted at 7127 South Danube Court, Centennial, CO 80016. Phone: (303) 796-7683. E-mail: robertjmarzano@aol.com.

Related ASCD Resources

At the time of publication, the following ASCD resources were available; for the most up-to-date information about ASCD resources, go to www.ascd.org. ASCD stock numbers are noted in parentheses.

CD-ROMs

Research-Based Strategies for Increasing Student Achievement (#503058)

Networks

Visit the ASCD Web site (www.ascd.org) and search for "networks" for information about professional educators who have formed groups around topics like "Arts in Education," "Authentic Assessment," and "Brain-Based Compatible Learning." Look in the "Network Directory" for current facilitators' addresses and phone numbers.

Online Course

What Works in Schools: An Introduction by John Brown (#PD04OC36)

Print Products

Classroom Instruction That Works: Research-Based Strategies for Increasing Student Achievement Robert J. Marzano, Debra J. Pickering, Jane E. Pollock (#101010)

Classroom Management That Works: Research Based Strategies for Every Teacher Robert J. Marzano, Jana S. Marzano, Debra J. Pickering (#103027)

Grading and Reporting Student Learning Robert J. Marzano and Tom Guskey (Professional Inquiry Kit; #901061)

A Handbook for Classroom Instruction That Works Robert J. Marzano, Jennifer S. Norford, Diane E. Paynter, Debra J. Pickering, Barbara B. Gaddy (#101041)

What Works in Schools: Translating Research into Practice by Robert J. Marzano (#102271)

Videotapes

Classroom Management That Works: Sharing Rules and Procedures (Tape 1; #404039)
Classroom Management That Works: Developing Relationships (Tape 2; #404040)
Classroom Management That Works: Fostering Student Self-Management (Tape 3; #404041)
What Works in Schools: School-Level Factors with Robert J. Marzano (Tape 1; # 403048)
What Works in Schools: Teacher-Level Factors with Robert J. Marzano (Tape 2; #403049)
What Works in Schools: Student-Level Factors with Robert J. Marzano (Tape 3; #403050)

For more information, visit us on the World Wide Web (http://www.ascd.org), send an e-mail message to member@ascd.org, call the ASCD Service Center (1-800-933-ASCD or 703-578-9600, then press 2), send a fax to 703-575-5400, or write to Information Services, ASCD, 1703 N. Beauregard St., Alexandria, VA 22311-1714 USA.